# Slavery and Freedom in the Shenandoah Valley during the Civil War Era

*Southern Dissent*

UNIVERSITY PRESS OF FLORIDA

Florida A&M University, Tallahassee
Florida Atlantic University, Boca Raton
Florida Gulf Coast University, Ft. Myers
Florida International University, Miami
Florida State University, Tallahassee
New College of Florida, Sarasota
University of Central Florida, Orlando
University of Florida, Gainesville
University of North Florida, Jacksonville
University of South Florida, Tampa
University of West Florida, Pensacola

# SLAVERY AND FREEDOM
## IN THE
# SHENANDOAH VALLEY
## DURING THE
# CIVIL WAR ERA

JONATHAN A. NOYALAS

Foreword by Stanley Harrold and Randall M. Miller

University Press of Florida
Gainesville · Tallahassee · Tampa · Boca Raton
Pensacola · Orlando · Miami · Jacksonville · Ft. Myers · Sarasota

26  25  24  23  22  21    6  5  4  3  2  1

Library of Congress Cataloging-in-Publication Data
Names: Noyalas, Jonathan A., author. | Harrold, Stanley, author of
    foreword. | Miller, Randall M., author or foreword.
Title: Slavery and freedom in the Shenandoah Valley during the Civil War
    era / Jonathan A. Noyalas ; foreword by Stanley Harrold and Randall M.
    Miller.
Other titles: Southern dissent.
Description: Gainesville : University Press of Florida, 2021. | Series:
    Southern dissent | Includes bibliographical references and index.
Identifiers: LCCN 2020044325 (print) | LCCN 2020044326 (ebook) | ISBN
    9780813066868 (hardback) | ISBN 9780813057798 (pdf)
Subjects: LCSH: African Americans—Shenandoah River Valley (Va. and W.
    Va.)—History—19th century. | Free African Americans—Shenandoah River
    Valley (Va. and W. Va.)—History—19th century. | Slavery—Shenandoah
    River Valley (Va. and W. Va.)—History—19th century. | Slavery—United
    States—History—19th century. | Shenandoah River Valley (Va. and W.
    Va.)—History—19th century.
Classification: LCC E185.93.V8 N69 2021 (print) | LCC E185.93.V8 (ebook)
    | DDC 306.3/6209755909034—dc23
LC record available at https://lccn.loc.gov/2020044325
LC ebook record available at https://lccn.loc.gov/2020044326

The University Press of Florida is the scholarly publishing agency for the State University System
of Florida, comprising Florida A&M University, Florida Atlantic University, Florida Gulf Coast
University, Florida International University, Florida State University, New College of Florida,
University of Central Florida, University of Florida, University of North Florida, University of
South Florida, and University of West Florida.

University Press of Florida
2046 NE Waldo Road
Suite 2100
Gainesville, FL 32609
http://upress.ufl.edu

Dedicated with love to the memory of my father—a man who epitomized persistence, courage, and love during his time on this earth

# CONTENTS

# FIGURES

# TABLES

# FOREWORD

The Shenandoah Valley region has long been a place of wonderment to travelers, settlers, and tourists. It also has been a place of mystery and myth that have hidden more than revealed the complicated—and often contradictory—social, cultural, and economic history of a "place" that was in fact many places. For centuries, in travel accounts, in folklore and song, in local histories, and in art and story, travelers and others have described the Shenandoah as a world of farms, ethnic and religious enclaves, and natural beauty that seemed to have little in common with "the South" of plantations and slavery. Even in twentieth-century scholarship, that view of the Shenandoah prevails. The influential historian Carl Bridenbaugh, in *Myths & Realities: Societies of the Colonial South* (1952), spoke for many historians in his descriptions of the Shenandoah as a pathway for thousands of Scots-Irish, Scots, Rhinelanders, Swiss, and other immigrants peopling the back country of the southern colonies, and a patchwork of farms rather than plantations. The variegated population supposedly retained many native tongues and Old World ways, in Bridenbaugh's words, with "each little group" resisting "with all its strength" the Americanizing process (pp. 131–132, 1971 ed.). In such rendering, the Shenandoah was a very diverse place but also a very white one.

One effect of casting the Shenandoah as a region of ethnic and religious diversity and farms, and unlike the Tidewater and other settled areas of "the South" where English and plantation culture ruled, was, paradoxically, to miss or ignore the extent to which that diversity included Africans and then African Americans who made up a significant part of the population in some areas of the region and lived and worked to some degree in all of it. As the story went for years, the Scots-Irish, German-speakers, and other immigrants and migrants who settled in the valley did not want or need African slaves to work their farms; for reasons of culture, conscience, and circumstance they supposedly kept slavery, and blacks, out. Such views of the Shenandoah dominated scholarship—until recently.

As Jonathan Noyalas reveals in his close study of the Shenandoah during the nineteenth century, blacks throughout the region were significant in numbers, the kinds of work they did, and the culture they created. Rather than anomalies, they were vital to the region's economic and cultural development. Whatever the degree of ethnic and religious diversity in the Shenandoah, race mattered in defining interest and identity. And enslaved Africans and African Americans and free blacks were not passive in the process.

In Noyalas's telling, the different kinds and places of work gave enslaved people in the region a nimbleness in being able to understand and adapt to new and varied circumstances. The alertness and awareness that came from working among whites, and learning their ways, positioned enslaved and free blacks to seize on the unsettlements and upheavals caused by the Civil War that came to the Shenandoah. The region's constant changing of hands as Union and Confederate forces fought to control it created openings for blacks to find freedom in the interstices of white control, and to create new ways to assert their freedom. Whether in running to Union lines or joining the Union army and an ostensible, if still conditional, "freedom," or staying in their home places, blacks, in Noyalas's careful accounting, knew their interests and acted accordingly. They also proved savvy in navigating the adjustments that came with the end of the war and efforts at Reconstruction. Their skill in negotiating to further their interests proved essential in carving out their place and building their own institutions—in defining "freedom" for themselves. White opposition was persistent, and white allies were not always supportive, but blacks did not give up on freedom.

In tracking the experiences of blacks in the Shenandoah during the Civil War era, Noyalas expands the scholarship on African American identity and interest by showing how place and circumstance counted in determining the scope and scale of dissent, resistance, and accommodation. He also points to the need to redraw the profile of "the slave" and then the "freedman" to work in the experiences of and consequences for many blacks who lived and worked among whites and learned their ways rather than on plantations that largely separated black from white and included a black community-building culture in the slave quarters. In the end, Noyalas insists there was no single South or single black experience during slavery, sectional conflict, and its aftermath. "Freedom" was always contingent and contested, and conditioned by circumstance. What this book shows is that for blacks to be free they needed to know their world and themselves and thereby be ready to seize freedom for themselves, whenever and wherever it came.

For all this and more, *Slavery and Freedom in the Shenandoah Valley during the Civil War Era* is a welcome addition to the *Southern Dissent* series.

*Stanley Harrold and Randall M. Miller*
*Series Editors*

# ACKNOWLEDGMENTS

No book is ever the work of a solitary individual. To those whom I express gratitude here, this book would not have been possible without your support, guidance, and encouragement: Adeela Al-Khalili of the Josephine School Museum, who has been a great friend, supporter, and sounding board; James Broomall, director of the George Tyler Moore Center for the Study of the Civil War at Shepherd University, a valued friend and colleague who improved this study through thoughtful comments on aspects of what eventually materialized into the chapter examining the postwar experiences of African Americans; Emmanuel Dabney, curator at Petersburg National Historical Park, who offered his time and talents in tracking down important information at the Library of Virginia and the Virginia Museum of History and Culture; Rebecca Ebert, archivist at the Stewart Bell, Jr. Archives, who has always supported my scholarly endeavors; Jake Gabriele, one of the best undergraduate research assistants I have ever had at Shenandoah University and who offered valuable assistance with this project; Penny Imeson, executive director of the Harrisonburg-Rockingham Historical Society; Hal Jespersen, who prepared the map of the Shenandoah Valley for this book; Norma Johnson of the Josephine School Museum; the staff at the Library of Virginia; Mary Morris, the font of knowledge for all things related to Clarke County's history; and colleagues of the Virginia Forum, who have offered splendid comments throughout the years on various aspects of this research.

Additionally, I wish to express my deepest gratitude to my wonderful colleagues in the history department at Shenandoah University: Jeff Coker (dean of the College of Arts & Sciences, who is among my biggest supporters at Shenandoah University), and Ann Denkler, Julie Hofmann, and Warren Hofstra, who have offered encouragement. I am especially grateful to Ann for all of the conversations we have had about slavery in the Shenandoah Valley. Those discussions with Ann have sharpened my thinking.

Special thanks are also due to Randall Miller and Stanley Harrold, who have been extremely supportive of this project and encouraged me along the way. Additionally, I am appreciative of the anonymous peer reviewers and the wonderful staff, especially Sian Hunter, at the University Press of Florida.

Last, but certainly not least, I wish to thank my family—especially my wonderful son Alex, my buddy who keeps me hopping, and the better part of me, my wife Brandy, a fine historian in her own right. Her thoughts and keen historical eye have made this book significantly better. I could not have completed this project without her and there is no one with whom I would rather travel through life's journey.

# ABBREVIATIONS

| | |
|---|---|
| AARFA | Abby Aldrich Rockefeller Folk Art Museum, Colonial Williamsburg Foundation, Williamsburg, VA |
| BRF&AL | Bureau of Refugees, Freedmen, and Abandoned Lands, National Archives and Records Administration, Washington, DC |
| CCHA | Clarke County Historical Association, Berryville, VA |
| EFPSU | Historical Collections and Labor Archives, Eberly Family Special Collections Library, Pennsylvania State University, State College, PA |
| HLHU | Houghton Library, Harvard University, Cambridge, MA |
| HRHS | Harrisonburg-Rockingham Historical Society, Dayton, VA |
| LOC | Library of Congress, Washington, DC |
| LVA | Library of Virginia |
| NARA | National Archives & Records Administration, Washington, DC |
| NHC | Newtown History Center, Stephens City, VA |
| OHS | Ohio Historical Society, Columbus, OH |
| O.R. | *Official Records of the War of the Rebellion* |
| RHMJCPL | General Robert H. Milroy Papers, Jasper County Public Library, Rensselaer, IN |
| SBAHL | Stewart Bell, Jr. Archives, Handley Regional Library, Winchester, VA |
| SHC | Southern Historical Collection, University of North Carolina, Chapel Hill, NC |
| UMO | University of Miami, Ohio, Oxford, OH |

| | |
|---|---|
| VDHR | Virginia Department of Historic Resources |
| VHS | Virginia Historical Society |
| WFJJC | Winchester-Frederick County Joint Judicial Center, Winchester, VA |
| WRCM | Warren Rifles Confederate Museum, Front Royal, VA |
| WRPLDU | William R. Perkins Library, Duke University, Durham, NC |

# Introduction

On a cold, rainy day in February 2018, I had the great fortune to lead a team of my students from Shenandoah University on an important mission in Middletown, Virginia, marking potential burial sites of enslaved people and mapping the Mount Zion African American Cemetery. For decades this cemetery, which contains the graves of enslaved individuals from the Civil War era, had been taken over by Mother Nature and largely forgotten until an effort by the Middletown Heritage Society, led by Ellen Gant, who has family members buried in the cemetery, and Joan Roche, started a movement to clean up Mount Zion. As I worked with students uncovering simple stones that denoted the graves of enslaved people, unfortunately unknown, it struck me that this cemetery's condition and location—situated in a wooded area, in the middle of a farm, hidden from plain sight—served as a metaphor for the story of African Americans during the Civil War era in the Shenandoah Valley.

Furthermore, the experience in Mount Zion underscored the value of examining the past through a more intimate lens. While the majority of grave markers in that cemetery were simple stones with no markings, efforts in that burial ground uncovered a more traditional tombstone, cracked from its base and over time pressed into the earth. A brush of the hand revealed the name Caroline Jenkins chiseled into the stone along with her death date of August 30, 1907, and the epitaph "God's finger touched her and she slept." Eighty-three years old at the time of her death, Caroline had been enslaved for almost the first four decades of her life in Middletown. For her final four decades Caroline, along with her husband Abraham, who had also been enslaved, attempted to realize freedom's potential in an environment where its meaning was frequently distorted and elusive. While the broad studies historians have produced that examine the African American experience during the Civil War era are significant, they can sometimes, as historian Edward Ayers noted, "blur into generalizations" and broad "categories," and lose sight of the personal battles of living, breathing human beings in the struggle to overcome oppression.[1] At times in a sweeping survey one can lose sight of the manner in which, as Gordon Rhea argued, seemingly "insignificant players" could "alter the course of history."[2]

The region in which Caroline Jenkins lived, labored, and died, the Shenandoah Valley, lends itself well as an inimitable laboratory to study the African American experience during the Civil War era. Not only does it afford an opportunity for a more intimate interaction with individuals long forgotten, but the Valley's wartime experience is arguably without parallel. Not only was the conflict omnipresent in the Shenandoah due to its importance as a source of provender for the Army of Northern Virginia, but also because of its strategic significance to Union and Confederate forces. For Confederates, the Shenandoah Valley served the role of diversionary theater of war and avenue of invasion. For the Union, the Valley served as a place from which to guard Washington, DC, and block invasion. By the summer of 1864, Union war planners recognized the necessity of seizing the Shenandoah Valley as an important step in crushing the Army of Northern Virginia. Caught in the midst of invading armies, tramping soldiers, occupations, destruction, and incessant fighting were the Shenandoah Valley's enslaved and free blacks. Studying the African American experience in the Shenandoah Valley brings greater clarity to how enslaved and free blacks during our nation's most tumultuous moment navigated life in an incessantly unsettled world where one day they could be in Union territory, the next Confederate, and the following in no-man's land. The lives of African Americans in the Shenandoah Valley sharply highlights the fact that emancipation was a contingent, individual process. That history also stresses that freedom was, and still is, extremely fragile.

Much has been written about the Civil War era in the Shenandoah Valley, that nearly 180-mile swath bounded on the west by the Allegheny Mountains and the Blue Ridge Mountains on the east, stretching from Harpers Ferry in the north to Rockbridge County in the south, but the story of how African Americans reacted to, were impacted by, and influenced events leading up to the conflict, during the Civil War, and in its immediate aftermath has largely been hidden. The African American story has remained concealed partially because it has been ignored, but also because various authors since the war's end have obfuscated historical reality for the Shenandoah's African Americans during our nation's defining moment.

Among those culpable for suppressing the historical reality of life for African Americans during the Civil War era was Joseph Waddell, publisher

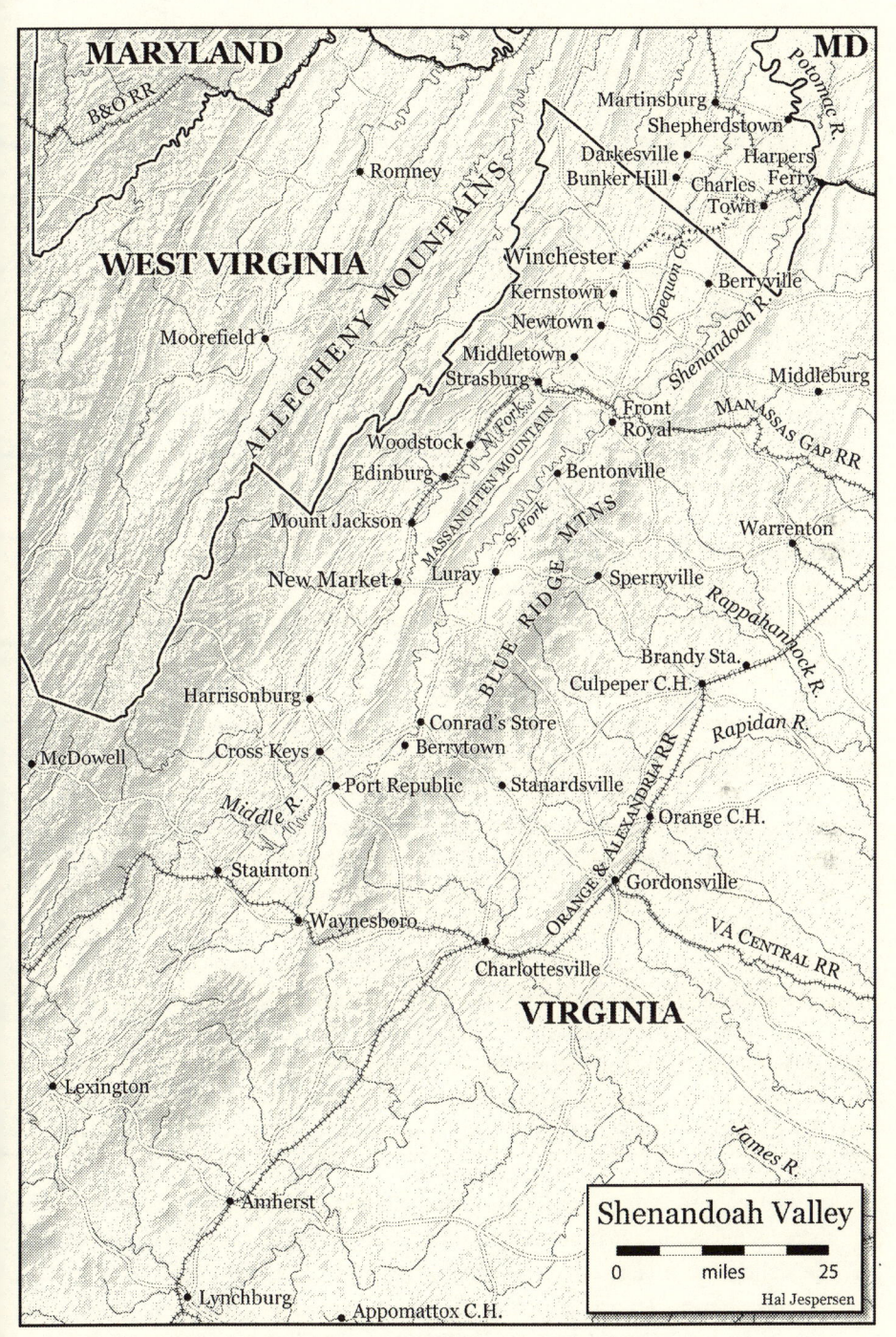

Figure I.1. Map of Shenandoah Valley (Courtesy Hal Jespersen).

of the *Staunton Spectator*, who enslaved three people at the Civil War's outset.[3] Two decades after the war's end Waddell published *Annals of Augusta County*, a book that proved a cornerstone of early scholarship on the Valley. Waddell informed readers that "the institution of slavery never had a strong hold" in Augusta County due to the fact that the Valley had largely been settled by people of Scots-Irish and German ancestry. "The Scotch-Irish race had no love for it [slavery], and German people were generally averse to it. Most farmers cultivate their own lands with the assistance of their sons," Waddell explained.[4] Twenty-one years after publication of Waddell's *Annals*, John Walter Wayland made similar arguments in his *The German Element of the Shenandoah Valley of Virginia*. "As a rule, the Germans of the Shenandoah Valley were opposed to slavery," Wayland concluded.[5] Without any critical analysis of her own, author Julia Davis accepted Waddell's and Wayland's conclusions as she repeated the claim in her 1945 book *The Shenandoah*. Davis penned, "The thrifty Germans found it [slavery] wasteful; the Scotch-Irish used but few."[6]

In the early 1980s W. Fitzhugh Brundage, then a PhD candidate at Harvard University, spent his time as the Mary Moody Northern Fellow at the Stonewall Jackson House in Lexington, Virginia, investigating attitudes toward slavery in antebellum Rockbridge County. Among the issues Brundage investigated was the myth of the Scots-Irish possessing an aversion to slavery. Brundage's careful analysis exposed a world vastly different from the ones described by Waddell, Wayland, and Davis. In Rockbridge, a place that boasted a minimum of two-thirds of its white inhabitants claiming Scots-Irish descent, Brundage discovered a vibrant slave economy, one that began to boom during the American Revolution as a result of the Continental Army's need for hemp.[7]

Similarly, Waddell's and Wayland's claims that few enslaved people lived and worked in the Shenandoah Valley echo through much of the literature. Davis mimicked Waddell and Wayland when she wrote that there "were comparatively few slaves along the Shenandoah . . . the Germans had never considered it economical to own Negroes."[8] Slightly more than two decades later Laura Virginia Hale, a local historian from Front Royal, Virginia, compiled a massive chronicle, *Four Valiant Years in the Lower Shenandoah Valley*. Her volume, which appears in many bibliographies of books published since its release in 1968, not only claims a lack of importance for slavery in the Valley, but makes broad statements that the relationship between enslaver and enslaved was always genial. Hale wrote, "The Valley was not a large slave-holding section . . . No two races ever lived in such harmony as the white and black people."[9] Robert Tanner's *Stonewall in the Valley*, published eight years after Hale's tome, also dismisses slavery's importance in the region and notes that by the time of the Civil War's outbreak "slavery had long been declining throughout the Valley, and what few slaves remained were among the best treated of the South."[10]

First and foremost, there were hardly "a few slaves" living in the Valley by the time the Civil War began, as Tanner suggests. Enslaved people comprised approximately 25 percent of the total population of the Shenandoah Valley's ten counties at the Civil War's outset, including Berkeley and Jefferson, which in 1863 officially became part of West Virginia.[11] As this book's first chapter shows, from the time of the first federal census in 1790 until 1860 the number of enslaved people steadily increased, with slight dips between 1830 and 1840 and 1850 and 1860. These declines, as addressed in chapters 1 and 2, might partially be a response to heightened anxieties in the wake of Nat Turner's revolt in 1831 and John Brown's attack on Harpers Ferry twenty-eight years later.

Furthermore, the claim that "slaves remained among . . . the best treated of the South" also proves problematic. Less than a decade after Confederate armies surrendered, the once-enslaved John Quincy Adams, who fled Frederick County, Virginia, for Pennsylvania during Union general John W. Geary's brief presence in the Valley in 1862, published his reminiscences—a rare account from one of the Shenandoah's formerly enslaved people. Adams wrote that his enslaver's daughters "were very good and kind to me." Adams even believed that had Virginia law not prohibited literacy among enslaved people, that they "would have taught me to read if they could have their way."[12] Proponents of the Lost Cause narrative of the Civil War era might undoubtedly see Adams's statement as evidence of slavery's benevolence; however, a full reading of his narrative reveals that although he believed some members of his enslaver's family treated him well, he still resented his enslavement. Adams, who never reported being beaten or family members being battered, regarded his owner and all those who enslaved human beings as "wicked people."[13]

Physical abuse has too often been used as the litmus test for measuring slavery's barbarity. Although it is difficult to quantify the extent to which enslavers employed physical abuse as a means of control, significant evidence exists which shows that violence against enslaved people did indeed occur in the Valley. One of the points of this book's first chapter, which provides an overview of slavery in the Shenandoah Valley stretching back to colonial times, is to highlight the physical abuse endured by enslaved individuals and establish that the treatment African Americans confronted during the Civil War and its immediate aftermath merely continued a long-established pattern in the area. Furthermore, it is important to keep in mind that abuse comes in many forms. Despite Adams's assessment that members of his enslaver's family treated him well, the experience of seeing his twin brother Aaron and sister Sallie "sold from us at Winchester" on the eve of the Civil War proved torturous—so much so that Adams, at least for a moment in his life, hoped for death as a means "to get rid of" his "sorrow and distress."[14] Like all enslaved people, Adams understood that torment took many forms. Even if an enslaved person did not suffer any physical or psychological torment—a rarity—the mere act of one human being owning another proved unconscionable. As Harriet Beecher Stowe wrote in *Uncle Tom's Cabin*, "the *thing itself* [slavery] is the essence of all abuse!"[15] Making statements then, as some historians have done previously, that enslaved people in the Shenandoah Valley enjoyed better treatment than elsewhere in the South is simply callous, cold-hearted, and reveals a lack of nuanced understanding of the complex relationship between enslaver and enslaved.

Some historians, such as Michael Mahon, have professed that the "employment of slaves was largely unnecessary" in the Shenandoah Valley by the time of the war's outbreak.[16] This too is in error. Historian Kenneth Koons, one of the most distinguished scholars of Shenandoah Valley agricultural history, provides convincing evidence through careful analysis of census and other data that enslaved laborers proved a crucial cog in the Valley's agricultural machine on the eve of the Civil War. "Slaves and free blacks formed a significant labor force in the antebellum Valley of Virginia," Koons argued. He continued: "Together, through their labor, free and enslaved African Americans contributed to the rise and continuing development of the Valley of Virginia as a highly productive agricultural region that a few years later would gain renown as 'the breadbasket of the Confederacy.'"[17]

As discussed in this book's opening chapter, slavery in the Shenandoah Valley might not be comparable to areas such as Virginia's Tidewater or South Carolina's Lowcountry in terms of the average numbers of people enslaved per household or the amount of acreage cultivated by enslaved people, but slavery proved important to the Shenandoah Valley's life and economy. Simply put, slavery was, as one historian concluded, "ingrained in the Valley's economy."[18] On the Civil War's eve one out of every five Valley residents was enslaved. Additionally, the number of enslaved individuals in the Valley increased by an unknown quantity at various points throughout the year as whites rented enslaved people to perform various seasonal tasks on farms and in local industries, most notably iron furnaces.[19] "The Valley," as historian Stephen Longenecker wrote, "was as typical on race and labor as any other Southern region . . . conditions for slaves were more similar to the rest of the South than different."[20]

While historians such as Koons, Longenecker, Edward Ayers, Jonathan Berkey, Susanne Simmons, Nancy Sorrells, and myself have made some gains in revealing elements of the complexity of the African American story in the Shenandoah Valley during the Civil War era, no single study exists that chronicles the African American experience in the Shenandoah Valley during our nation's most tumultuous moment. To date the best resources for understanding aspects of the African American experience are Edward Ayers's two outstanding volumes, *In the Presence of Mine Enemies* and *The Thin Light of Freedom*. As important as both of these studies are, however, they only reveal insights into the African American experience in Augusta County—located in the southern, or upper, Shenandoah Valley—as part of a broader study about how the Civil War era impacted all individuals living in Augusta and Franklin County, Pennsylvania. Ayers's instant classics do little to shed light on the experiences of African Americans in the northern, or lower, Shenandoah Valley, where on January 5, 1863, Union general Robert Milroy began enforcing President Abraham Lincoln's Emancipation Proclamation. Additionally, the lower Valley experienced the bulk of significant military operations during the conflict and thus African Americans who lived there experienced the conflict differently than those in Augusta County, an area less in a state of flux throughout the war. Although part of the same Shenandoah Valley, the experiences of African Americans in the northern Valley compared to its southern reaches made it seem as if they were a world away.

While this history builds on earlier works such as Ayers's studies and other scholars mentioned previously, I have made extensive use of untapped primary material in constructing this volume. Anyone who researches African American history understands the difficulties inherent in the task. In his outstanding study *The Calculus of Violence*, historian Aaron Sheehan-Dean notes that historians who explore African American history are customarily relegated to using "the passing observations of soldiers and civilians" to reconstruct the lives of enslaved individuals and free blacks.[21] While this study indeed utilizes letters and diaries of white soldiers and white civilians, Union and Confederate, it also employs previously untapped evidence that offers a compelling look into the lives of the Valley's African Americans. Underutilized or never before used primary material such as interviews

Union soldiers conducted with enslaved people who fled enslavers in late 1861 and early 1862 housed in General Nathaniel P. Banks's papers at the Library of Congress, thousands of documents from the Freedmen's Bureau's operations in the lower Shenandoah Valley, and service records of United States Colored Troops who hailed from the Shenandoah Valley inform this study. Although extremely rare, freedom narratives from two people once enslaved in the Shenandoah Valley, Bethany Veney and John Quincy Adams, lend an African American voice. Valley historians have used Veney's *The Narrative of Bethany Veney: A Slave Woman*, published in 1890, to better understand the African American experience in the Valley. While powerful, her narrative covers the experiences of African Americans prior to the conflict. Adams's *Narrative of the Life of John Quincy Adams: When in Slavery, and Now as a Freeman*, published in 1872, presents a firsthand account of his experience and that of his family during the conflict in Frederick County. Despite the richness of Adams's narrative, it has been neglected by scholars. Use of these materials, along with newspapers and analysis of census data, comprise the corpus of evidence utilized to chronicle the African American experience in the Shenandoah Valley during the Civil War era.

This study aims to examine the various ways enslaved people in the years leading up to and during four years of war resisted their enslavement. Sometimes that resistance took rather overt forms, from arson in the wake of John Brown's raid, a moment that various historians contend elicited little response from the Valley's enslaved population, to planning insurrection against Confederate forces that occupied Winchester in the war's opening months or fleeing bondage.[22] At other times this book reveals that some enslaved people chose more passive options during the era, such as gambling or killing an enslaver's livestock.

Additionally, this work illuminates the uncertain nature of freedom and how the region's African Americans navigated that ambiguity in a region that experienced numerous battles, occupations, skirmishes, and raids—326, by one accounting.[23] This study illustrates that uncertainties about freedom appeared not only during Confederate occupations but Union ones as well, particularly General Robert Patterson's presence in the Valley in the spring and summer of 1861. Collaterally, this study offers insight into not only how enslaved people viewed Union troops, but traces the evolution of Union policy toward African Americans in a region war-planners in Washington, DC, deemed important to the capital's safety as well as the broader Union war effort.

As this book contends, however, while the region's African Americans certainly viewed Union troops and the federal government as great allies in their quest for freedom during the conflict and its immediate wake, they were not passive in their pursuit of emancipation. Quite the contrary. Whether fleeing bondage to enlist in United States Colored Troop regiments, serving as spies for Union officers in the Valley, working as laborers, teaching in Freedmen's Schools after the war, raising money to support those schools, or organizing Emancipation Day celebrations, the region's African Americans were active participants in their quest for liberty.

For all of their efforts and any progress they might have made in resisting injustice and inequality, the Valley's African Americans confronted numerous obstacles during the Civil War era. Whether free blacks, as evidenced in chapter 4, were captured by Confederates and enslaved, or contended with angry former Confederates who tried to erect impediments to education in the conflict's aftermath, as examined in chapter 7, the challenges the Shenandoah Valley's African Americans confronted seemed at times insurmountable. However, patience, persistence, and a firm belief that they stood on the right side of history kept hope alive.

From this book rise new heroes, individuals long forgotten and now resurrected—Robert Orrick, Thomas Laws, Edward Hall, and Caroline Jenkins, to name a few. This study reveals stories of determination among people who suffered unquantifiable horrors and injustice. Finally, from this book comes confirmation, as one former Shenandoah Valley slave observed after the conflict, that "nothing is more glorious to know" than that an individual is "free."[24]

# 1

## "In the Land of Bondage"

In 1727, at a time when the first white settlers began trickling into the Shenandoah Valley to establish permanent settlements, the first enslaved people came to the Valley—not to labor for an enslaver, but seeking freedom. This group of fifteen enslaved people fled their master east of the Blue Ridge Mountains and settled near Lexington, Virginia. For a time, they enjoyed freedom, built homes, and farmed the land. Unfortunately, they were discovered and returned to slavery. However, as slavery increased in numbers and importance in the ensuing decades, enslaved people no longer viewed the Shenandoah Valley as a refuge, but as place from which to escape.[1]

Although it is extremely "difficult to document" enslaved people in the colonial era in the Shenandoah Valley, as Warren Hofstra, one of the most preeminent scholars on settlement in the Shenandoah Valley noted in his groundbreaking study *The Planting of New Virginia*, evidence indicates the presence of a growing number of enslaved people living and laboring in the Valley decades prior to the American Revolution. Some of the first enslaved people sent to labor in the Shenandoah Valley came from Virginia's Tidewater—the surplus labor of enslavers such as Robert "King" Carter and his heirs, who owned 60,000 acres in the lower Shenandoah Valley by the time of Carter's death in 1732.[2] Records, such as a 1754 census of tithables for Frederick County, which at the time covered the area of the present-day Virginia counties of Frederick, Clarke, Shenandoah, and Warren and the West Virginia counties of Hardy, Hampshire, Berkeley, and Jefferson, reveals that among the approximately 9,380 inhabitants of Frederick, 680 were enslaved.[3] Slavery's importance in the Valley increased during the American Revolution as a result of the Continental Army's need for hemp.[4] In Rockbridge County, which at the time of the Revolutionary War was part of Augusta County, 600 enslaved people were counted among the county's 3,700 inhabitants by war's end.[5]

Table 1.1. Shenandoah Valley enslaved population, 1790–1860

| Census Year | Enslaved Population | Percentage of total population enslaved |
| --- | --- | --- |
| 1790 | 10,715 | 16.7% |
| 1800 | 14,493 | 18.7% |
| 1810 | 18,611 | 23.7% |
| 1820 | 23,105 | 25.9% |
| 1830 | 25,745 | 26.1% |
| 1840 | 24,495 | 25.5% |
| 1850 | 27,402 | 24.4% |
| 1860 | 24,779 | 20.4% |

*Sources*: The figures in this table are derived from "Population of Virginia in 1790," accessed June 1, 2019, http://www.virginiaplaces.org/population/pop1790numbers.html; "Population of Virginia in 1800," accessed June 1, 2019, http://www.virginiaplaces.org/population/pop1800numbers.html; "Population of Virginia in 1810," accessed June 1, 2019, http://www.virginiaplaces.org/population/pop1810numbers.html; "Population of Virginia in 1820," accessed June 1, 2019, http://www.virginiaplaces.org/population/pop1820numbers.html; "Population of Virginia in 1830," accessed June 1, 2019, http://www.virginiaplaces.org/population/pop1830numbers.html; "Population of Virginia in 1840," accessed June 1, 2019, http://www.virginiaplaces.org/population/pop1840numbers.html; "Population of Virginia in 1850," accessed June 1, 2019, http://www.virginiaplaces.org/population/pop1850numbers.html; "Population of Virginia in 1860," accessed June 1, 2019, http://www.virginiaplaces.org/population/pop1860numbers.html.

By the time of the first census of the United States in 1790, enslaved people accounted for 16.7 percent of the Valley's population—10,175 out of a total population of 85,502. Over the ensuing decades the Valley's enslaved population steadily increased. By 1820 the number of slaves counted among the Shenandoah's populace more than doubled, to 23,105. Enslaved people now accounted for 25.9 percent (23,105 out of 111,401) of the region's total population. That percentage increased slightly during the following decade to 26.1 percent (25,745 out of 124,094). The steady growth prompted a reporter for the *Richmond Examiner* to state in 1845 that as the number of enslaved people swelled in the Valley the divide between eastern and western Virginia closed. "The Valley region and the East are now identified in interest, so far as slave property is concerned . . . Indeed, in the whole Valley, the slave population [is] greatly augmented," the correspondent noted.[6]

By 1850 the Valley's enslaved population reached 27,402; however, by 1860 the number dipped to 24,709. While that decline could be superficially interpreted as a sign of slavery's decreasing importance in the region, it might also be attributed to heightened anxieties of slave insurrection in the wake of John Brown's attack on Harpers Ferry in 1859, something examined in much greater detail in the next chapter. The only other time the Shenandoah Valley recorded a decline in its enslaved population was between 1830 and 1840. Over that time span the number of slaves decreased by 1,250. That decline could have been partially a result of intensified concerns in the wake of Nat Turner's Revolt in the summer of 1831.[7]

Sometimes, whether during the decades when slavery declined or during periods when the number of enslaved people increased overall, cases exist of enslavers selling their enslaved not because enslavers developed a spontaneous moral aversion to slavery, but because it proved economically necessary. For instance, in January 1858, Newtown merchant George W. Lemley sold three people whom he enslaved (Martha, an adult female and her two children, George and Jennie) to Joseph Long to avoid financial ruin.[8] Other enslavers manumitted slaves upon their death, among them Frederick County wagon-maker John Grove. In his will Grove ordered that his enslaved laborer Jesse Helms "shall be free at the decease of myself and wife and that one hundred dollars be paid to him out of my estate by my executors as soon as convenient."[9] While Grove's manumission might be superficially interpreted as a benevolent act, the fact that Helms's freedom would not come until both John Grove and his wife passed might also be construed as Grove's attempt to reduce Helms's risk of escape while enslaved. As historian T. Stephen Whitman concluded in his examination of manumission in Maryland, the act of manumission by will "may well have been motivated . . . by desire to forestall flight and secure further uninterrupted service."[10]

Despite the fluctuations that occurred from 1790 to 1860, enslaved people accounted for approximately one-quarter of the Valley's population from 1820 until the Civil War's outbreak. Remarkably, despite that statistical evidence, the perspective that slavery never took hold in the Shenandoah Valley, nor proved an integral component to its economy, persists. In the early 2000s historian Ann Denkler, during research for *Sustaining Identity, Recapturing Heritage*, interviewed individuals from Page County whose families once enslaved individuals and discovered that people either denied that their ancestors did so, or "underplayed the institution in the county." Denkler regularly received the response from individuals to whom she spoke: "There just weren't many slaves here."[11]

While it is true that the numbers of enslaved people counted between the first United States census in 1790 and 1860 are comparatively less than Virginia's Tidewater region, where enslaved individuals accounted for more than half of the total population, the fact that fewer enslaved people lived and labored in the Valley should not singularly discount its importance, enslaved peoples' sufferings, and their desire for freedom. Additionally, utilizing the decreases in the enslaved population between either 1830 and 1840 or 1850 and 1860 as an indicator of slavery's importance is simplistic, and does not fully capture slavery's significance. For example, in 1850 Augusta County's Rev. Francis McFarland enslaved four individuals who aided in operating his 135-acre farm, Rosemont. By 1852, for reasons not entirely clear, McFarland divested himself of his human property. However, although McFarland no longer enslaved people, he still relied on the labor of enslaved individuals and rented enslaved laborers—a practice that occurred in the Shenandoah Valley as early as the 1740s.[12]

Reconstructing rental practices is rather difficult, because, as historians J. Susanne Simmons and Nancy T. Sorrells noted in their groundbreaking essay on the hiring of enslaved laborers in Augusta County, agreements made between an enslaver and a renter "were private rather than public agreements, often written on scraps of paper."[13] Fortunately, some of those scraps exist. On December 28, 1850, Thornton McLeod, a resident of Newtown (present-day Stephens City), entered into an agreement with Joseph Long, a wealthy farmer and one of the community's largest enslavers, to rent a female slave, Ann, for one year. McLeod agreed to pay Long $10.[14] Although scholarship indicates that hiring contracts such as the one between McLeod and Long proved typical in terms of duration—one year—some whites rented enslaved laborers for shorter stints during the most labor-intensive moments of the year. For wheat growers in the Shenandoah Valley, June and early July, harvest time, and late December to early January, when threshing occurred, proved popular hiring times for those who did not enter into annual agreements.[15]

In addition to variations in the duration of hiring agreements, the locales from which whites rented enslaved laborers varied. While Thornton McLeod rented from an enslaver in his community, other Valley residents rented from enslavers in other Valley counties. For example, Hamilton Gibson, a Frederick County wagon-maker, rented enslaved laborers from Eliza Page in neighboring Clarke County.[16] Others hired enslaved laborers from other parts of the Old Dominion.[17]

The fee renters paid also varied. While the female McLeod rented from Long commanded only $10 annually, a hired male farm laborer could cost as much as $120 per year in the mid-1850s.[18] Enslaved laborers rented by owners of the Valley's many iron forges cost between $80 and $110 annually.[19] Female enslaved laborers commanded between $60 and $75 and young girls anywhere from $20 to $45 in the decade prior to the Civil War.[20]

Slave-hiring not only proved cost-effective for renters, but proved financially lucrative for enslavers too. Renting provided enslavers an opportunity to earn extra income from surplus enslaved laborers.[21] In January 1857, Winchester's Mary Greenhow Lee advertised that she had "for the present year, a smart active BOY between thirteen and fourteen years of age" available "for hire."[22] Although unclear if anyone ever rented the unnamed male, Lee could have earned as much as $80.[23] For some enslavers, finding someone to hire their enslaved laborers proved critical to their financial security. Staunton's Dr. E. Berkeley noted in a letter to his brother Robert in early March 1850 that in addition to his medical practice, he depended upon the income he received from hiring out his enslaved.[24]

Because the hires of enslaved people proved critical to their annual income, enslavers took steps to ensure their enslaved laborers were properly cared for during the duration of the agreement. Owners demanded that enslaved laborers be properly fed, clothed, and cared for. When Newtown's Joseph Long entered into an agreement with Thornton McLeod he demanded that his enslaved woman Ann receive "sufficient diet, lodging and the usual clothing and . . . a new suit of strong winter clothes [and] blanket."[25] Some enslavers even attempted to break hiring contracts when they believed the person to whom they rented placed the enslaved laborer at risk. For instance, when E. M. Eskridge, an enslaver from east of the Blue Ridge Mountains in Fauquier County, learned that one of the enslaved laborers he rented to William Weaver's iron furnace in Rockbridge County had suffered a leg injury, he demanded the enslaved man not return to work until completely healthy.[26]

Perhaps occurrences such as this one fueled statements from chroniclers such as Waddell, Wayland, and Davis that the Valley's enslaved population was "well treated."[27] While evidence corroborates that enslavers looked out for the health of their enslaved laborers, whether they rented them or utilized the labor themselves, the question should be asked: Why did white enslavers express that concern? While some enslavers, as historian Todd Savitt argued, might have done so for humanitarian reasons, protecting one's investment also motivated enslavers to demand laborers they rented be cared for properly.[28]

Enslavers in the Shenandoah Valley also did things that could be interpreted as treating their enslaved well, when in actuality they were done to protect their investment. Evidence shows that Augusta County's Rev. McFarland purchased a basket from an individual whom he enslaved and tipped another person working on a stagecoach. Offering enslaved individuals financial rewards proved not only beneficial to the enslaved, but the enslaver. Rewards, as J. Susanne Simmons and Nancy Sorrells have concluded, helped promote "orderliness and discipline" among enslaved people and lessened the likelihood that enslaved individuals would flee.[29] Like the concern enslavers exhibited about the health of rented enslaved laborers, these rewards were meant to protect an investment. Enslaved individuals utilized the small financial rewards to purchase items that made their existence in slavery slightly better. Matthew Greer, who is engaged in a multi-year archaeological investigation at Belle Grove Plantation in Middletown, Virginia, notes that in his examination of ledgers from various merchants in the northern Shenandoah Valley between 1795 and the start of the Civil War, enslaved people used money they received from enslavers either as financial rewards or compensation for the purchase of products, such as alcohol, sugar, molasses, and textiles.[30] Archaeological evidence uncovered by Greer and his team also reveals that enslaved people purchased other items, including buttons, jewelry, and ceramics.[31]

Among the handful of accounts that survive from the Shenandoah Valley's enslaved, some note that from a material perspective, their enslavers did indeed take care of them. John Quincy Adams, an enslaved male from Frederick County born in 1845, wrote in his *Narrative*, published in 1872, that his enslavers, the Calomese family, "were very good and kind to me."[32] Similarly, Bethany Veney, an enslaved female from Page County who had been enslaved by various individuals, explained in her *Narrative* that some of those who enslaved her were "kind to me."[33] A former enslaved person from Augusta County, identified as "Mrs. Mary E.— Wsey," told an interviewer working for the WPA Slave Narrative project that her enslavers, William and Susan Marshall, treated all of those whom they enslaved "good."[34]

If examinations of the treatment of enslaved individuals in the Shenandoah Valley stopped with those statements, then assertions promulgated by authors such as Waddell, Wayland, and Davis, who minimized slavery's importance in the Shenandoah Valley and wrote that enslavers treated enslaved people kindly, would be valid. However, accounts left by the same enslaved individuals who attested to being given what they needed materially recognized that kindness had its limits. Although Mrs. Mary explained that her enslavers treated her and other enslaved people well, the Marshalls only did so in order to protect the investment they made in slave property. Mary noted that so long as those the Marshall family enslaved were healthy and could work, they gave them all they needed. When any of the enslaved people became ill or too old to perform their tasks the Marshalls sold the enslaved person, squeezing out one final profit from their human chattel. After Mary informed the interviewer, "Yes, they were good when you could work but when you got sick they sold you," she related a story about her aunt. After being stricken with some type of fever, Mary recalled that her aunt became "feeble minded." No longer able to work, Marshall "sold her" to an unidentified slave trader. Mary never saw her aunt after that moment.[35]

John Quincy Adams too recognized that his enslavers treated all of their slaves well not necessarily out of a sense of humanity, but in an effort to protect an asset. Adams recalled that at various moments his enslavers went "around sometimes and put their hands on one of the little negroes, and say, 'here is $1,000, or $1,500 or $2,000.'"[36]

In short, the "kindness" that existing narratives record was limited to really providing the basic necessities of life—food, shelter, and clothing to protect an enslaver's property. Bethany Veney wrote that while she was enslaved she defined kindness dramatically different than what she enjoyed after she attained her freedom in 1858. "I then counted kindness, never whipping or starving me; but it was not what a free-born white child would have found comforting or needful."[37] Like other enslaved people throughout the Shenandoah Valley, Veney also enjoyed a modicum of freedom in her mobility, being allowed to move "for a good distance about the country" so long as she carried a pass signed by her enslaver at the time, David McCoy, permitting her to travel for various errands. The pass she carried allowed her to journey from one place to another within a defined geographic space, but also marked her as McCoy's property, offering some safeguard from someone kidnapping and selling her. While Veney admitted that this pass allowed her "a good degree of freedom," it was still limited freedom. The more she carried that pass on various errands the more she "desired . . . a life where" she would "need no pass written by a human hand to insure my safety as I went from place to place, but where the stamp of my humanity, imprinted by the Infinite . . . Father of all, should be an all-sufficient guarantee in every emergency."[38] Discussions of kindness then do not necessarily reveal an enslaver's humanity toward an enslaved person, but expose

Figure 1.1. Bethany Veney (*The Narrative of Bethany Veney*, 1889).

the various methods enslavers employed to secure their investment in slave property.

When those efforts did not yield the results enslavers desired, evidence indicates that some turned to abuse. Melinda Ruffin, an enslaved female from Waynesboro born in 1839, recalled that various members of her family, "Ant Polly, Uncle Bob, Henry," were whipped "every morning before they eat [a] mouthful." Their backs had been so terribly beaten that Ruffin stated her mother had to rub "grease" on their "back to git de shirt on" and to "keep it from sticking" to the wounds.[39] Even Bethany Veney, who wrote that some of her enslavers treated her with kindness, could not escape physical abuse. As a young girl she had been badly beaten by David Kibbler. After Veney's original owner, James Fletcher, passed away, she became the legal property of Fletcher's daughter Lucy. After Lucy's sister Nasenath married Kibbler,

Lucy moved in with Kibbler and took Veney with her. Although Lucy's property, Veney recognized that as part of Kibbler's household she "was really under his direction and subject to his control, almost as much as if he and not Miss Lucy had owned me."[40] Regarded by Veney as "a man of most violent temper," she noted that one day, when she was approximately nine or ten years old, she "was awkward" and did something to enrage Kibbler. Incensed, Kibbler took a "nail-rod" and beat Veney, making her "so lame." After Veney complained to Lucy, someone she described as "kind and tender-hearted," about what Kibbler had done, Lucy confronted Kibbler. Although no record of this discussion exists, it infuriated Kibbler that Veney complained. Angry, he confronted Veney and "beat" her "severely" with a rod in retaliation for speaking to Lucy about the first beating.[41] An enslaved person identified as Emily had done something to enrage her enslaver so much that he struck her over the head with a board. The crack proved so severe that she "developed symptoms of derangement" shortly after she suffered the blow. After eight years of suffering she was taken to the Winchester Medical School, where surgeons tried to fix the fracture to her skull and alleviate her symptoms. The efforts proved futile and Emily died soon after surgery.[42] Augusta County enslaver John M'Cue reportedly "tied up his slaves and whipped them" each Sunday before he left for church, "and left them bound" while he was away.[43]

When David Stallard, an enslaver from Shenandoah County, learned that one of his enslaved males who fled had been captured and was being held in the jail in Woodstock, he intended to punish him in the severest manner possible. After Stallard and another unidentified man took the enslaved man from the jail, they tied him to one of the horses and prepared to drag him home. A white individual identified as "Spillman" witnessed what occurred next. On a "day that was excessively hot," Spillman explained, the enslaved man tried to keep up at first, but "they rode so fast, dragging the man by the rope behind them, that he became perfectly exhausted—fainted—dropped down, and died."[44]

On occasion, the brutality enslavers exhibited toward enslaved individuals prompted some whites to take action. One morning, on an undetermined date prior to 1839, a carpenter from Harrisonburg, Virginia, identified as Kyle, was awakened early to the sounds of the "most piteous moaning and shrieking." When he looked out his bedroom window he saw "a colored woman nearly naked tied to a fence" while the man for whom he performed some repair work, Benjamin Lewis, "was lacerating her." Unnerved by the vicious scene, Kyle "instantly commanded" Lewis to cease, but he refused.

Lewis informed Kyle that he possessed "jurisdiction over his slaves." Lewis also informed Kyle that if he continued to interfere he "would punish him for his interference."[45]

In 1811, John Vance "was returning from [a] mill, in Shenandoah county" when he "heard the cry of murder." The shrill cries also caught the attention of John Morgan and Michael Siglar, who along with Vance hastened toward the sound. As they looked out into a field they spied "a man named Painter . . . beating a negro with a tremendous club, or small handspike, swearing he would kill him." Without hesitation, the men rushed Painter and stopped the beating. When the three white men questioned Painter as to why he acted so brutally he told them that he "had commenced flogging the slave for not getting to work soon enough." Painter also shared that when he initially chastised the enslaved person and alerted him that he was going to be beaten, the enslaved man took "refuge under a pile of rails that were on some timbers up a little from the ground." Painter set the rails on fire to coax the slave out. According to Vance the white men convinced Painter, who swore "he would kill him," to sell the slave "to another man."[46]

Beatings and other forms of extreme physical abuse aside, enslavers abused those whom they enslaved in other ways in an effort to exert dominance. For instance, in 1838 Staunton merchant Robert McDowell had become so incensed with one of his enslaved females leaving to visit her children who were enslaved by someone else that he placed "an iron collar around her neck, with horns or prongs extending out on either side, and up, until they met at something like a foot above her head, at which point there was a bell attached." McDowell hoped that this "degraded" form of punishment, oftentimes used by enslavers, would inhibit her "from running away" to see her children.[47]

Abuse of enslaved people could be viewed on a broader scale each autumn as slave traders moved enslaved people south through the Shenandoah Valley to be sold in markets outside of Virginia. In 1812 Marie Carr, a resident of Harrisonburg, observed the horrific scene: "Negro men were driven through the town chained together going South to be sold—women and children following in wagons singing the most mournful songs." Coming from the column Carr heard the enslaved people singing "Look down, look down that lonesome road/Hang down y head an' cry/The best of friends must part sometime/then why not you—and I."[48] Jonas Graybill, an elder in the Brethren Church, observed the ghastly scene of enslaved humans being driven south through the Shenandoah Valley. "In the fall of each year large droves of slaves were taken south . . . the men were handcuffed on the sides

Figure 1.2. "Slave Trader, Sold to Tennessee" by Lewis Miller (The Colonial Williamsburg Foundation. Gift of Dr. and Mrs. Richard M. Kain in memory of George Hay Kain).

of a chain forty or fifty feet long. Each one was just given enough room to walk and to lie down at night to sleep."[49] John Quincy Adams, enslaved in Frederick County, also viewed the horrific spectacle of enslaved humans chained together in large groups and being moved south to markets elsewhere. "I have seen droves of men, women and children, all handcuffed together," Adams wrote, "going to Richmond, Virginia, to be sold again and to hear their cries and groans would make ever tender-hearted man or woman shed tears." Adams further noted that "their masters' hearts were so hard they never cried only when they did not get the price they asked for what they called their property."[50]

When Lewis Miller, an artist from Pennsylvania, passed through the Shenandoah Valley in 1853 he sketched enslaved people marching from Staunton to market in Tennessee. In addition to the powerful image of approximately twenty enslaved individuals being driven south by two white men on horseback, Lewis included a lengthy caption at the bottom of the image. "The company going to Tennessee from Staunton, Augusta County, the law of Virginia suffered them go on. I was astonished at this boldness," Lewis wrote, "the carrier Stopped a moment, then Ordered the march. I Saw the play it is commonly in this State, with the negro in droves Sold."[51]

Evidence indicates that enslaved people did not passively accept their enslavement and varying forms of abuse—they resisted. Some resistance proved extreme. For example, on Valentine's Day, 1842, Martin and Captain, two males enslaved by Page County's John Wesley Bell, murdered Bell. How much planning went into it is unclear, but when Bell checked on Martin's and Captain's progress in cutting bushes, Martin struck Bell in the head with an axe. After killing Bell, the two men threw Bell's body into the Shenandoah River. At first authorities ruled Bell's death an accidental drowning, however, further investigation revealed that Martin and Captain murdered Bell. A court presided over by Colonel Daniel Strickler found Martin and Captain guilty and ordered their execution by hanging.[52]

Although not as extreme as murder, some enslaved individuals used arson as a mechanism of resistance. On February 4, 1780, Violet, an Augusta County woman enslaved by Sampson Sawyers, set fire to her enslaver's home. An Augusta court found Violet guilty and ordered "that she be hanged by the neck until she [was] dead." After the execution, the court ordered that she be "cut down" and "her head be severed from her body by the neck and stuck upon a pole in the public place near Staunton."[53]

Other enslaved people in the Shenandoah Valley rebelled by bolting from their enslavers. Although it is difficult to determine the number of enslaved who fled enslavers from the time of the Republic's founding until its dissolution in 1860–61, existing newspaper advertisements reveal that enslaved people fled on a weekly basis. For example, existing copies of *The Torch Light and Public Advertiser* from the spring of 1828, a newspaper published weekly in Hagerstown, Maryland, contain announcements from enslavers in Frederick, Shenandoah, and Rockingham Counties, seeking the return of enslaved people who fled.[54] Peachy Grattan, an enslaver from Rockingham County, offered a $50 reward for the capture of two enslaved males, Henry (aged thirty-one) and Harry (aged twenty-seven). Grattan believed "it . . . probable they are making their way to Pennsylvania or Ohio."[55] On June 19, Frederick County's David Timberlake offered a $50 reward for the capture of his enslaved male, William Jackson. Timberlake surmised

## RUNAWAY.

WAS committed to the jail of Washington county, on the 5th of April, inst. a negro man who calls himself ALLEN, about thirty years of age, tolerably black ; had on when committed a coarse drad home-made roundabout and pantaloons, an old wool hat, and an old pair of lace boots—says he belongs to a Mr. Jacob Cooper, in Winchester, Va. The owner is requested to come forward, prove property, pay charges and take him away, otherwise he will be discharged according to law.

Wm. H. FITZHUGH, Sh'ff.

April 26—3w

Figure 1.3. The above notice appeared in the April 26, 1833, issue of *The Mail*, a Hagerstown, Maryland, newspaper alerting Winchester's Jacob Cooper that a man he enslaved, Allen, had been apprehended by authorities in Washington County, Maryland (author's collection).

that before Jackson journeyed to some point north, he might first visit his "relations, near Charles-Town, Jefferson County" and then flee "with his brother."[56]

Sometimes those efforts to flee ended abruptly when authorities seized them. In the spring of 1833 an enslaved man identified as Allen fled his enslaver, Jacob Cooper, in Winchester. Allen made it as far as Washington County, Maryland, when Sheriff William Fitzhugh seized him. Fitzhugh placed Allen in the county jail and directed Cooper to "come forward, prove property, pay charges, and take him away."[57]

Where enslaved people ventured, how many fled annually, whether they made it safely to their destination, or whether their efforts failed are all difficult questions to answer. However, there is indeed proof that some enslaved people who bolted from enslavers in the Shenandoah Valley made it to their destination and finally enjoyed freedom. In the late 1830s the slave Joseph Taper, along with his wife and at least one of their children, fled Newtown enslaver Joseph Long. Taper first fled to Erie, Pennsylvania, in 1837. When he arrived in Erie, he noted that he met others who had escaped from that part of the Shenandoah Valley. Taper remained in Erie for two years, but when he learned of the presence of slave catchers he gathered his family and ventured north to Canada. He arrived there in August 1839. Slightly more than one year later Taper wrote a letter to his former enslaver explaining that no matter how kindly Long might have treated him and his family, living a life in freedom proved infinitely better. "Since I have been in the Queens dominions I have been well contented, Yes well contented for Sure, man is as God intended he should be. That is, all are born free & equal . . . I have enjoyed more pleasure with one month here than in all my life in the land of bondage," Taper wrote on November 11, 1840. As Taper closed the letter he wrote: "My wife and self are sitting by a good comfortable fire happy, knowing that there are none to molest or make afraid."[58]

Although Bethany Veney did not have the experience of running away, but was instead freed after G. J. Adams, a copper mining speculator from Providence, Rhode Island, purchased and then manumitted her, Veney felt reborn after she moved to Providence. "A new life had come to me. I was in a land where, by its laws, I had the same right to myself than any other woman had. No jailer could take me to prison, and sell me at auction to the highest bidder. My boy was my own, and no one could take him from me," Veney explained.[59]

There is no denying that on the surface, compared with eastern Virginia or other parts of the plantation South, slavery looked different in the Shenandoah Valley. Slave-owners frequently worked alongside those whom they enslaved, something that eastern Virginia's slaveholding elites dared not do, as keeping distance proved a way of distinguishing themselves from yeomen-class farmers.[60] Statistically, enslaved people did not comprise as large a percentage of the total population as they did east of the Blue Ridge. However, the fact that enslaver and enslaved worked side by side or that the numbers of enslaved people in the Valley did not compare statistically with places such as Nottoway County or Amelia County, Virginia, where slaves accounted for more than 70 percent of the total population by 1860, should not diminish the reality that slavery existed in the Valley or proved an integral part of the area's economy.[61] Advertisements for enslaved people who fled, freedom narratives, and interviews with people once enslaved—sources not consulted by the earliest chroniclers of Shenandoah Valley history—reveals that slavery in the Valley mirrored slavery elsewhere. Simply put, as historian Warren Hofstra noted, "life for . . . slaves" in the Shenandoah Valley "would not have been much different from what it was for blacks growing tobacco elsewhere in Virginia."[62] If anything, particularly in slavery's earliest decades in the Valley, life for enslaved people could be viewed as being more difficult as enslaved individuals lived in greater isolation and lacked access to broader communities of friends and relatives that made life slightly more tolerable on larger plantations east of the Blue Ridge.[63]

Since the first enslaved people arrived in the Valley in colonial times they suffered in myriad ways, resisted however they deemed appropriate, and above all desired freedom. While freedom proved elusive and a mere daydream for most, slavery's wedge widened the chasm between free and slave states to an almost unbridgeable point by the 1850s. Little did the Valley's enslaved population realize that events at the end of the decade would push the nation to a conflict that would ultimately provide opportunities to resist, flee, assume an active role in slavery's annihilation, and thrust open freedom's gate.

# 2

## "The Effect Was Immediate"

Wesley Harris from Martinsburg, Virginia (now West Virginia), enslaved by Philip Pendleton, had had enough of his life in bondage by 1853. For most of Harris's existence as an enslaved male, Pendleton rented him annually. In 1853, Harris labored for the "proprietress of the United States Hotel," Mrs. Carroll. Although Harris spoke "in very grateful terms" about Carroll and recalled "that she was kind to him," he found the hotel's manager "cruel." In the autumn of 1853 the hotel's manager informed Harris that he was going to "flog him" for "some trifling cause." Instead of being docile and accepting the punishment, Harris snatched the whip from the manager's hands and flogged the manager. Perhaps fearful for his life, the manager did not resist but instead informed Pendleton of his behavior. Incensed, Pendelton decided to sell Harris by "the following Christmas." When Harris discovered the plan he "began to contemplate how he should escape the doom which had been planned for him." Harris, along with three other enslaved individuals, "set out for the North." Although Harris confronted obstacles during his escape—including being discovered by authorities near Terrytown, Maryland; being shot in the left arm; being recaptured and confined for several weeks in Maryland; and then bolting once more—he eventually made his way to Canada, "the so-called Promised Land," where he found employment as "a brakesman" on the Great Western Railroad.[1]

While the story of an enslaved person becoming disgruntled with their situation and running away was oft-repeated in the Valley by the time Harris bolted, the assertiveness Harris demonstrated against the manager seemed on the rise among slaves in the Shenandoah Valley and across Virginia throughout the 1850s. During that decade, when debates about slavery's westward expansion intensified and widened the canyon between free and slave states, enslavers, as historian William Link noted, believed that the apparent increase in enslaved people's insolence resulted from the fact "that slaves' aspirations for freedom were connected to developments in white

Figure 2.1. Wesley Harris's fight for freedom (William Still, *The Underground Railroad*, 1871).

electoral politics."[2] In the late autumn of 1856 and early months of 1857, following Democrat James Buchanan's victory over Republican John C. Frémont, Winchester's Robert Young Conrad believed there was a "frequent" and "numerous" increase in the amount of arson in the area perpetrated by slaves, free blacks, and abolitionists.[3]

The extent to which enslaved people's boldness actually increased during the tumultuous 1850s is difficult to determine, but slavery's supporters certainly perceived an increase. That sensitivity fueled whites' paranoia of insurrection. In short, as historian David Blight noted, "perception was becoming reality" during the tumultuous 1850s.[4] As threats increased, slavery's supporters took measures to further restrict the lives of enslaved people and free blacks during the 1850s. For example, in the early 1850s authorities in Berkeley and Augusta Counties imposed an annual tax on dogs in an attempt to greatly reduce the number of African Americans who owned them. Customarily the tax rate was $1 per dog. In the Valley and across the Commonwealth enslavers purported that dogs owned by African Americans were largely responsible for the death of livestock.[5] Near the end of the decade citizens from Frederick, Jefferson, and Clarke Counties petitioned the Virginia Senate and House of Delegates to end the "immoral practice" of enslaved people raising hogs for their personal use. The petitioners contended that enslaved people would "steal such provisions" required to feed the hogs. Furthermore, once the hogs reached maturity and were butchered, it would be "impossible . . . to prove that any bacon found in their possessions is stolen property."[6] In the summer of 1857 citizens in Frederick County petitioned the state legislature to remove "idle, trifling, thieving free negroes, who incite well-disposed slaves to steal and to perpetrate other punishable offences."[7] Three years earlier Newtown's town council passed an ordinance regulating the "playing of Ball and marbles within in the Corporation on the Sabbath." This rule not only illustrates the petty lengths to which whites were willing to go in order to subjugate African Americans, but the dramatically different worlds in which whites and blacks lived in the Shenandoah Valley. While the law prohibited both white and free black children from playing ball and marbles on Sundays, the punishment for disobedience proved markedly different. Newtown's authorities imposed a fine of "one dollar [for] each free white person offending." Free blacks who broke the rule received "not less than five nor more than fifteen lashes in force."[8]

The various measures taken to further restrict the lives of African Americans, however, did little to calm whites' fears. By 1856 fears of insurrection, as historian William Link argued, "were common" throughout Virginia and the broader South.[9] Those fears would reach their crescendo in mid-October 1859, as abolitionist John Brown attempted to strike a major blow against slavery at Harpers Ferry.

Born in 1800, Brown devoted his life to ameliorating life for African Americans and slavery's destruction. By the mid-1850s Brown's abolitionism turned extremely militant. Following the Pottawatomie Creek Massacre in Kansas in 1856, where Brown and his "Liberty Guards" killed five pro-slavery settlers, Brown began formulating a plan to begin a crusade against slavery in the state that boasted the largest number of enslaved people, Virginia. Situated at the confluence of the Potomac and Shenandoah Rivers, Harpers Ferry proved an ideal starting point for Brown. As an important transportation hub and location of the United States Arsenal and Armory as well as Hall's Rifle Works, Harpers Ferry could provide Brown with the material support he required in order to wage a war against slavery, as well as the transportation routes necessary to carry out his abolitionist campaign. Furthermore, the town's proximity to Maryland, which contained the largest population of free blacks in the South, further enticed Brown, as he hoped they might join his army of liberation. After approximately two years of planning and garnering support, Brown and a contingent of twenty-one men launched the attack on the evening of October 16, 1859.[10]

The following morning the sound of pealing courthouse and church bells in communities throughout the northern Shenandoah Valley tolled not to summon congregations to prayer, but to alert local militia units to muster. As the sound of the bell ringing "wildly" from the Jefferson County Courthouse in Charles Town, Virginia (now West Virginia) cut through the crisp autumn air, resident Lucy Ambler wondered what it meant. "Rumors flew more wildly," Ambler noted as area inhabitants gathered what tidbits of information they could.[11]

When area citizens learned that the United States Arsenal and Amory at Harpers Ferry had been attacked, tales about what transpired ranged from the extraordinary to the unbelievable. One outlandish claim prompted some to believe that Harpers Ferry had been attacked by the British as their first step to reclaim what they lost during the American Revolution. One Jefferson County resident penned that some throughout the area "conjectured that it was the British who had seized Harpers Ferry."[12] Some reports that filtered into various communities throughout the Shenandoah Valley stated that a group of approximately 150 African Americans attacked Harpers Ferry. The Associated Press reported that "an insurrection has broken out at Harpers Ferry where an armed band of Abolitionists has full possession of the government arsenal . . . The insurrectionists number about 250 whites and are aided by a gang of negroes."[13]

While rampant imaginations and sensationalized reports attempted to make sense of what transpired at Harpers Ferry, reality came into focus by day's end—that Harpers Ferry had been attacked by John Brown and a small contingent of white abolitionists and African Americans. Although Brown's efforts to first strike a blow against slavery in the Shenandoah Valley and then launch a broader campaign to eradicate slavery ended abruptly on the morning of October 19, when twenty-seven US Marines commanded by Lieutenant Israel Greene stormed a small fire engine house, forever dubbed "John Brown's Fort," Brown's attack had widespread consequences for the Shenandoah Valley, Virginia, and the nation. As a correspondent for the *Richmond Enquirer* explained, it fueled "the cause of Disunion, more than any other event that has happened since the formation of the Government."[14]

In the raid's immediate wake, anxieties increased among the Shenandoah Valley's white citizens. For some the mere mention of the word "abolitionist" conjured unquantifiable angst. Shenandoah Valley resident Jennie Chambers, a child at the time of Brown's attack, feared going outside of her home because she believed that abolitionists lurked around every corner and might capture her. "I didn't know what minute an Abolitionist might jump out from behind a tree," Chambers explained.[15] Robert Conrad observed that in Jefferson County where Brown's attack occurred and in neighboring Clarke County "dread and alarm" was "felt . . . the ladies especially are in a condition of nervousness."[16]

As news of Brown's raid spread throughout the Shenandoah Valley's communities the region's whites contemplated whether or not Brown's activities might energize the area's African American population, whether enslaved or free, to strike their own blow against slavery. Thomas Ashby, a white resident of Front Royal, noted that when the white inhabitants of his community learned the reality of what transpired they "were thrown into a great state of excitement."[17] Ashby believed Brown's attempt to "arouse the negro and create race antagonism" would undoubtedly create "distrust and animosity in the mind of the negro toward his master" and prompt some enslaved people to be "moved by the hope of freedom to become restless and turbulent."[18]

While the region's whites feared that enslaved people "moved by the hope of freedom" might rise up, anxieties rose further as reports circulated that abolitionists planned to liberate Brown from his jail cell in Charles Town. Approximately one month after Brown's attack a reporter in the region noted that white residents, particularly in the northern Shenandoah Valley, "were . . . thrown to a state of great excitement [and] alarm in consequence of flying rumors . . . that a large body of armed men were on the march to that vicinity."[19] Molly Walls, a Newtown resident, penned her brother on December 1, 1859, that the community's inhabitants "are kept in a continual state of excitement day and night . . . There are continual reports of all kinds that keep the people frightened to death."[20] Elizabeth Conrad wrote that she "can't help feeling some anxiety" about abolitionists' potential efforts to free Brown.[21]

Among the reports that "frightened" the region's white inhabitants "to death" was one that came out of Clarke County in late November. With enslaved people and free blacks comprising slightly more than half of Clarke County's population, officials and white inhabitants were no doubt startled when news circulated that "a fight occurred . . . between some citizens and a party of strangers" near the dairy farm once owned by John Curtis Underwood.[22] Throughout the preceding decade Clarke's pro-slavery citizens harbored great distrust of Underwood, a staunch Republican, abolitionist, and New York native. Some area inhabitants surmised that Underwood's farm, situated near the village of Blue Ridge, served as the epicenter of abolitionist activity in Virginia. Although Underwood left Virginia and returned to

New York in 1856, some of Clarke County's residents believed he supported Brown and had sent abolitionist literature to the Valley to be circulated in the aftermath of the attack on Harpers Ferry.[23]

While the Clarke Guards proceeded to Underwood's farm a militia company from Alexandria, Virginia, that had recently arrived in the area "scour[ed] the country round" Berry's Ferry searching for a reported 250 abolitionists. When the militia arrived at Underwood's they found no abolitionist literature, no fight, and no abolitionist mob. They encountered two northern laborers deemed "suspicious characters" and removed them from the property.[24]

To journalists not from the slaveholding South who covered Brown's trial and execution, the anxieties displayed by many of the region's white inhabitants bordered on the absurd. One reporter believed that "all the asylums in Christendom could not hold the multitude of lunatics prevailing" in the region.[25] However bizarre the reactions might have seemed to those not from the Shenandoah Valley, the fear among the Valley's whites was palpable. This apprehension, however, existed not only in the Shenandoah, but across the South.[26]

That trepidation prompted demands to increase the number of slave patrols, which had operated throughout the South since colonial times to restrict the movements and activities of African Americans.[27] Patrol duties in the aftermath of Brown's attack, as historian Sally Hadden notes, were fulfilled by a variety of groups—local militia, patrols established under the supervision of local officials, vigilante groups, and "paramilitary corps."[28] While slave patrols roamed the Valley's communities twenty-four hours a day, their vigilance heightened during the night. Charles White, a Presbyterian minister from Clarke County, noted that the patrols were quite conspicuous after sunset. On November 10, White wrote to his brother-in-law John Felt in Salem, Massachusetts, "We have patrols out every night."[29] Slave patrols throughout the Shenandoah Valley made a concerted effort to visit the residences of African Americans, whether enslaved or free, at least once a week. Mager Steele Sr., a Frederick County justice, directed members of the county's slave patrol to "visit within the bounds of the said County at least once a week all negro quarters and other places suspected of having therein unlawful assemblies of such slaves as may stroll from one plantation to another to another."[30]

Slave patrols in the Shenandoah Valley received the widest latitude to enforce order in the aftermath of Brown's raid. Even if they uncovered no evidence of an insurrection, slave patrols could arrest any African Americans who were "strolling" around and simply looked suspicious.[31] Officials directed Frederick County's slave patrols "to take any . . . slaves so found strolling before some Justice near the place of capture, to be dealt with according to law."[32] Approximately one month after Brown's attack, officials in Shenandoah County arrested two African Americans on suspicion of "being insurgents."[33] The only evidence members of that slave patrol offered as justification for the arrest of the "insurgents" was that they appeared to be "stragglers" who looked out of sorts walking about "almost naked and bare-footed." Shenandoah County officials, who might have believed the two were fleeing their enslaver, questioned them. With no evidence they had fled an enslaver or intended to do anything illegal, county officials released them. An African American detained by a slave patrol in Rockingham County in late November on a similar charge was not so lucky. Officials there seemed reluctant to release the unidentifiable person. A correspondent for the Washington, DC-based abolitionist newspaper *The National Era* noted simply that the "straggler . . . in Rockingham county . . . is still in jail there."[34]

While slave patrols attempted to closely monitor the region's African Americans and restrict their movement by not allowing "them [to] go from one place to another without a pass," it did not completely curb the desire of some of them to assert themselves in aggressive and violent ways in the aftermath of Brown's raid.[35] For example, several weeks after the Harpers Ferry raid, Joe, enslaved by Clarke County's Colonel Francis McCormick, planned to burn buildings in Clarke County owned by enslavers. Additionally, he wanted to aid abolitionists' attempts to free Brown from his jail cell in Charles Town. A newspaper correspondent noted that when "Joe . . . had heard that an army was coming on to take him [Brown] out of jail" he wanted to "join them" to help Brown get "out."[36] For his role in the conspiracy Joe "was sentenced to transportation," meaning that he "was ordered to be sold out of the state."[37]

Another man enslaved by McCormick, Jerry, seventy-five years old at the time of Brown's raid, noted that he was "glad to hear of" Brown's effort. Jerry admitted that had he known about Brown's plot he would have journeyed to Harpers Ferry with his four sons. Although Jerry missed the opportunity to aid Brown, he believed that he could continue Brown's work at least in Clarke County by "burning" the homes of those who either enslaved human beings or favored slavery.[38] Among the places Jerry targeted was the home of Daniel Sowers, a forty-seven-year-old farmer who enslaved thirteen slaves ranging in age from one to seventy-five.[39] After Jerry and a handful of other enslaved individuals carefully "made a plot," they set out to burn Sowers's residence. Jerry and his followers knew that if they had any chance of carrying out their mission they needed to avoid the slave "patrole [that] had been out."[40]

Fortunately for Sowers, Jerry never had a chance to carry out his campaign of arson, because Alfred Castleman encountered Jerry and his followers "along the road" and stopped him. Authorities promptly arrested Jerry. During Jerry's trial in December 1859, presided over by five magistrates, a witness testified that Jerry did attempt to purchase matches in Berryville, "but could not get any." After the magistrates considered the "able arguments from each side, and duly" deliberated "the evidence and arguments," they "unanimously found the prisoner guilty of plotting and conspiring to excite the slaves to rebel and make insurrection." The court, in compliance with Virginia law, ordered Jerry to be executed on February 17, 1860.[41]

After the court sentenced Jerry, it recommended that Virginia's newly inaugurated governor John Letcher extend "mercy."[42] Some of Clarke County's white residents also appealed to Letcher to spare Jerry's life. Others, however, could not fathom why anyone would implore Letcher to commute the sentence. One area resident believed that Jerry, although not officially part of Brown's contingent, was still part of "the wicked and diabolical conspiracy of which John Brown, the 'murdered-martyr,' was but the nominal head," and deserved death.[43] After considering the requests, Letcher commuted Jerry's sentence on February 10, 1860.[44] Although Letcher reprieved Jerry from execution, he did not let him go unpunished for his role in "conspiring with slaves to rebel and make insurrection."[45] Letcher condemned Jerry to hard labor.[46]

While superficially it might seem that petitions to stay Jerry's execution derived from some sort of admiration for him, ulterior motives fueled pleas for leniency. Those who appealed to Letcher argued that if the state carried out the execution it would prove that enslaved people in the Shenandoah Valley did support John Brown.[47] This ran counter to the narrative that many Virginia officials and white residents expounded in the raid's aftermath.

In the wake of Brown's raid officials and white residents throughout the region touted the "loyalty" of the Shenandoah Valley's enslaved population. One newspaper correspondent contended that the region's enslaved remained not only loyal to their enslavers, but preferred their life in bondage to one in freedom. "The negroes . . . did not rally to the black standard" and support Brown's campaign because "they were unwilling to risk the consequences of a conflict where the benefits it could confer, if successful, were no greater than those already enjoyed," the journalist wrote.[48] Several weeks after the raid, Virginia senator James Mason, who resided in Winchester, wrote that the only emotion the region's enslaved people felt in the aftermath of Brown's attack "was alarm and terror." Mason asserted that not "a slave escaped or attempted to escape during the tumult . . . Virginia was saved by insurrection among her slaves only by the loyalty of her slaves."[49] An Augusta County newspaper boasted that "the hope" abolitionists had "that thousands of discontented slaves" would "flock" to Brown's "standard" mustered support from "NOT ONE" African American in the region.[50]

Frederick County's Thomas Cartmell, perhaps best-known among Shenandoah Valley historians as the author of *Shenandoah Valley Pioneers and Their Descendants*, also believed that the lack of support among the area's enslaved for Brown offered tangible evidence of loyalty to one's enslaver. Cartmell stated that "the poor down-trodden slave" refused to support Brown because the "negroes . . . could not be tempted by what meant evil to those with whom they had mingled since infancy—forming a relation between the races that can never be understood by those unfamiliar with slavery . . . But for their loyalty, the story of John Brown's raid would be differently told."[51]

In the aftermath of Brown's raid statements such as those by Mason, Cartmell, and various journalists throughout the Shenandoah Valley were more about masking the insecurity of slavery's supporters than presenting an accurate portrayal of the reactions of enslaved people to Harpers Ferry. Numerous scholars have shown that enslavers wanted to believe their slaves were "content," "loyal," and "docile."[52] Events such as Brown's attack and the reactions of African Americans to it challenged that paradigm. Not only in the aftermath of events such as Brown's raid, but following events such as Nat Turner's revolt, slavery's advocates stubbornly restated the claim that enslaved people enjoyed their lot, were intensely loyal to their enslavers, and would only rise up when, as historian Donald Reynolds argued, they were seduced by abolitionists who wished to lure enslaved people "from the natural loyalties and use them to destroy the South and its social system."[53]

Interestingly, even some northern newspapers promulgated the idea that enslaved individuals refused to join Brown's army out of loyalty to their enslaver and contentment with their lot. For example, *Harper's Weekly* published an image in its November 26, 1859, issue that helped fuel the loyalty narrative. The image—titled "A Premature Movement"—depicted Brown with a Sharps carbine in his left hand and a pike in his right. As Brown of-

**A PREMATURE MOVEMENT.**

JOHN BROWN. "Here! Take this, and follow me. My name's Brown."
CUFFEE. "Please God! Mr. Brown, dat.is onpossible. We ain't done seedin' yit at our house."

Figure 2.2. Depiction of imagined encounter between "Cuffee" and John Brown in November 26, 1859, issue of *Harper's Weekly* (author's collection).

fered the pike to the enslaved man, the artist invented a conversation that took place between the two: "Here! Take this, and follow me. My name's Brown," the image's caption read. The enslaved person, labeled by the artist as "Cuffee," responded negatively to Brown and asserted: "Please God! Mr. Brown, dat is onpossible. We ain't done seedin' yit at our house."[54]

Although true that the throngs of area enslaved people Brown hoped would journey to Harpers Ferry and swell the ranks of his abolitionist army never showed up, it did not mean that loyalty to one's enslaver or satisfaction with being a slave fueled an enslaved person's refusal to join him. First, on a practical level, most enslaved people did not know about Brown's plot until after it ended. While Brown's plan could only succeed with the support of significant numbers of the region's enslaved, his plan also needed to remain clandestine in order for it to have any chance of success. While large numbers of enslaved people did not rally to Brown's standard, evidence indicates that a handful of enslaved people learned about Brown's intentions and journeyed to Harpers Ferry. Unfortunately for Brown they did not arrive until after the raid.[55] Additionally, even if some enslaved people did know about Brown's plot, they needed to consider if this was some sort of trap. If it indeed proved genuine enslaved people needed to consider the consequences of their involvement not only to themselves, but to friends and family who remained behind. Perhaps some possessed Frederick Douglass's mindset and believed that although Brown's desire to strike a decisive blow against slavery was well intentioned, the effort seemed destined to fail.[56] A correspondent for *Frank Leslie's Illustrated Newspaper* mused less than a month after Brown's raid that the area's enslaved did not join Brown's army because "they have too much common sense to be heroes."[57]

Not only did officials hope to cultivate the idea that Brown's raid elicited no desire among the region's African Americans to rise up, some wished to convey that a portion of the Shenandoah Valley's African Americans desired to stop John Brown's raid. Chief among those touted by the Valley's white inhabitants as a "loyal" African American was Heyward Shepherd. A free black from Winchester who worked on the Baltimore & Ohio Railroad at Harpers Ferry as a baggage porter, Shepherd was the raid's first casualty. Just as a train arrived at Harpers Ferry at 1:25 a.m., Shepherd walked toward the bridge spanning the Potomac River in search of William Williams, the bridge watchman. As Shepherd approached, two of Brown's men ordered Shepherd to halt. When he refused and turned around to head back to the depot, shots rang out. One bullet struck Shepherd in the back, just below his heart.[58] Dr. John D. Starry, who lived nearby and tended to Shepherd in the railroad office, noted that Shepherd "had been out on the railroad bridge, looking after a watchman who was missing" when one of Brown's men "ordered [him] to halt." Instead of obeying, Starry informed a special select US Senate committee charged with investigating Brown's attack, Shepherd "turned to go back to the office, and as he turned they shot him in the back."[59]

Some whites lauded Shepherd as a hero, willing to stand up to Brown and his crusade against slavery. Less than two weeks after the raid the *Shepherdstown Register* portrayed Shepherd as an advocate of slavery, murdered because he refused to join Brown's army, not because he failed to comply with a simple order to halt. "Hayward Shepherd," the *Register* reported, "was shot by the insurrectionists at Harpers Ferry because he would not join them."[60] Soon, whites throughout the Shenandoah Valley promulgated that perspective in personal correspondence. For instance, Mason Anderson, a resident of Clarke County, wrote in a letter to his brother Cornelius on December 11, 1859, that Shepherd was shot by one of Brown's men after he refused to relinquish keys to Brown. "When they [Brown and his men] came to the gate upon the bridge they found it locked and the keys in possession of a servant. They wished to enter the town very quietly and told the servant they had come to liberate the slaves and set them free . . . He told them they would not do it," Mason explained to his brother. In Mason's imaginative account, after Shepherd refused to turn over the keys, "they immediately fired on him and wounded him badly . . . and left him in dying condition . . . He was the first man killed by the friends of the Negro."[61] Through embellishment and manipulation of historical reality, Heyward Shepherd was transformed into an African American champion of slavery. In an attempt to further "dramatize . . . affection for blacks who had spurned" Brown's efforts, Shepherd's remains were transported to Winchester and "buried . . . with the honors of war."[62] Shepherd's funeral included prominent officials, a band, and three militia companies.[63]

The manipulation of Heyward Shepherd's mortal wounding proved not only useful for white officials in the aftermath of Brown's raid, but became important as advocates of the Lost Cause touted the loyalty of African Americans during the Civil War era. In 1931 the United Daughters of the Confederacy erected a monument to Shepherd at Harpers Ferry. The monument, controversial ever since its dedication on October 10, 1931, immortalized Shepherd as an "industrious and respected Colored Freedman . . . mortally wounded by John Brown's raiders. In pursuance of his duties . . . became the first victim of this attempted insurrection."[64]

Despite the efforts of some who tried desperately to convey that the Shenandoah Valley's African Americans were in no way motivated by Brown's raid, evidence indicates otherwise. While some such as Clarke County's Charles White believed that "the majority of servants" possessed "no evil intentions—or desire any movement" in the aftermath of Harpers Ferry, he acknowledged the reality that Brown's actions emboldened some enslaved people to lash out violently. In a letter to his brother, White noted somewhat disconcertedly that in the weeks after Brown's attack "several masters have been beaten or attacked by their servants."[65]

Seemingly more widespread than attacks against enslavers was arson. While eminent historians such as John Hope Franklin and Loren

Figure 2.3. Heyward Shepherd monument (photo by author).

Schweninger have long contended that setting "fires to outbuildings, barns, and stables" proved commonplace forms of "day to day" resistance and occurred in the Valley in the decades prior to Brown's raid, as noted in the previous chapter, arson did occur in the immediate aftermath of the raid as well.[66] The challenge is determining the frequency of incendiarism compared to earlier periods. In *Twice Condemned: Slaves and the Criminal Laws of Virginia, 1705–1865*, Philip Schwarz contends that Brown's raid sparked "a wave of slave arson."[67] Some evidence exists to bolster Schwarz's conclusion. Although citing no specific amount of incendiary activities, one newspaper correspondent reported on November 15, 1859 that there were "numerous incendiary fires in the neighborhood" of Charles Town, a clear indicator "that emissaries of old Brown are still lingering about."[68] In mid-November one newspaper reported five acts of arson between November

11 and 17 within a fifteen-mile radius of Charles Town.[69] On November 18, the *Winchester Republican* noted that by the month's midpoint six "conflagrations of the kind [arson]" had already occurred in Jefferson, Clarke, and Berkeley Counties.[70] The following day a reporter for the *Alexandria Gazette*, as part of a broader article about the rise in arson in the wake of Brown's raid, wrote that "incendiary fires are becoming very frequent in various parts of the country . . . Incendiary burnings have lately occurred in Jefferson and Clarke counties."[71] Near the end of November, Robert Conrad noted "several firings of barns & stockyards" in the northern Valley, but interestingly, he did not believe cases of arson to be as frequent as they had been in years past.[72] Some Virginia newspapers, such as the *Charlestown Independent Democrat*, believed the reports of a significant increase in arson inaccurate.[73] Whether arson significantly rose as a result of Brown's raid or reports were exaggerated, it did indeed occur with enough frequency to raise alarm.

Among those victimized were three men who served as jurors in Brown's trial—John Burns, George H. Tate, and Walter Shirley. All three men enslaved people. A newspaper reported in mid-November that the "barns, stacks, yards, and implements, amounting to several thousand dollars" owned by Burns, Tate, and Shirley "have been burned."[74] Judge Richard Parker, who presided over Brown's trial, reported arson on his approximately 1,100-acre plantation, the Retreat, located east of Berryville along the banks of the Shenandoah River.[75] While it could not be proved conclusively that African Americans—either enslaved people or free blacks—carried out these specific campaigns of arson, some local white inhabitants certainly blamed them for it. When Murat Halstead, a newspaper reporter from Ohio, arrived in Jefferson County he saw by "the roadside there were marks of fire, the burning of stacks" and a makeshift sign that proclaimed to passers-by "The n[—] have burned the stacks of one of the jurors who found Brown guilty."[76] Members of the Clarke Guards, a militia company, arrested "several slaves . . . on suspicion of having been the incendiaries" near the end of November.[77]

Journalists who covered events in the Shenandoah Valley that autumn of 1859 noted that while many acts of arson devastated property owned by the "prominent and wealthy" throughout the region, some of those who carried out the fiery destruction did so indiscriminately.[78] While some enslaved individuals such as Jerry wanted to focus their fiery campaign exclusively on enslavers, evidence indicates that those who committed arson sometimes did not distinguish between whites who enslaved people and those who did not. About one month after the Harpers Ferry raid one newspaper reported: "Numerous acts of incendiarism have destroyed much property . . . of the poorer people."[79] Regardless of who suffered property damage, acts of arson appeared to be a regular and almost nightly occurrence throughout parts of the Shenandoah. "Night after night the heavens are illuminated by the lurid glare of burning property," noted one journalist.[80]

Additionally, some enslaved individuals reportedly lashed out by killing livestock—another common form of day-to-day resistance among slaves. William Turner, a Jefferson County resident who enslaved eighteen people, reported that at the time of Brown's execution "several" of his "horses had died very suddenly, and also some sheep." Turner "supposed they had been poisoned and intended to have their stomachs analyzed." Others also reported that their "stock . . . had also died very mysteriously" at the time of Brown's hanging.[81]

Regardless of what means African Americans utilized to show support for Brown's efforts, news of each incident raised fears among the Shenandoah Valley's whites.[82] Visual evidence of destruction, along "with the exaggerated reports flying through the country," one journalist penned, "increase[d] the excitement."[83] Even though they might have wanted to believe enslaved people loyal, a correspondent for the *Richmond Examiner* succinctly captured how attacks and fires unnerved white inhabitants in the Valley: "The inhabitants are not by any means easy in their minds as to the temper of the slaves and the free negroes among them."[84]

The uneasiness of slavery's supporters after Brown's attack was not exclusive to the Shenandoah Valley. Scholars who have studied this tumultuous period in other states clearly show that paranoia gripped enslavers as far away as Texas. In the months that followed Brown's attack reports of fire, whether real or imagined, intensified fears among whites of some grand conspiracy to incite slave insurrection across the South. Furthermore, as historians such as Donald Reynolds and Dale Baum have noted, Brown's attempt fulfilled "the paranoid prophecies" of pro-slave voices in the South who continually raised alarms that abolitionists would eventually infiltrate the South and prompt otherwise "docile slaves" to insurrection.[85]

While attacks, arson, and killing livestock seemed the most unnerving to slavery's supporters in the Shenandoah Valley, enslaved people also asserted themselves in more passive ways. One white resident of Warren County recalled that in the aftermath of Harpers Ferry some "of the more restless of the younger negroes showed a disposition to leave their homes after night and to meet in unfrequented places where, not infrequently, they drank and gambled."[86] Both vices had long been employed by enslaved people as a form of resistance and a means of reclaiming, if but for a moment, control over their bodies and their life.[87] Some of the Shenandoah Valley's enslaved showed solidarity with Brown's attempt by simply not working as hard. One of the region's white inhabitants noted "that a great change came over the slaves immediately after the Raid . . . the slaves were not as reliable as before."[88]

Additionally, enslaved people throughout the region rebelled by holding clandestine gatherings. A resident of the lower Shenandoah Valley wrote: "Up to that time they had not been allowed to hold meetings," but in the wake of Brown's attack the area's enslaved "would congregate without the knowledge of their owners."[89] When officials in Warren County learned that slaves "were away from home without permission" they intensified slave patrols to break "up this growing habit of meeting." In the estimation of one resident, the patrols effectively curbed the gatherings. "After the arrest of a few negroes . . . the negroes soon gave up their night wanderings and remained home," Thomas Ashby recalled.[90]

Although it is difficult to quantify how much of the Shenandoah Valley's enslaved population participated in some form of resistance, either overt or covert, in the aftermath of Brown's raid whites possessed a greater level of distrust of those whom they enslaved.[91] Questions about the extent to which enslaved people could be trusted to care for the property and the lives of whites consumed the minds of enslavers.[92] One Valley inhabitant recorded that after that tumultuous autumn "the master began to doubt the loyalty of his slave . . . a mutual distrust began to express itself."[93] Another resident explained simply that "masters were uneasy."[94]

That uneasiness prompted some enslavers, such as Caroline Bedinger, to ponder whether they might need to rid themselves of their slaves and utilize either rented enslaved laborers or hire free labor.[95] Although difficult to determine precisely how many enslavers might have pursued this course, the number of enslaved people in the Valley declined slightly by the time of the 1860 census. Eight counties in the region saw a decline in enslaved people between 1850 and 1860, including Jefferson County—the place where Brown's raid occurred. Only Rockingham and Augusta Counties saw an increase in the enslaved population between 1850 and 1860. Rockingham's enslaved population increased by fifty-six, while Augusta saw a significant increase, with 563 more enslaved people in 1860.[96] In areas where the enslaved population declined over that ten-year span, great difficulty exists in precisely determining when enslavers rid themselves of people they enslaved and what motivated them to do so. While some might have divested themselves of slaves after Brown's raid out of fear, others might have done so, as discussed in the previous chapter, because it proved more economically viable to rent enslaved labor rather than own. Additionally, manumission upon an owner's death accounts for some of that decline. For example, twelve slaves in Winchester and Frederick County gained their freedom in the wake of Harpers Ferry as a result of manumission upon an enslaver's death.[97]

Regardless of how many enslavers possessed Bedinger's perspective and actually sold people whom they enslaved, some enslavers remained resolute, refusing to be cowed into selling their chattel. One Valley newspaper noted that many of the region's enslavers "will [fight] to the last gasp" to "protect and defend" their right to enslave people "from the lawless miscreants and abolitionists."[98] Perhaps in an effort to deter any insurrectionary activity, one Shenandoah Valley enslaver took one of his young slaves with him to witness Brown's execution. Decades after the event the former slave from Jefferson County recalled that his "Old Master . . . a Democrat" who "was glad" he "owned slaves . . . carried me there to see him hung . . . [as] a slave . . . I had to obey what they told me to do." When interviewed decades later during the Great Depression, the formerly enslaved male remembered that the event made little impression on him. In fact, he remembered being excited to see a hanging, as he never before witnessed one. "Oh, I was happy to see a hanging; I never seen one before," the former enslaved person recalled.[99]

Brown's attack on Harpers Ferry not only galvanized the Shenandoah Valley's enslaved population to resist in some way, but also inspired some of the region's whites who favored slavery's destruction to speak out against the institution. For example, following Brown's raid a resident of the Valley identified simply as Haines openly proclaimed his desire for slavery's destruction in Harrisonburg. One Valley inhabitant recalled that Haines "got to throwing out some of his abolitionist sentiments."[100] Soon a "committee" formed "to wait upon" Haines. With tensions at a fevered pitch following Brown's raid and various reports of violence and resistance, the "committee" prepared to execute Haines without trial. Abraham Spengler explained to his brother that after Haines made his comments "he had the rope put around his neck and was about to be strung up." A local official, Judge Kenney, intervened and ordered Haines released. Haines apparently recanted his statements and according to Spengler, "Haines is a perfect changed man now; he admits that he *did* support abolitionist principles, but he would not any longer, he is as good a democrat as anybody."[101]

In Page County, officials arrested David Bumgarner on suspicion of making comments about the benefits of slavery's eradication. Confined in a jail cell, officials interrogated him, but Bumgarner "denied . . . what he was accused of saying." Satisfied that Bumgarner posed no threat, officials released him.[102]

Some arrested on suspicion of being an abolitionist did not deny the accusation. When officials arrested a supposed abolitionist near the Chesapeake and Ohio Canal several days prior to Brown's execution the unidentified male did not refute his hatred of slavery. As officials arrested him he warned, somewhat prophetically, that if Virginia carried out Brown's hanging it would "unleash the bloodiest war ever known."[103]

As the new year of 1860 dawned, some of the region's inhabitants hoped that they could put Brown's raid and the fallout that followed behind them. Nine days after Brown's execution Mason Anderson, a resident of Clarke County, optimistically penned his brother who lived in Ohio that "the very great excitement" caused by the Harpers Ferry raid appeared "pretty well over for the present."[104] Anderson's observation proved somewhat naïve. Excitement and fear prompted a wave of militarism throughout the Shenandoah Valley and Old Dominion as new militia companies formed and reinvigorated Virginia's weak and somewhat dysfunctional militia system.[105] A resident of Augusta County noted that the attack on Harpers Ferry "created a great deal of military enthusiasm . . . and was the handwriting upon the wall."[106]

Although the immediate excitement created as a result of Brown's raid might have "subsided," it became evident to many who lived in the Shenandoah Valley—black or white, free or enslaved—that the gap between free and slave states over questions related to slavery had widened to an unbridgeable point.[107] To John Allstadt, an enslaver who petitioned Virginia's legislature for financial compensation for two enslaved people lost as a result of Brown's attack, what transpired at Harpers Ferry was the beginning of "a Civil War."[108] Another of the region's inhabitants reflected that "the Brown Insurrection was the beginning of more serious . . . complications . . . secession and civil war would soon be the final solution to the conditions that confronted the slaveowning States."[109]

As slavery continued to tear the nation apart, the leaders of the Methodist Episcopal Church held their annual meeting in the Shenandoah Valley in

June of 1860. As church leaders gathered in Winchester, discussions about slavery dominated the proceedings. Keenly aware of the effect of Brown's raid and the manner in which African Americans responded to it, church leaders adopted a series of resolutions aimed at ameliorating the environment in the region. Church leaders stated that they "sincerely deplore the agitation of the slavery question, both in the Church and State, and earnestly hope and fervently pray that this discreditable and disastrous strife may speedily cease." Although the clergy gathered in Winchester "solemnly remonstrate[d] against the continual discussion of the slavery question" and stated that it would "preach the Gospel of the Son of God both to master and slave, and devote . . . ourselves wholly to our appropriate work of winning souls to Christ," it did nothing to condemn slavery.[110] After proclaiming they possessed "the least sympathy with abolitionism," church leaders stated they "opposed . . . any inquisition upon the motives underlying the relation of master and slave."[111]

While the leaders of the Methodist Episcopal Church gathered in Winchester and prayed for peace, one that protected slavery, the Shenandoah Valley's enslaved hoped for slavery's end. Fourteen years old at the time of the Harpers Ferry raid, John Quincy Adams, enslaved by the Calomese family of Frederick County, Virginia, recalled that as a child his parents attempted incessantly to buoy his spirits and those of his siblings by telling them "that we would not be always slaves."[112] Adams tried to remain optimistic that he "would be free some day or other." Although Adams tried to remain hopeful that freedom would come at some point in the future, the scenes he witnessed as a child from his vantage point in the lower Shenandoah Valley undoubtedly chipped at his resolve. Adams witnessed enslaved people "murdered . . . [and] starved to death. Husband and wife parted . . . seen droves of men, women and children all handcuffed together . . . to be sold."[113] Depressed beyond imagination, Adams believed only death could relieve his distress. "I thought, though but a boy," Adams explained, "if I could just die to get rid of my distress, I would be satisfied. I could do no good, but suffered day and night for months and years."[114] Sadly, Adams's feelings were all too common among enslaved people.[115]

Tormented by his status as a slave, Adams seemed resigned to his fate by the time of Brown's raid. Although the attack on Harpers Ferry did not inaugurate the Civil War, it pushed the country much closer to the tipping point. In the interim between Brown's raid and the Civil War's opening shots, African Americans, as historian James Oakes argued, paid close attention to the nation's political climate and believed their fate ultimately rested with

Abraham Lincoln's election.[116] Lincoln's victory at the polls, which precipitated the secession crisis and thus led to the Civil War's opening shots in Charleston Harbor in April 1861, brought a renewed sense of optimism to enslaved individuals such as Adams that one day he would be free. He penned simply: "Bright hopes are coming now. The war commenced."[117]

With the war's outbreak the Shenandoah Valley's African Americans would soon have opportunities to attempt to seize "freedom." The region's enslaved population, however, would soon come to learn that any "freedom" they achieved became not only difficult to define, but nearly impossible to maintain in a region that experienced the conflict incessantly as Union and Confederate armies vied for control of the strategically vital Shenandoah Valley.

# 3

## "To Call on All the Blacks"

When the Civil War began in the spring of 1861 the Shenandoah Valley's African Americans did not fully comprehend how the conflict would affect them or their status, but they sensed that in some way it would have an impact. As Virginia militia marched through Charles Town en route to Harpers Ferry to form regiments for Confederate service, throngs of civilians, including free blacks and enslaved people, lined the streets and watched the spectacle. For those African Americans, like others throughout the Valley and the broader South who witnessed similar scenes, the spectacle of parading soldiers prompted them to pause and ponder how this might affect them. As the troops paraded through Charles Town, Unionist David Hunter Strother observed the parade and the reactions of the African Americans in the crowd. To Strother, the enslaved people and free blacks who watched had a look of wonder on their faces. Strother thought that he "could discern in the eyes of some of the older and wiser Negroes . . . a gleam of anxious speculation, a silent and tremulous questioning of the future."[1]

In the Civil War's early months, prior to the presence of any federal troops, the Shenandoah Valley's enslaved population needed to determine how best to use the conflict as an instrument to seize their freedom. On May 26, 1861, a contingent of nineteen enslaved individuals and an unidentified white man from Massachusetts attempted to start an uprising near Winchester. Confederate forces in the area quickly subdued it. A correspondent for the *National Anti-Slavery Standard* wrote: "A feeble attempt at insurrection was made in the vicinity of Winchester . . . but the Southern army encamped there soon quieted the affair." While mention of this attempted insurrection is nonexistent in Confederate reports, a newspaper correspondent reported that Confederate troops "shot" three "negroes and a white man." The remaining sixteen who participated in the revolt were "lodged in the jail" in Winchester.[2] Unfortunately the final fate of these sixteen enslaved people is absent from any records.

Although not as extreme as carrying out an insurrection, evidence indicates that hundreds of enslaved people from the northern Shenandoah Valley used the war's outbreak to flee their enslavers for Pennsylvania. While some enslaved people might have been motivated simply to leave as a result of the conflict, coupled with an understanding, as historian Edward Ayers noted, of "the opportunity the chaos of war offered," the prospect of being sold and separated from family members as enslavers considered how best to protect their chattel might also have compelled some enslaved people to bolt.[3] The Civil War's outbreak encouraged enslavers living on what historians Ira Berlin, Barbara Fields, Thavolia Glymph, Joseph Reidy, and Leslie Rowland referred to as "the exposed periphery of the South," to take various measures to protect their slave property.[4] Enslavers in the Shenandoah Valley, especially those who lived in its northern reaches, certainly lived on the periphery and weighed their options as how to best secure their investment in slaves. Some enslavers sent those they enslaved to points in the Confederacy away from the "periphery" or rented them to other enslavers in areas farther removed from the border. Other enslavers decided to sell their enslaved people for whatever price they would yield. In the war's early months Dolph White, a slave trader from Newtown, Virginia, scoured the area around his Frederick County community for enslavers willing to sell their slaves. At a time when the average price of an enslaved person stood at $1,500, White offered $500 per slave.[5]

While no evidence exists as to the precise numbers of men, women, and children who ventured north or what precisely motivated them to flee, newspaper accounts reveal that sizable numbers of enslaved people fled the Shenandoah Valley in the conflict's opening months before any Union soldiers neared the area. A correspondent in Harrisburg, Pennsylvania, reported on June 7, 1861, that "over one hundred fugitives from labor, from the neighborhood of Winchester, arrived here on Wednesday and Thursday nights . . . the last arrivals were in a wretched plight." Those freedom-seekers who spoke to newspaper correspondents in Harrisburg informed them that the journey from the Valley to Harrisburg took them ten days. Refugees from slavery also informed journalists that Pennsylvania's officials should ready themselves for a steady stream of runaways, as "the mountains of Virginia are full" of enslaved people escaping bondage.[6] Enslaved individuals from the Shenandoah Valley were indeed, as one journalist recorded in early June, "daily escaping over the border into Pennsylvania. Harrisburg is the retreat of many of them."[7]

Some of the Shenandoah Valley's enslaved who escaped into Pennsylvania in the spring of 1861 confronted obstacles from some local authorities, such as the constable in Chambersburg, who arrested freedom-seekers.[8] If refugees from slavery had any hope of true freedom in 1861 they needed to not merely make it to a free state, but to Canada. Aware of the uncertainties freedom-seekers confronted in Pennsylvania, abolitionists in Harrisburg stood at the ready to aid refugees who made it to the Keystone State's capital in continuing their journey across the United States' northern border. After a contingent of refugees from Frederick County, Virginia, arrived in Harrisburg in early June, abolitionists there "supplied" them "with provisions, and sent [them] on their way rejoicing toward the promised land—Canada."[9]

Not all of the Shenandoah Valley's enslaved believed open rebellion or running away the best means to secure freedom in the war's opening months. Enslaved individuals such as John Quincy Adams noted that his father thought it best to remain, labor for their Frederick County enslaver, and wait until conditions to make a successful escape improved. While Adams did not see the point in remaining, his father seemed more pragmatic. "We knew how we were treated," John Quincy wrote in his postwar narrative, "but father told us that we must be good to them, work for them in the day-time and take care of them at night."[10]

Actions such as those taken by John Quincy Adams's father supported enslavers' beliefs that those whom they enslaved preferred bondage to a life in freedom. A white resident of Warren County wrote after the conflict that the fact that enslaved people "remained" with enslavers and were "obedient, and loyal as though a war for liberation was not in progress" proved that "the negroes were, in the main, a happy and contented people, unwilling to assume the responsibilities that their independence would bring them."[11] However, recent scholarship indicates that enslaved people who opted to initially remain with their enslavers did so for various reasons, the least of which was an enslaved person's love of being enslaved. In the war's opening months enslavers throughout the South, keenly aware of the fear enslaved people had of being sold and separated from loved ones, spread rumors that Union soldiers intended to capture them and sell them to enslavers in other nations, including Cuba.[12] For enslaved people who did not fear being sold, other factors influenced their decision to remain with their enslavers, chief among them the notion that outward displays of loyalty might, as historian Ira Berlin contended, "earn them new privileges."[13] Some enslaved people simply remained because they wanted to wait for the best situation that would allow them to flee successfully.[14] In the end, then, what enslavers interpreted as enslaved people being loyal was in reality the enslaved being loyal to themselves.

For those enslaved in the Shenandoah Valley's northern counties, it seemed that the best opportunity they might have thus far in the conflict to flee appeared on the horizon as a Union army commanded by General Robert Patterson approached the region in mid-June 1861. By the time Patterson's force entered the Valley, Union general Benjamin F. Butler had given refuge to enslaved people seeking his protection on the Virginia peninsula at Fortress Monroe. Butler, who believed it acceptable to retain enslaved people whose enslavers supported the Confederacy and whose labor therefore supported the Confederate war effort, issued his "contraband order" on May 27, 1861, which offered protection to enslaved individuals once within Union lines.[15] How aware the Shenandoah Valley's enslaved were about Butler's order, widely covered in newspapers, remains unclear, but hope existed that Patterson's army might offer an opportunity to break their bondage.[16]

As Union troops marched into Jefferson County in mid-June it did not take long for the area's enslaved to learn of the federal soldiers' presence and appeal to them for protection.[17] Near Smithfield, a contingent of approximately twelve enslaved people approached Patterson's troops and appealed to them for protection. "About a dozen negroes, men and women, had come out of the adjoining fields equipped for travelling with their Sunday clothes and bundles," one Union soldier wrote.[18] In David Hunter Strother's estimation it did not appear that the enslaved people's decision to flee was last-minute, but rather planned. To Strother, it seemed that when this particular group of enslaved individuals learned of Patterson's approach, they packed their meager belongings and fled at the first sight of federal troops. "They had evidently prepared themselves beforehand and waited the approach of the army," Strother explained.[19] One of the enslaved males approached a soldier and asked "if this was not the army that was come to set them free." The soldier's response must have shocked the enslaved man. "No, my man," the unidentified soldier from Massachusetts stated, "we have come here solely to execute the laws. To set you free, or to do any thing contrary to the law of the land, is not our mission." Not only did this federal soldier inform this group of enslaved people that they had not come to the Shenandoah Valley to free them, but urged that they return to their enslavers and serve them "faithfully, and be content to know that you are in all probability better off under his protection than if you were free."[20] The enslaved man seemed flabbergasted. "The negro looked alternately at the speaker and at the armed host that was sweeping by with an expression of mingled perplexity and disappointment," recalled Strother.[21] While the Massachusetts soldiers remarks rendered the enslaved man speechless, a female from the group confronted the Union soldier and inquired as to the Union army's purpose, if not to aid in freeing those enslaved. Boldly, the "girl," described by a Union officer as having a "shining face," asked if their only purpose then was "burnin people's fences and spoilin dere corn?"[22] After the exchange the Union troops urged the enslaved people to return to their enslavers. Whether they did or not remains unclear, but Strother wrote that they "slowly turned away, looking perplexed, like one who has been awakened from a long-cherished dream."[23]

Similar interactions between Patterson's army and the area's enslaved continued on a daily basis during Patterson's tenure in the Shenandoah Valley, which ended on July 25. On a regular basis enslaved people sought refuge with federal troops, but Patterson ordered them returned to enslavers. To some, such as the 2nd Massachusetts Infantry's Henry Newton Comey, Patterson's directive proved disconcerting. Soon after the regiment arrived in Harpers Ferry in mid-July a contingent of thirteen refugees from slavery appealed to the regiment's commander, Colonel George Gordon, for protection. Not long after they reached Harpers Ferry some of their enslavers showed up demanding their immediate return. Gordon, sympathetic to the enslaved people's plight in the Shenandoah Valley, as evinced by his actions in 1862 discussed in the next chapter, asked Patterson for guidance. Patterson responded that Gordon "must turn over the slaves to their masters with all due haste. The law considered them as 'property,' and we had no choice but to obey the law." An irate Captain Comey wrote that Patterson's order "upset" him "because I believe no human being should be owned by another."[24] Dumbfounded by Patterson's directive, the regimental chaplain, Alonzo H. Quint, wrote: "The fugitives were sent back to their rebel owners. That same week, the battle of Bull Run was fought; and the owners of some of these very slaves were in the rebel army that day."[25]

Some in Patterson's command believed returning those who fled their enslavement not only morally objectionable, but militarily unwise. Instead of returning enslaved people to work for enslavers who supported the Confederate war effort, there were those who served in the Union army in the Shenandoah Valley during the summer of 1861 who believed employing refugees from slavery as soldiers would restore the Union more expeditiously. Lieutenant Robert Gould Shaw, who served in the 2nd Massachusetts Infantry in the Valley that summer and eventually organized and commanded the 54th Massachusetts Infantry, contended that the Lincoln administration needed to "make use of the instrument that would finish the war sooner than anything else . . . the slaves. I have no doubt they could give more information about the enemy than any one else . . . What a lick it would be at them [the Confederates], to call on all the blacks in the country to come and enlist in our army."[26] Chaplain Quint concurred. "And if our government be wise," Quint wrote, "besides its immense armies, in the fear of the Southern heart John Brown's ghost is worth a hundred thousand men."[27]

Although some in Patterson's army disapproved of their chieftain's "miserable business . . . to send back fugitives," it should have not surprised anyone under his command. On June 3, 1861, Patterson issued a proclamation to his command in Chambersburg, Pennsylvania, as it prepared to move south. In it Patterson informed his troops that as they moved into Virginia to "meet the insurgents" that every soldier in his army "must bear in mind you are going for the good of the whole country, and that while it is your duty to punish sedition, you must protect the loyal, and, should occasion offer, at once suppress servile insurrection."[28] Patterson made it eminently clear that his men should not in any way encourage enslaved individuals to flee and if enslaved people sought refuge with the Union army they should be immediately returned to their enslaver. If the enslaver could not be identified, then Patterson ordered the freedom-seekers jailed until enslavers could be located.[29]

The guidelines under which Patterson's command operated in the northern Shenandoah Valley in the late spring and early summer of 1861 were not of his devising, but instead kept with broader Union policy toward dealing with refugees from slavery in the conflict's early months. While true that President Abraham Lincoln supported General Butler's handling of freedom-seekers at Fortress Monroe, it proved the exception rather than the rule. From General William Harney's Department of the West, to General George B. McClellan's command in western Virginia, and of course Patterson's force, Union armies followed federal policy dictating that Union troops should not in any way interfere with slavery.[30] Political leaders in Washington, DC, who advocated such policy believed noninterference with slavery important for various reasons. In addition to President Lincoln's concern about alienating Northern Democrats and border states, he also believed that a lack of Union interference with enslaved people in the seceded states might encourage more pro-Union sentiment in those areas. Members of Lincoln's cabinet such as Attorney-General Edward Bates also disapproved of Union armies aiding enslaved people to flee enslavers, as he believed it might foment a bloody insurrection.[31] Congress too weighed in and supported noninterference. With an overwhelming majority, Congress approved the Crittenden-Johnson resolution that stated "this war is not waged upon our part . . . [for the] purpose of overthrowing or interfering with the rights or established institutions of those States, but to defend and maintain the supremacy of the Constitution and to preserve the Union."[32]

Although refusing to aid enslaved people seeking refuge with Patterson's army kept with, as David Strother noted, "the proclaimed policy of the Government [that] fugitives would be returned to their masters from the camps, and that in a military point of view they could not be tolerated," it did not deter enslaved people from fleeing to Union lines. Routinely, throughout Patterson's time in the Shenandoah Valley, enslaved people fled to Union camps, as they had done in other areas where Union troops had a presence in 1861, with the hope that they could trade something beneficial to Union forces in exchange for their freedom.[33] Oftentimes enslaved people offered foodstuffs to Union soldiers, as they did to a contingent of twenty-five soldiers from the 2nd Massachusetts Infantry during a foraging expedition between Charles Town and Harpers Ferry on July 21.[34]

Enslaved people sometimes offered their labor to Union forces, such as one identified by soldiers in the 13th Pennsylvania Infantry as "Skinner," who proposed he labor for the regimental staff as a "waiter, cook, hostler, and errand boy."[35] Patterson knew nothing of Skinner's employment by the 13th Pennsylvania until soldiers in the army's provost guard arrested Skinner after they saw him riding a horse, wearing "an old uniform, pants, with military cap, of the Pennsylvania order" and carrying "a trusty old sword," through the streets of Martinsburg while running errands for the regiment's commander, Colonel Thomas Rowley. Although aware of Patterson's policy toward enslaved people, the regiment's chaplain, Rev. A. M. Stewart, believed Skinner's arrest blasphemous. "Has he killed a secessionist, insulted some pompous military official; or acted upon some other military wickedness?" Stewart inquired. Skinner's apprehension resulted not only from the fact that he was a freedom-seeker, but that he wore portions of a Union uniform.[36] Concerned that the sight of an African American wearing a Union uniform might unnerve area white Confederates, Patterson issued an order which stipulated that if any African American legally labored for the Union army, under no circumstances should they wear any piece of a Union uniform. The directive stipulated that "no darkie, being an attaché of the army, should wear any article of military dress, or carry any kind of weapon offensive or defensive."[37]

On other occasions, some enslaved people offered military intelligence to Patterson. When pickets from the 11th Pennsylvania Infantry encountered a freedom-seeker near Darkesville, located in southern Berkeley County, he revealed that he had some information that might interest Patterson. The enslaved man, believed by the regimental chaplain, William Henry Locke, to be enslaved by a Mr. Byerly, had occasion to eavesdrop on a conversation between Confederate officers in General Joseph E. Johnston's command and his enslaver. When the enslaved man, identified simply as George, arrived at Patterson's headquarters in Martinsburg, he informed the commanding general "that the principal part of the Southern force was at Winchester, throwing up intrenchments [sic] that the Yankees were coming."[38] During the course of Patterson's interrogation George also revealed that Johnston impressed enslaved people in the area to work on the defenses being constructed on Winchester's northern outskirts. One of the 11th's members recalled that he heard George tell Patterson "that many of the colored people had been sent there to help on the work."[39] George hoped that after he divulged what he knew to Patterson, that he would be permitted safe passage northward. That proved a fantasy. After taking the information, Patterson confined George to a jail cell in Martinsburg until he could be reunited with his enslaver. "The colored man's face was turned toward the Potomac," Chaplain Locke explained, "and when the general and his staff had ceased to question him, he begged to be permitted to pursue his journey. But in reward for revealing what he knew he was sent to the guardhouse, and confined as a runaway slave."[40]

Patterson never had the chance to return George to his enslaver. When Patterson's army left Martinsburg on July 16, 1861, and marched south toward Bunker Hill, George somehow managed to escape. Whether or not George's break from the guardhouse benefitted from the kindness of a sympathetic Union soldier is unclear. Once free from his confinement, George considered his next step; although he had initially hoped to flee north, various thoughts coursed through his mind. He wondered if other Union soldiers might snatch him and lock him up. Even if he avoided capture, George contemplated how he would survive. For the moment he believed it best to return to his enslaver and wait for a better opportunity to escape north. Noting that he "was afeard ob de Yankees," George remained "close at home." George thus did not return to his enslaver or remain with him for the time being out of loyalty, but rather out of allegiance to himself. He simply bided his time and waited for an occasion that would offer the best chance of success. Fortunately for George that occasion came in late May 1862, when Union general Nathaniel P. Banks withdrew his army from Winchester north to Williamsport, Maryland, following his defeat at the First Battle of Winchester. Inspired by the sight of "a good many colored people" whom he knew, George finally fled his bondage and ventured successfully to Pennsylvania.[41]

For some in Patterson's command the manner in which Patterson handled cases like Skinner and George proved difficult to comprehend. Those like the 13th Pennsylvania's Rev. Stewart could not fathom why Patterson cared about not upsetting the Valley's enslavers, the large majority of whom supported the Confederacy. Stewart concluded that Patterson did it to "pander to this inexorable spirit of Slavery—in order to sooth these F.F.V.'s, these traitor slaveholding secessionists among whom we are now."[42]

Patterson's staunch stance against aiding freedom-seekers not only frustrated portions of the federal force in the Valley that early summer of 1861, but prompted some of them to take action. Although difficult to determine precisely how many of Patterson's approximately 18,000 men abhorred his policy of returning enslaved people or imprisoning them, evidence suggests that a contingent of his force cared little about current military policy, instead favoring humanity and justice. In a scene that played out in all areas where Union troops encountered refugees from slavery in the conflict's early months, some Union soldiers could not bring themselves to turn away those who sought freedom.[43] "Slaves," the chaplain of the 13th Pennsylvania wrote, "endeavored to find shelter from oppression within our camp."[44] The 2nd Massachusetts Infantry's Major Wilder Dwight, who remarked in a letter shortly after his regiment's arrival in the Shenandoah Valley that the presence of Union soldiers should mean "freedom" to enslaved people in the area, understood Patterson's policy, but could not bring himself to enforce it.[45] When "a lot of negro fugitives" sought refuge with the 2nd Massachusetts near Harpers Ferry on July 23, Dwight knew "we are obliged to stop them," but he could not. "It went against my grain to throw obstacles in their way," Dwight explained in a letter the following day. According to Dwight they let all but one of the freedom-seekers continue on their northward journey. The one who did not continue north was a male enslaved by Captain William Baylor, an officer in the 5th Virginia Infantry. Whether or not the enslaved person, identified as "Bob," served as a body servant for Baylor and fled his enslaver at some point during the regiment's tenure in the northern Shenandoah Valley that summer, or he escaped from Augusta

County and made his way north, is unclear. The 2nd Massachusetts' regimental staff hired him "as a waiter" and determined to "retain his services until Colonel Baylor returns to his allegiance."[46]

The daily encounters individuals such as Major Dwight had with freedom-seekers only hardened perspectives that any opportunity they had to aid enslaved people on their path to freedom should be seized, even if it meant defying Patterson's orders to not do so. The day after Dwight allowed a group of enslaved people to continue northward, a freedom-seeker from Charles Town appeared at regimental headquarters. When Gordon inquired if he was enslaved, the man answered in the affirmative. Major Dwight was dumbstruck, as the man's complexion was nearly white. "Nothing could have been more unexpected than this reply. The fellow says he has brothers and sisters as white as himself, and all slaves," Dwight wrote.[47] When the enslaved man informed Gordon that his "father was a white man," Dwight seemed confirmed more than ever before of slavery's evils and the responsibility of Union soldiers to help enslaved people. "O, this is a beautiful system," Dwight explained, "in its practical details—a firm basis for a Christian commonwealth! It is an order of things worth fighting for! Bah!"[48]

While some of the Valley's enslaved found sympathetic Union soldiers once they arrived in a Union camp, evidence indicates that some of Patterson's command actively sought out enslaved people and encouraged them to seek refuge with Union troops. When "several" runaway slaves appeared at Colonel George Thomas's headquarters in Martinsburg shortly after his brigade arrived in Berkeley County, he was shocked to learn that they "were persuaded to present themselves at his headquarters." Keenly aware that this violated Patterson's order, Thomas promptly issued a directive to his men "that he will punish any of his men who tamper with or induce slaves to leave their masters."[49] Directives such as these seemed to have little impact on those Union soldiers who believed slavery wrong, and returning those seeking freedom outrageous. On the very day Thomas issued his reminder, James Hooff, a Jefferson County resident, recorded that "Federal troops . . . begged them [enslaved people] to go along with them offering any inducement, it is supposed about forty or fifty have been persuaded off."[50]

Those in Patterson's army who aided enslaved people bolting for freedom seemed astounded at the amount of effort Patterson expended on finding and returning refugees from slavery. A regimental chaplain from Pennsylvania wrote bluntly, "this is contemptible . . . a posse of soldiers carefully searching through the tents of soldiers where the trembling bondsman had vainly endeavored to hide himself, dragging him out and conveying him to

Martinsburg jail, there to be claimed at leisure by his master."[51] Chaplain Alonzo Quint concurred. "Shame on the miserable business our army had, to send back fugitives!"[52]

Patterson's program of returning freedom-seekers might also explain why some enslaved people in areas occupied by his command exhibited signs of greater loyalty to their enslavers when soldiers in Patterson's army threatened white owners. For example, on the morning of July 4, 1861, soldiers from the 7th Pennsylvania Volunteer Infantry entered the Boyd home on Queen Street in Martinsburg in search of Confederate contraband. Belle Boyd explained that the soldiers "broke into our house and commenced their depredations . . . for the purpose of hunting for 'rebel flags,' with which they had been informed my room was decorated." According to Boyd, when the Union soldiers announced their intent, her "negro maid promptly rushed up-stairs, tore down the obnoxious emblem, and before our enemies could get possession of it, burned it."[53]

Although in compliance with Union military policy, Patterson's practice of incarcerating enslaved people or returning them to enslavers did not sit well with anti-slave leaning members of Congress. When reports of it reached abolitionist Owen Lovejoy, he was appalled. Although Lovejoy, whose brother Elijah was murdered by a pro-slavery mob in Alton, Illinois, in 1837, did not believe in doing anything to alienate the border states, he believed returning freedom-seekers, who could in some way be used to support the Confederate war effort, ludicrous.[54] On July 8, 1861, Lovejoy introduced a resolution condemning practices such as Patterson's and urged the House of Representatives to pass a resolution that would shift Union policy and also repeal the Fugitive Slave Law. The House tabled the vote. Undaunted, the following day Lovejoy introduced another resolution, this time removing his call to abolish the Fugitive Slave Law but continuing in his demand that "it is no part of the duty of the soldiers of the United States to capture and return fugitive slaves." The resolution passed the House by a vote of ninety-three to fifty-five, but it was not a law, merely a condemnation of practices such as Patterson's and a reaffirmation of Butler's policy.[55]

Sixteen days after Lovejoy's resolution, authorities in Washington, DC, relieved Patterson of command of the Department of the Shenandoah and replaced him with General Nathaniel P. Banks.[56] War-planners removed Patterson not as a result of his policy of returning those who fled their enslavement, but because of his inability to prevent General Joseph E. Johnston's Confederates from escaping the Shenandoah and going to the aid of General P.G.T. Beauregard at Manassas Junction. When Banks arrived at

Harpers Ferry his primary concern was to take measures to prevent Maryland's secession.[57] Although keeping Maryland in the Union was his principal focus, Banks could not ignore the Shenandoah Valley's enslaved people who sought refuge with his command. When Banks assumed command of the Department of the Shenandoah, official military policy still dictated that Union troops return freedom-seekers or detain them. That practice took a major blow less than two weeks after Banks arrived at Harpers Ferry. On August 6 President Lincoln signed the First Confiscation Act, which stated that all property, including enslaved people, used to support the Confederate war effort was "declared to be lawful subject of prize and capture wherever found" by Union soldiers.[58] While the First Confiscation Act did not officially grant freedom to enslaved people who bolted from enslavers or prohibit Union soldiers from returning them to enslavers whose loyalties rested with the Union, it did allow Union soldiers authority to keep enslaved individuals from enslavers who in any way supported the Confederate war effort.[59]

As refugees from enslavement arrived at Harpers Ferry in the wake of the First Confiscation Act, some of Banks's officers believed he should consider doing more than merely offering the freedom-seekers protection or safe passage to points north. Some, such as Robert Morris Copeland, an abolitionist from Roxbury, Massachusetts, who served as the quartermaster of the 2nd Massachusetts, believed Banks should consider using them in some capacity as spies or soldiers. Copeland, who by early August was, in the estimation of Robert Gould Shaw, "always fuming and raging about" slavery, discussed the possibility "about making use of the negroes against the Secessionists" with Banks. Although opposed to slavery, Banks did not consider it.[60]

Whether or not news of the First Confiscation Act trickled down to the Shenandoah Valley's enslaved population, enslavers such as Winchester's Benjamin F. Brooke, the minister of the Market Street Methodist Church, noted that by the end of the second week of August that those whom he enslaved appeared defiant in a manner not yet exhibited up to this point in the conflict. A careful examination of Brooke's journal notes no insolent behavior among his enslaved laborers until August 15, 1861. "Much provoked with the servants—they take advantage of me now," Brooke wrote.[61]

While enslaved people such as those enslaved by Rev. Brooke might have been galvanized by the First Confiscation Act to be more assertive, evidence indicates others might have believed the timing right to flee to Banks's camps near Harpers Ferry, a reaction historian Ira Berlin contends was rather typical in the wake of the First Confiscation Act.[62] The decision, however, for an enslaved person to flee after the First Confiscation Act correlated directly with their proximity to Banks's army. Although records specifying the detailed reports of freedom-seekers coming to Harpers Ferry do not exist for the summer and autumn of 1861, reports of refugees from enslavement arriving at Harpers Ferry in February and early March 1862 reveal that nearly 60 percent of the enslaved people who made it to Harpers Ferry came from Jefferson County, with the remainder fleeing from nearby Clarke, Berkeley, and Frederick Counties.[63]

The scene of freedom-seekers streaming into the environs of Harpers Ferry greatly heartened Union soldiers who detested slavery and had been forced to return enslaved people during Patterson's tenure. Major Wilder Dwight gleefully wrote in early 1862 from his camp near Charles Town: "I saw a sight that I would gladly photograph . . . A large wagon full of negro men, women, and children, overrunning like the old woman's shoe. It had come in from the farm, near town, of some disloyal Rebel."[64] When freedom-seekers arrived on a daily basis some simply offered their name, name of their enslaver, and the place from where they had fled. Others provided Union soldiers with details of their enslaver's barbarity. When forty-year-old Edmund Cook arrived at Harpers Ferry he stated that his enslaver "Abraham Isler . . . knocks me around and abuses me unmercifully." A ten-year-old boy identified simply as "Ned" informed one of Banks's men that he "ran away" because his "master whipped" him. Other enslaved people who sought sanctuary with federal troops reported that they fled out of threats their enslavers made against them. A twenty-one-year-old enslaved male who identified himself to Union authorities as "John Brown" explained to authorities that he fled because the "overseer was going to whip me." Similarly, Orange Smith, a forty-year-old enslaved man who journeyed from Clarke County, explained that he "ran away to avoid being whipped master was going to school me."[65]

Other freedom-seekers told Union officials where their enslavers hid foodstuffs to aid the Confederate war effort or where they secreted military goods or Confederate symbols. Twelve-year-old John Quincy Adams (not the same John Quincy Adams mentioned earlier in this volume) "told the soldiers of flour concealed in cellar," while an enslaved person who fled from Clarke County told one of Banks's men that "Master has a secession flag."[66] Edmund Cook, aside from discussing the abuse he suffered, informed a Union soldier that his "master has a gun and sword and pistol hid between two feather beds in some bed room up stairs."[67]

Some enslaved individuals who fled from the vicinity of Winchester in early 1862 brought more than insight as to why they bolted or information about where their enslavers hid Confederate contraband; they carried vital military information about Confederate general Thomas Jonathan "Stonewall" Jackson's army and defenses around Winchester. This information proved particularly useful to Banks as he advanced south toward Winchester during the first week of March. After Henry Dilworth, a twenty-five-year-old enslaved male who escaped his enslaver approximately five miles north of Winchester, informed Union authorities that he fled "to avoid being sold in Richmond," he offered a detailed report about Jackson's defensive works. Dilworth informed Union officers that Jackson's men had taken "R[ail] R[oad] ties, set endwise in [the] ground" around the perimeter of Fort Collier located on Winchester's northern outskirts. He also provided information about the location of artillery pieces and that Jackson, anticipating an advance by Banks's command, had begun to remove his supplies from Winchester. "9 field pieces 4 miles from town, near Winchester, some iron, some brass . . . one large gun on hill near Pughtown Road—one other gun on hill back of Winchester. The store of goods have been removed from Winchester," Dilworth explained.[68] Another freedom-seeker, twenty-five-year-old Dennis Taylor, whose enslaver lived several miles north of Winchester, also provided a detailed description of Fort Collier and also offered information about Jackson's defensive works east of town. "Have seen the fort on Stine's farm," Taylor informed one of Banks's men. Taylor noted that the fort on Stine's farm, Fort Collier, contained "large guns between two banks—banks made of flour barrels with dirt thrown against them . . . have seen the earthwork on the Berryville Pike—looks as if in [a] circle."[69]

While the reports from enslaved people aided Banks as he marched toward Winchester, the movement of 35,000 Union soldiers against a city defended by 3,500 Confederates helped enslaved people, who opted to remain with their enslavers up to this point in the conflict, reconsider their pragmatism. During the war's first eleven months two enslaved people from Jefferson County, one identified as Aunt Chloe and the other her eighteen-year-old son George, believed it best to stay put. Although the sight of a massive Union army marching south did little to dissuade Aunt Chloe, her son George believed it presented the best opportunity to date for freedom. When the 2nd Massachusetts' Wilder Dwight encountered Aunt Chloe during the first week of March he noted that although his mother suffered "great affliction" at his going, George bolted because he "wanted to be free, instead of following [any] longer the apron-string and status of his mother."[70]

While the Valley's enslaved population would have to wait and see how events played out in 1862, some in Banks's command believed that as Union forces marched further south more of the Shenandoah Valley's enslaved people would follow George's example. To Major Dwight it seemed, after learning of George's departure, "The leaven is working, there is no stopping it."[71]

# 4

"The Servants . . . Could Not Be Conveniently Stored Away"

Throughout the day on March 11, 1862, as Union occupation of Winchester became imminent with Stonewall Jackson's army marching south, Winchester's white Confederates hid their valuable possessions. The one item, however, they could not easily secret away were those whom they enslaved. Laura Lee lamented that throughout the afternoon the white inhabitants of the Lee household on Market Street "were busily putting into place of safety, silver, papers, swords, flags, military clothes, war letters, in short everything contraband, except the servants, who could not be conveniently stored away."[1] While individuals such as Lee recognized the impossibility of hiding enslaved people, some who lived in Winchester's vicinity understood that while they could not conceal enslaved individuals in the communities where they resided, they could safeguard them by sending them south—a commonplace practice among enslavers in the South throughout the conflict. Frank Mead, who lived near Millwood, about a dozen miles southeast of Winchester, decided to do just that. When Mead learned of Banks's approach he hastily prepared to send those whom he enslaved to Charlottesville, Virginia. At least one of those enslaved people, thirteen-year-old Adam Griffith, fled when he learned of Mead's intentions. When Griffith reached Union troops he explained that he "ran away because [he] was whipped" and Mead "was going to send me to Charlottesville" because Mead feared that the "Yankees would get us all."[2]

The spectacle of 35,000 Union soldiers marching into Winchester on the Martinsburg Pike on March 12 seemed almost apocalyptic to the community's Confederate sympathizers, but to the community's African Americans it offered hope. John Peyton Clark confided to his journal on that day, "The town during the entrance presented a sad and sullen appearance . . . [but] negro men and women . . . congregated on the corners of the streets for the purpose" of greeting the Union troops.[3] Clark also noted "eleven negro women" standing on the porch of the Taylor Hotel, a place frequently used by slave traders to broker deals in the years prior to the conflict, to greet Banks's command.[4] One Union soldier wrote that as Union troops arrived that day "the town [was] alive with negroes."[5]

While Union soldiers noted numbers of African Americans coming out to welcome them, they also discovered a level of distrust among some enslaved people. Four days after Banks's army entered Winchester, Samuel Sexton, the assistant surgeon of the 8th Ohio Infantry, met several enslaved people he believed possessed "a peculiar dread" of Union soldiers and seemed "very reserved and uncommunicable."[6] Federal troops also encountered enslaved individuals who seemed content to remain on their enslaver's property to safeguard it, despite the fact that their enslavers had fled. To Major Wilder Dwight this made little sense. After the 2nd Massachusetts Infantry established its camp "near a fine old farm-house," Dwight conversed with "the negro servants" who had been charged with watching the property after "its Rebel owner left with haste."[7] "This leaving one kind of property in possession of another kind of property hath in it a certain logical and natural inconsistency," Dwight wrote. He pondered why the enslaved people would not "learn to make free with" themselves and leave.[8] What Dwight did not understand, however, was that enslaved people who decided to remain on an enslaver's property customarily did so because, as historian Jonathan Berkey concluded, it permitted "the slave" to enjoy "a de facto freedom."[9] Staying also created an opportunity for those enslaved people to aid the Union war effort through providing supplies to soldiers. This was certainly the case with the enslaved people Dwight encountered near Winchester, who gave Union troops all of their enslaver's "hams and the other fixings."[10] Furthermore, enslaved people who remained not only had the opportunity to provide supplies to Union troops, but also profit from it. For example, Morgan Coxen remained on his enslaver's property in Clarke County after he ventured south in 1862. Coxen sold various pieces of his enslaver's property, including horses and foodstuffs, and kept the earnings.[11] What Union soldiers such as Dwight believed incomprehensible ultimately proved a form of resistance: one that permitted enslaved people to assert themselves, support the Union war effort, and remain in the place with which they held deep connections. The behavior of the Shenandoah Valley's enslaved who opted to remain on their enslaver's property was not atypical as enslaved people determined how best to secure their freedom. For instance, in his study of enslaved people in Georgia during the Civil

War, historian Clarence Mohr concluded that enslaved people "maintained a strong sense of local identity and a bittersweet affinity for the land of their birth." Personal affinity "for the land of their birth" aside, enslaved people had to consider more than their personal situations, but also had to contemplate other factors as they determined whether or not they should flee or remain.[12] As Mohr aptly noted, enslaved people confronted "an almost bewildering array of emotions and private considerations" as they weighed fleeing's impact on family and friends and potential prejudices they might confront from Union soldiers.[13]

Enslavers who remained noticed that the presence of Banks's troops prompted those whom they enslaved to become, as one Winchester enslaver noted, "very impudent."[14] For example, shortly after Banks's army entered Winchester a female enslaved by Elijah McDowell, a carriage maker, reportedly "had been insolent to and actually struck" McDowell's wife for some unknown reason.[15] Enraged at the treatment this enslaved woman accorded his wife, Mr. McDowell promptly sought revenge and "struck the women to make her behave herself." When a Union officer questioned why he hit her, McDowell stated that the "laws of Virginia permit him to punish his servant." Furthermore, McDowell admitted he only "gave her a light tap."[16] McDowell's claim that he acted in accordance with Virginia law held little sway with Union authorities who investigated the incident. Colonel John S. Clark, Banks's aide-de-camp, chastised McDowell and told him that "was not the proper way to manage a servant." When McDowell asked Clark how would he recommend handling one, Clark responded simply, "by love."[17] While Union officials did not punish McDowell, it proved an instructive moment to him and every other enslaver in the area that Banks's men placed African Americans, whether enslaved or free black, on an equal plane with whites and expected that whites treat them not like property, but like human beings. On the day of the hearing, a Winchester resident wrote that Banks's "policy in regard to slaves is the theme of conversation today. This policy is unquestionably the entire emancipation of all the slaves in the country."[18]

While existing evidence indicates that the behavior of Elijah McDowell's female slave was uncommon, enslaved people fleeing Valley enslavers once Banks's troops entered Winchester proved commonplace. Not only in the Shenandoah, but across the South, nothing proved, as historian Yael Sternhell noted, a more "important factor [in] instigating the movement of slaves" than "the advance of the Union army."[19] Winchester's white inhabitants filled their diaries with daily accounts of friends and acquaintances whose enslaved people fled. For instance, on March 23, 1862, Mary Greenhow Lee wrote: "Numbers of servants have gone off . . . two of ours & many more that I have forgotten."[20] Four days earlier Robert Young Conrad noted, "Many in town have lost servants."[21] Winchester also became a magnet for enslaved people escaping bondage from surrounding counties. Two days after Union troops entered Winchester, five individuals enslaved by Samuel Cook, a resident of Warren County, fled to Winchester. When they arrived all five told the same story: they had escaped to free themselves from Cook's brutality. One of those enslaved by Cook, forty-two-year-old Milford Thomas, reported to Union authorities they fled because Cook "beated" them "very badly, gave us not half enough to eat . . . whipped [us] by tying hands up and feet down—using a raw hide on naked skin." Moses Williams, twenty-two years old, echoed of Cook's treatment, "Master is very cruel, did not feed us well, worked us hard, whipped us undeservedly."[22] Two days after those enslaved by Cook arrived in Winchester, twenty-year-old John Carter, who had been taken by his enslaver Strother Jones into the Confederate service as a body servant, escaped when opportunity presented itself when Stonewall Jackson's command halted near Mount Jackson, forty-five miles south of Winchester.[23]

Although freedom-seekers who for bolted for Winchester in March 1862 usually came from areas closer to Winchester, news of enslaved people escaping to Winchester might have motivated enslaved individuals from as far as Augusta County, located approximately one hundred miles from Winchester in the Shenandoah Valley's southern end, to flee. On March 23, two enslaved men, Thornton and David, rented from an enslaver in Caroline County, Virginia, to work at the Mossy Creek Iron Works, escaped. In both the April 1 and April 15 issues of the *Staunton Spectator* Daniel Forrer ran advertisements seeking these "Two Runaways!" Unfortunately, no records exist detailing Thornton's and David's ultimate fate.[24]

While no accurate figures exist enumerating how many enslaved people escaped to Winchester on a daily basis in the early spring, local diarists estimated it to be in the hundreds. Two days after Union troops occupied Winchester, Rev. Benjamin Brooke recorded that he "looked out and hundreds of negroes were in the streets shouting: 'Massa Abe has set us free.'"[25] While Laure Lee did not offer a numerical estimation, she wrote in her journal one month later: "The streets are filled with runaways who have flocked to town from all around the country."[26]

As enslaved people fled, enslavers came to Winchester in search of them. Robert Conrad noted that on March 18, 1862, a number of enslavers from Clarke and Warren Counties journeyed to Winchester in the hope that

Union soldiers, as they had in the conflict's opening months, might aid in locating and returning freedom-seekers. This, however, was not 1861. In addition to the First Confiscation Act, which Banks's aide-de-camp Colonel Clark vehemently believed Union forces "must put through," a Congressional resolution passed by both the House of Representatives and Senate on March 13, 1862, explicitly prohibited Union soldiers from returning enslaved people seeking freedom.[27] The "Act to make an additional Article of War" clearly articulated that "All officers or persons in the military or naval service of the United States are prohibited from employing any of the forces under their respective commands for the purpose of returning fugitives from service or labor, who may have escaped from any persons to whom such service or labor is claimed to be due." Beyond prohibiting Union soldiers from returning refugees from slavery, it promised immediate dismissal from military service for "any officer who shall be found guilty by a court-martial of violating this article."[28] When enslavers arrived in Winchester and appealed to Union authorities to return those once enslaved by them the reply to each enslaver, according to one Winchester resident, "was that if their negroes wished to be free they should be as free here as in Penn[sylvani]a."[29]

In addition to the throngs of enslaved people who journeyed to Winchester, reports from Banks's command note that a contingent of free blacks also ventured there in search of security. When Stonewall Jackson's army retreated from Winchester on March 11, 1862, Jackson not only arrested scores of white male Unionists, but also seized an undeterminable number of enslaved people and free blacks.[30] On March 20, David Hunter Strother spoke with a Unionist resident of Newtown, located six miles south of Winchester, who informed Strother that as Jackson's men withdrew south "the Southern troops" seized "Negroes, and white men . . . without remorse."[31] Among the free blacks Jackson's troops seized were John William Martin and Sylvester Jordan. Having already disregarded their status as free, Martin and Jordan undoubtedly understood that Jackson intended to use them as enslaved laborers. At what point Martin and Jordan must have realized this and cut loose for Winchester is unclear, but both men arrived in Winchester on March 16. The thirty-three-year-old Martin informed Union soldiers in Winchester that Jackson's soldiers "took me away last Monday." Jordan, thirty-five years old and from Winchester, similarly informed Union authorities that Confederates "took me away with Jackson's army."[32] Free blacks, such as eighteen-year-old James Sestro who lived near Strasburg, fifteen miles south of Winchester, had not been captured by Confederates, but feared he might and so broke for Winchester when he "saw the enemy in motion."[33]

Once in Winchester, African Americans who came there in the first month of spring 1862 asserted themselves in various ways. For example, on March 14, a group of African Americans held a meeting at the Market Street Methodist Church and proposed resolutions aimed at subduing Confederate sentiment. Rev. Brooke wrote that "[at] night, the colored people held a meeting at the church and passed resolutions that 'no white man should preach to them who did not go in for President Lincoln and the war for the liberty of the slaves.'"[34] Others simply affirmed their sense of independence by moving freely about the city. One of Winchester's white inhabitants witnessed "servants, who walk the streets boldy."[35] Similarly, Laura Lee penned in her diary: "The sauciness of the servants is very hard to bear. The streets are filled with runaways who have flocked to the town from all around the country."[36]

Shipley, enslaved by a Maryland enslaver, but rented to Newtown's Dr. J. William Walls, asserted his independence by demanding his wife's release from bondage. At the time Banks's army entered Winchester, Dr. Walls had subleased Shipley to someone there. After Shipley bolted from his temporary Winchester enslaver, whose identity is unfortunately unknown, he sought support from Banks's men to aid in securing his wife's freedom. "With a wagon and escort of 25 Yankee soldiers," Mary Walls wrote, Shipley "showed up one morning . . . to get Mary."[37] In addition to his wife's freedom, Shipley demanded that she be permitted to take the furniture she used while in the Walls's home and her clothing. As Union soldiers helped Shipley and his wife load the wagon, one of Banks's men ordered Mrs. Walls to give Shipley and his wife one hundred pounds of flour and fifty pounds of meat to hold them over until they found suitable employment. Shipley, however, interceded and told the soldier not to bother. His intervention came not due to any affinity he had for the Walls, but out of his desire to provide for his family on his own. Mrs. Walls explained that "Shipley then spoke up and said he did not need it as he could support his wife."[38] Once Shipley claimed his wife, they journeyed to Baltimore. Unfortunately Mary, according to one account, died "soon after they" arrived there.[39]

For some who escaped, like Shipley, Winchester proved only a momentary stop on the path to freedom. Although scores of African Americans arrived each day, scores also departed for areas where they believed their freedom more secure. Some made their way to Washington, DC, escorted by Union soldiers. For instance, in April 1862 "a large number of male contrabands followed" Colonel Simon Hoosick Mix's 3rd New York Cavalry from Winchester to the nation's capital. When the refugees from slavery arrived in Washington many remained with the regiment for as long as they could. Lieutenant James R. Chamberlain took an interest in an unidentified "fine-looking boy of about 20 years." This particular freedom-seeker performed camp chores and groomed Chamberlain's horse while in the Shenandoah Valley. When they arrived in DC, Chamberlain gave the refugee some "money to purchase an extra supper out of camp." The twenty-year-old man cared little about extra meals and instead used the money and "invested in a spelling-book." Recognizing education's role as a critical step on the path to true freedom, he "studied it intently every leisure hour, and although perfectly ignorant of the alphabet one week ago, he is now master of his letters."[40]

Other freedom-seekers used Winchester as their springboard to Pennsylvania. A correspondent for the *National Anti-Slavery Standard* reported that ninety "contrabands . . . from Winchester have recently settled in the neighborhood of . . . Bucks County."[41] Similar numbers of formerly enslaved people from Winchester's vicinity journeyed to Philadelphia and attempted to put down roots. When they arrived in Philadelphia many appeared in a deplorable state. A correspondent there wrote that as "many as a hundred have arrived in a single week . . . Some of these black ones reach our borders without shoes, their feet torn and bloody by tramping over frozen roads—not hats for some, no shirts for others; and as for food, emaciated from anxiety and famine, for they have travelled by night, and had no money with which to purchase food." People once enslaved by Senator James Mason, the author of the 1850 Fugitive Slave Law, were among those who arrived in the City of Brotherly Love. Mason penned a letter to his wife on December 12, 1861, following his capture during the Trent Affair, stating that he was "much gratified" to learn that those whom the family enslaved maintained their loyalty.[42] Several months later the enslaved people Mason believed loyal bolted for Philadelphia when Banks's "capture of Winchester broke down their prison doors and let them go free, never to be reenslaved."[43] When refugees from slavery arrived in Philadelphia, local African American families provided them the basic necessities and assisted them in finding suitable employment, usually working for farmers. Now for the first time in their lives these former slaves "receive[d] wages" for their labor.[44]

Although the area around Philadelphia became a new home for untold numbers of the Shenandoah Valley's refugees from slavery, they never lost sight of the fact that significant numbers of freedom-seekers remained in the region. Cognizant of the challenges they confronted if they remained in Virginia—or would encounter if they continued northward—a group of twenty-seven formerly enslaved women who from came from the area around Harpers Ferry and now called Philadelphia home organized a relief association that sent clothing to those in the Valley who needed it. With support from the Women's Aid Committee of the Friends Freedmen's Association, this group of women sewed new clothing to benefit those who remained in the Shenandoah.[45]

Regardless of why they remained or how long they stayed, General Banks mandated that enslaved people who escaped enslavers and opted to stay in the Valley could not be idle. As had been the case wherever Union armies went, the large numbers of freedom-seekers strained an army's resources. Banks wanted to make certain that did not happen in the Valley. Instead, Banks wanted to capitalize on that labor source to support his operations. His approach was not a new one. Since the moment the war began and enslaved people sought protection of federal soldiers, Union generals searched for efficient, cost-effective methods to provide basic necessities for refugees from slavery. Following in the footsteps of officers such as Union general John Wool, who in the autumn of 1861 ordered that all enslaved people who sought the protection of Union forces on the Virginia peninsula needed to labor for the Union war effort, General Banks issued Special Orders No. 50, which directed that refugees from slavery who remained in the Shenandoah Valley should be employed by the quartermaster department.[46] These African Americans supported the quartermaster's operations around Winchester in a variety of ways from serving as teamsters, unloading wagons, distributing supplies, or performing various camp chores. Females found employment as laundresses and cooks.[47] John Mead Gould, an officer in the 10th Maine Infantry, wrote of the multitude of tasks refugees from slavery performed: "They do all the work around town such as cleaning up the filth and ruins and unloading Quartermaster stuff."[48] Union officials sent some to Harpers Ferry to work on the Baltimore & Ohio Railroad.[49] Additionally, although not noted in official documents, evidence indicates that Banks employed some freedom-seekers as spies, particularly to track the activities of the area's Confederate civilians. Winchester's Mary Greenhow Lee observed that "they get the servants to watch who will not pass under the Union flags that are hung out in various places & a regular system of espionage is kept up."[50]

While labor from refugees proved important to Union operations and

Figure 4.1. Photograph by John P. Soule of contraband camp at Harpers Ferry in 1862 (Library of Congress, LOT 4164, no. 212).

offered an opportunity for freedom-seekers to earn wages, the disparity in compensation created bitterness among some. In her prodigiously researched book on contraband slaves, historian Amy Murrell Taylor notes that the wages Union authorities paid refugees from slavery varied tremendously. Some labored for wages of one dollar per month, while others received ten. Disparate wages aside, labor agreements were never committed to paper and without any legal contract, as Taylor argues, Union officials were bound by "no legal compulsions . . . to guarantee the actual payment of wages."[51] This unfairness compelled some to leave the Union army's employ. In some instances, when disgruntled refugees from slavery left they journeyed back to their enslavers. While statistical data as to how many of the Shenandoah Valley's refugees from slavery felt slighted by their labor conditions and decided to go back to their enslavers is nonexistent, at least two instances exist of contrabands who returned to their enslavers in the spring of 1862 due to a lack of being paid by Union authorities. At some point during the spring of 1862 two enslaved males from Rockingham County, one enslaved by Jacob Strayer and the other by Samuel Hence Lewis, escaped with Banks's army as it moved from Rockingham County north to Shenandoah. They offered their services as teamsters and were promised wages, but they never received "a cent for their services." As the two pressed the issue, one Union officer reportedly told them to "steal their wages from the rebels." Dissatisfied with this response, the two returned to Strayer and Lewis. Whether or not these two enslaved men departed at a later point during the war or remained for its duration is unknown; however, episodes such as this underscore the difficult labyrinth the Shenandoah Valley's enslaved people sometimes had to navigate after they made it to what they believed was the security of Union lines.[52] Even after Union military policy transformed in a manner that provided some protection and employment opportunities for enslaved people who sought safety with federal forces and opted to remain in the area in which they were once enslaved, making it to Union lines guaranteed nothing. The case of the two enslaved men from Rockingham County also elucidates the primary concern for enslaved people. While enslaved individuals wished for freedom, the desire for survival proved paramount. Sometimes satiating that basic human instinct for survival meant doing the unthinkable and returning to one's former enslaver.

In addition to the variety of labors performed by refugees from slavery, one of Banks's staff officers, R. Morris Copeland, believed Banks should also consider organizing an African American regiment to bolster his army's ranks in the Valley. When Copeland raised the idea, one he proposed to Banks shortly after Banks took command in the Valley, Banks did not immediately reject it. Instead, as Copeland remembered, Banks greeted it "with characteristic caution, neither approved nor objected to it." Banks permitted Copeland and Robert Gould Shaw to take a "leave of absence" to venture to Washington, DC, to seek the advice of Secretary of War Edwin Stanton. Unfortunately, Copeland's effort failed.[53]

By the end of March, the military situation in the Shenandoah Valley required Banks to push his army south in pursuit of Stonewall Jackson. As Union regiments marched south, the scenario that played out during the second week of March, as Union troops advanced from Harpers Ferry to Winchester, replayed itself as Banks's command moved seventy miles south toward Harrisonburg. As word of Banks's approach reached the ears of enslaved people, some enslavers reported that those whom they enslaved asserted themselves in manners they had not witnessed before and became "more insolent and lazy" as Union forces approached.[54] Union general Alpheus Williams, one of Banks's division commanders, wrote on April 29, 1862, from a camp near Harrisonburg: "The Negro population increases as we go south . . . They seem glad at our coming and probably think some great benefit is to accrue to them."[55] Four days earlier, from the army's camp twenty miles north of Harrisonburg, near New Market, Chaplain Alonzo Quint observed that "contrabands are frequent. All tell the same story, all desire to be free, all seem ready to work" for the Union cause.[56]

While diaries and letters from soldiers in Banks's army note that freedom-seekers arrived in their midst frequently, those accounts do not specifically quantify the number of enslaved people who sought refuge with the Union army as it moved south. However, extant reports filed by enslavers with the Commonwealth of Virginia as a result of the state legislature's efforts to "enquire into and ascertain, as far as practicable, the number of slaves that have escaped to the enemy during this war, and have not been recovered" offer a glimpse into the amount of enslaved people who escaped during Banks's southward march.[57] In Shenandoah County, twenty-two enslavers reported a total of sixty-four slaves who fled to Banks's army in April—thirty-seven male and twenty-seven female ranging in age from one to sixty. While most of the twenty-two enslavers lost one or two enslaved people, eighteen enslaved people escaped from John Strayer and eleven from Jacob Zirkle.[58] Further south in Rockingham County, twenty-six enslavers reported forty-eight slaves went "with Bank's [sic] Army." The report from Rockingham County enslavers also reveals that while some enslaved might not have sought refuge with Banks's troops in May 1862, they fled the following month when General John C. Frémont's army passed through the area. For example, Dr. A. M. Newman reported that only one person he enslaved, a nineteen-year-old male named John, escaped to Banks's army on April 27. However, Newman reported that eight of those whom he enslaved fled to Frémont's command on June 8.[59] In Page County, situated east of Shenandoah County, enslavers reported fifteen enslaved people slipped away during Banks's movement south.[60]

What Union soldiers also discovered as they moved south was that Stonewall Jackson continued his practice of seizing free blacks to labor for the Confederate war effort. In April 1862 Colonel George Gordon, 2nd Massachusetts Infantry, encountered "a neat-looking free negro" woman who lived near Edinburg, forty miles south of Winchester. Although Gordon never recorded her identity, he learned that Stonewall Jackson's men "had

Table 4.1. Enslaved people from Shenandoah, Page, and Rockingham Counties who escaped to Union forces in spring and summer of 1862 and were not recovered by enslavers as reported to Commonwealth of Virginia

| County | Number of Slaves Reported Escaped | Number of Enslavers Who Reported Slaves Fled |
| --- | --- | --- |
| Page | 104 | 46 |
| Rockingham | 61 | 32 |
| Shenandoah | 65 | 22 |

*Source*: Information in this table is derived from Page County: Records of Slaves that Have Escaped to the Enemy During the War [1861–1863], Runaway Slave Records, 1794, 1806–1863, Box 2, Folder 6, Library of Virginia, Richmond, VA; Rockingham County: Records of Slaves that Have Escaped to the Enemy During the War [1861–1863], Runaway Slave Records, 1794, 1806–1863, Box 2, Folder 7, Library of Virginia, Richmond, VA; Shenandoah County: Records of Slaves that Have Escaped to the Enemy During the War [1861–1863], Runaway Slave Records, 1794, 1806–1863, Box 2, Folder 7, Library of Virginia, Richmond, VA.

taken her two sons away from her." The Confederates who seized the boys, one of whom was "a poor cripple," reportedly used them to drive wagons and "haul off sick soldiers of Jackson's army." Whether or not these two free black men survived or escaped is unknown, but their mother certainly possessed no hope for a reunion. Noting the pain in her voice, particularly regarding the fate of her debilitated son, the woman pessimistically informed Gordon simply "I shall never see him again."[61]

Free blacks' concerns extended beyond seizure and impressment into Confederate service by Jackson's troops. They also feared reprisals by local white Confederate civilians if in some way they aided the Union war effort. As Banks's army moved south, David Hunter Strother encountered an "old bedridden mulatto" in Shenandoah County who told him that "free Negroes were shot down like dogs" if local Confederate sympathizers spied free blacks speaking with Union soldiers or exhibited even "the slightest disobedience or restiveness."[62]

As Union troops maneuvered throughout the Valley that spring they witnessed firsthand the brutality some enslavers exhibited toward those whom they enslaved. Richard Eddy, the chaplain of the 60th New York Infantry, was mortified when he saw an enslaved female being "beat" and "most shamefully whipped" by a white female in Middletown.[63] South of town, near the banks of Cedar Creek, a contingent of New York soldiers encountered an enslaved male who informed them that his life "was very hard at times . . . he had been badly whipped." As this unidentified slave continued in his conversation he informed the contingent of Union soldiers that "he thought that sometimes he could feel thick places on his back where the whip had been." Outraged at what this young enslaved male told them, the New Yorkers requested he remove his shirt. When he did the sight of the man's scarred back appalled them. "We had all read of scarred backs," one New Yorker wrote later, "but this surpassed all description. It was one continuous scar, and the ridges, thick as our fingers, which the whip had made, crossed it in all directions!"[64]

Horrifying sights such as the ones witnessed in Middletown compelled some Union soldiers to shift their attitudes about the destruction of slavery as a war aim. While historian James McPherson has offered compelling evidence that a significant number of Union soldiers did not wish at this point in the conflict to transform the war for union into one of abolition, sources indicates that some Union soldiers who campaigned in the Valley during the spring of 1862, who might not have initially viewed slavery's destruction as a war aim, softened their stance once they encountered slavery's horrors in the Shenandoah Valley.[65] For instance, the 2nd Massachusetts' Alonzo Quint never fancied himself an abolitionist; however, after various encounters with enslaved people in the Valley his attitudes about Union armies being agents of freedom changed. Even if enslaved people did not suffer brutal treatment, Quint believed the mere act of one human being owning another, with the enslaver having the right to exert all suzerainty over enslaved people, an unpardonable sin. "It is slaveholding itself that is the sin . . . it perverts the conscience, warps the intellect, brutalizes the heart," Quint wrote from Winchester on March 22, 1862. He continued in disgust in the same letter, "Believe no such nonsense as that 'the slaves are contented.' They . . . long to be free. Nor is there any difficulty in settling the slave question so far as our armies go."[66] Lieutenant Melzer Dutton, 5th Connecticut Infantry, echoed Quint when he wrote his mother from a camp near Edinburg in early April: "Am becoming an abolitionist fast."[67]

The encounters Union soldiers had with enslaved people did more than merely alter their attitudes toward slavery; some were prompted to use personal financial resources to aid some enslaved people escape the Valley for points north. So distraught was Chaplain Eddy after examining the scarred back of the young enslaved boy south of Middletown that he, along with two others from the regiment—Lieutenant George M. Gleason and Sergeant David M. Robertson—planned to help the boy and another male enslaved by the Stickley family escape. "We at once determined further action," Eddy wrote. The plan required the three New Yorkers to meet the two individuals in a wooded area at night. When the trio arrived at "the appointed place" the two enslaved males were nowhere to be found. Whether they had second thoughts or did not meet the New Yorkers because they learned "that rebel cavalry had been seen in that neighborhood" is unclear. However, after they did not show, Eddy, Gleason, and Robertson boldly went to Stickley's residence, located adjacent to where the Valley Pike crossed Cedar Creek. One of them called out and demanded the boys, but only one was there—an enslaved male the New Yorkers called George. While no record exists regarding the fate of the other enslaved person, the New Yorkers hoped to send George to New York, but sickness required them to send him to a Union hospital in a location which Eddy simply noted was "out of Virginia."[68] Unfortunately, George's ultimate fate is not known.

Although George's eventual fortunes remain unclear, the case of an enslaved female identified as Peggy and her child "Topsy" illustrates that some enslaved people who received support from Union soldiers during the spring campaign in the Valley did enjoy a fresh start in the North. Peggy and her child sought refuge with Colonel George Gordon's 2nd Massachusetts Infantry when the regiment passed through New Market. For a time during the campaign Peggy worked as a cook for the regimental staff, but in mid-June 1862, Gordon secured safe passage for Peggy and her child to Washington, DC, where he then purchased them two train tickets to Boston. "I readily gave my bond, secured the tickets, placed the bewildered woman and child in charge of a faithful expressman." According to an account Gordon wrote twenty years after the conflict's end, Peggy continued to live in "prosperity" in Massachusetts.[69]

While refugees from slavery like Peggy benefitted from the kindness of Union soldiers, the Shenandoah Valley's enslaved population did not merely sit passively and wait for Union soldiers to come carry them away to freedom. That proved the exception rather than the rule. Most enslaved people, as they had elsewhere in the South, understood that the best hope of attaining freedom rested with ultimate Union success. While this chapter has already established the important work enslaved people who fled to Winchester performed for Banks's command, diaries, journals, letters, and regimental histories are filled with examples of enslaved people in other portions of the Shenandoah Valley throughout the 1862 Valley Campaign doing what they could to weaken the Confederate cause. As portions of Banks's army moved south through Frederick County, various enslaved individuals informed Union troops that Confederates destroyed the bridge over Cedar

Creek and that Jackson's command rendezvoused near Harrisonburg.[70] As Union forces moved further south that spring and passed through Shenandoah County a contingent of enslaved people brought messages to Union troops about the whereabouts of Confederate forces.[71] The same proved true when federal regiments entered Rockingham County. Assistant Surgeon Samuel Sexton, 8th Ohio Infantry, wrote his wife from the regiment's camp near Harrisonburg in early May, "Many fine Negroes are leaving their rebel masters and seeking employment in the army . . . The most reliable information we get is from these colored fugitives from the rebel lines. They will tell the truth."[72]

While sometimes the information enslaved people offered Union soldiers regarded the whereabouts of an entire Confederate army, on other occasions it pointed Union soldiers to a handful of Confederate soldiers who took time out to visit with friends and family during the 1862 spring campaign. For instance, in June 1862, Emma Cassandra Riely Macon, a resident of Winchester visiting friends in Luray, noted that the enslaved laborers kept a close eye on everything. When they noticed food being carried upstairs they surmised that it was being fed to Confederate soldiers. The enslaved laborers quickly alerted Union soldiers who searched for the Confederate soldiers for two days. Unfortunately for the federal troops, they could not find any Confederate soldiers.[73]

Aside from taking information to Union forces the region's enslaved population supported the Union war effort that spring in other ways. After Stonewall Jackson's command annihilated a small Union garrison of approximately one thousand troops under command of Colonel John Kenly at the Battle of Front Royal on May 23, an enslaved person attempted to set fire to the depot there to hinder Confederate operations, but was arrested by Jackson's men.[74] As Union troops passed through Newtown, another refugee from slavery, employed by a Union officer, recognized someone dressed as a civilian "counting and noting down the number" of Union soldiers who passed through the town. Although none of the federal troops took notice, the refugee from slavery recognized the individual as a local who had gone off and enlisted in a Confederate artillery unit. After the refugee informed Union authorities, they promptly arrested the Confederate officer in disguise.[75]

Although enslaved people flocked to Union forces as the 1862 campaign ebbed and flowed throughout the Shenandoah and provided valuable assistance, it is important to note that some of the Valley's enslaved population still harbored reservations about fleeing and doubted the intentions of

Union soldiers. General Alpheus Williams noted at the end of April that "many of them are afraid of us . . . probably from big stories of cruelty that are told them."[76] While some of the Valley's enslaved exhibited, according to a newspaper correspondent attached to Union general John C. Frémont's army which entered Harrisonburg on June 6, "unmistakable signs of pleasure at seeing the National troops coming round" with one enslaved female so overjoyed that she "clapped her hands and threw them up in [the air] in an attitude of glory, hallelujah," others doubted the reality of the freedom Union soldiers promised.[77]

For instance, in April 1862 Colonel Gordon, who believed "it was the right as well as the duty of our armies to declare to the Southern slaves we found around us that they were forever free," ordered that as many enslaved people as could be found in the vicinity of Mount Jackson be brought to him so he could share the good news. Although official Union policy had not yet granted Union armies authority to declare enslaved people free—things for which Frémont had been chastised for attempting in Missouri in 1861 and General David Hunter been lambasted for doing in South Carolina in 1862—Gordon gathered an undeterminable number of enslaved people in the parlor of a home he commandeered in Mount Jackson and informed them "that from do-day, for all your lives, you are free. You belong to no one, you need work for no one unless you wish." After Gordon made his pronouncement he noted that "this motley gang of dark and ragged creatures gazed at me in wonder . . . there was no movement, not a word reply." Gordon offered further explanation, but still it elicited no reaction. "Still not a word was uttered; but instead there was an anxious, earnest, painful look of inquiry, as if the mind could not grasp the subject." Now for a third time, Gordon—perhaps somewhat befuddled by the lack of reaction—pressed the group assembled before him and asked, "Can you do nothing, to show that you are glad?' Can't you even turn a summersault in reply?" This time, an elderly enslaved man named George attempted a summersault but "flopped over with an awkward thud."[78]

As Union forces coursed throughout the Shenandoah that spring and encountered enslaved people reluctant to leave their enslavers, federal troops informed them that if they remained with their enslavers Stonewall Jackson would murder them. "There is the greatest panic among the servants," Winchester's Laura Lee wrote in May. "The Yankees have assured them that Jackson is murdering all the Negroes as he advances, even cutting the throats of the babies in their cradles."[79] Another white Valley resident noted of the panic that gripped African Americans in late May, "They had been told by the Yankees that Jackson's men would have no mercy on them but that they would be put to the most cruel death."[80] Although no evidence exists to corroborate the claim, fear of what Confederate soldiers might perpetrate sparked panic as Jackson's victories mounted and Banks's force retreated north.

In addition to the fear that Jackson's troops might murder enslaved people, anxiety also gripped the Valley's free blacks as Banks's army withdrew north toward Winchester in late May, as they feared the possibility of being captured by Confederate soldiers and sold to compensate enslavers whose enslaved fled during Banks's tenure in the Shenandoah. "There is a panic amongst the free blacks," Winchester's Mary Lee wrote, "who have heard that when Jackson comes back, they are to be sold to indemnify those whose slaves have absconded."[81] While no evidence exists to corroborate the claim, as in the case of rumors about Jackson murdering enslaved people, perception was reality.

By the time Banks's force reached Strasburg in mid-May his army had attracted hundreds, if not thousands, of African Americans. David Hunter Strother wrote that "negroes of all ages, from the gray-haired sire and dame to the child that can barely run, homeless, wandering, and pitiable" had attached themselves to the Union army.[82] Some came with only the clothes on their backs, while others followed Banks's command with wagons filled to the brim with all types of furniture and articles.[83] Among those who attached himself to Banks's command was an unidentified enslaved male from Rockingham County. During a conversation Strother had with the enslaved person on May 23 in Strasburg, the individual, labeled by Strother as a "poor creature . . . so dazed," told Strother that while he did not initially flee with Union forces moving north out of fear of what might happen to his family, the dread that if he fell into Confederate hands and could be "impressed" by Confederate authorities "into the service at Richmond, or sold into the cotton states" ultimately outweighed any initial angst the enslaved man possessed about bolting. Those fears "induced him to run away when our army fell back," Strother explained. Although this enslaved person attached himself to Banks's army, anxieties about loved ones who remained in Rockingham County remained. In fact he explained to Strother that once the situation stabilized in the Valley he "was hoping to get back to his family in Rockingham somehow."[84] While freedom proved his long-term goal, this enslaved person's immediate concern—like that of all African Americans who followed Banks's army—was keeping pace with Union troops and avoiding capture by Confederates.

The day after Strother's conversation with the enslaved male from Rockingham, Banks, learning of Jackson's victory at Front Royal, ordered his command north to Winchester.[85] As Union forces departed Strasburg around 9:00 a.m. on May 24, several thousand African Americans, by some accounts, headed north on the Valley Pike riding in wagons and on foot. As Union forces moved along the fifteen-mile stretch from Strasburg to Winchester, the numbers of enslaved people and free blacks grew.[86] However, not all who sought refuge with Union forces made it to Winchester. Refugees from slavery employed by the army's quartermaster as teamsters panicked as they neared Newtown and learned of the presence of a detachment of Confederate cavalry commanded by General George H. Steuart. Fearing capture or murder, many of the African American teamsters turned their wagons around, bolted south, and scattered. Some Union soldiers believed their behavior cowardly, but others understood the decision. A New York soldier wrote sympathetically, "They . . . knew that they had everything to lose in being captured. There was some excuse for them to act as they did."[87]

The sight of Union troops, thousands of African Americans arriving, and the likelihood of Stonewall Jackson defeating Banks's numerically inferior command compelled some African Americans who remained in Winchester to pack up what belongings they could carry and head for the Potomac River. "On the approach of Jackson the negroes, who had, many of them left their homes and were living in the town, began a flight," Cornelia McDonald observed.[88] For African Americans who opted to remain in the hope that Banks might be able to defend Winchester, the sound of Confederate artillery fire cutting through the air around 5:40 a.m. on May 25 forced them to confront the impending reality of Confederate victory and the dire consequences it might bring with it. With rumors continuing to course through the ranks of African Americans in Winchester "that Jackson's men would have no mercy on them" and that "they would be put to the most cruel death," thousands hastily gathered what possessions they could and dashed north. To one white resident who witnessed the scene unfold they appeared "a terror-stricken mob."[89] Shortly after the First Battle of Winchester's opening salvos James H. Brewster, a soldier in the 5th Connecticut Infantry, saw "an old colored woman with a big bundle on her head and two or three small children clinging to her hands and dress" trying "the best she could for freedom and the North." Unfortunately, a Confederate artillery shell landed in the midst of this woman and her children and killed them. Brewster penned of the horrifying scene, "but when the rebel battery opened up the first shell struck her, and the whole family, bundles and all, disappeared."[90] David Hunter Strother, near the Taylor Hotel when the battle began, spied an African American man and a few women "in the greatest trepidation, hustling some trunks and bundles into a light wagon."[91]

The scenes Brewster and Strother witnessed played out throughout Winchester as the battle opened. By 7:30 a.m. the situation intensified as Banks's army broke from its positions on Bowers Hill and Camp Hill. As Union soldiers hastily fled through the gauntlet of Winchester's streets, being shot at by angry Confederate civilians, thousands of frantic freedom-seekers "thronged" the Union retreat.[92] Rufus Mead, the 5th Connecticut regiment's commissary sergeant, estimated that as "high as 2 or 3,000" African Americans "of every age and color" hastened out of Winchester that morning.[93] With Union soldiers dashing north and thousands of frightened African Americans mixed amongst Banks's troops, the already chaotic scene became horrifying when Confederate artillery lobbed shells into the retreating mass. Each time a cannon fired the mere sound intensified fears. Union soldiers heard cries of "O Lord . . . save us! Please don't leave us behind! They gwine to kill us—they gwine to kill us!"[94] In one instance David Hunter Strother saw a female refugee from slavery so frightened by the concussion of artillery that she dropped her infant child.[95] Children unable to keep up with the frenzied pace were abandoned alongside the Martinsburg Pike leading out of Winchester "until some soft-hearted soldier would gather up the little foundling."[96] Although some Union soldiers reportedly aided refugees from slavery, some saw them as a liability to their own safety. "The exigencies of a moving army are remorseless," David Hunter Strother wrote. During the retreat from Winchester, north to Williamsport, Strother saw evidence that Union soldiers had pushed aside the wagons and carts of African Americans to secure safe passage of federal troops and artillery. "At every point in the road we found the vehicles of these poor fugitives thrust aside, broken, and overturned, their goods scattered, and the family weeping in despair."[97]

As Banks's army retreated north the number of African Americans following it increased. "At every step," David Hunter Strother wrote, "droves of negroes . . . thickened the column."[98] Uncertain how far north Confederate soldiers might go, evidence indicates that enslaved people in the swath of territory between Winchester and Williamsport, Maryland, fled their enslavers when they learned of Banks's retreat. Susan Nourse Riddle, a resident of Martinsburg, wrote in her diary on May 25, "'Banks *Grand Retreat*' from Winchester. Confederates here in the evening. Darkies gone."[99] Sarah Morgan McKown, another Berkeley County resident, penned her in diary that as the federal troops retreated "there was a great excitement" and that a

Figure 4.2. David Hunter Strother's "Jordan is a Hard Road to Travel" depicting African Americans during Union general Nathaniel P. Banks's retreat from Winchester (Strother, "Personal Recollections," *Harper's New Monthly Magazine*, 1866).

male whom they enslaved, identified as "Jim," ran "off."[100] Accounts such as these underscore the fact that the decision of an enslaved person to flee was sometimes a spur of the moment decision.

By the evening of the 25th untold numbers of African Americans made it to the Potomac River's north shore. As David Hunter Strother approached Williamsport that evening he "passed a cart-load of negroes who were singing, merrily, 'Jordan is a hard road to travel.'"[101] Those who made it to Williamsport did not remain long. Some continued their journey northward into Pennsylvania. Less than two weeks after Banks's retreat a newspaper correspondent noted that "numbers" of freedom-seekers sought refuge with African American families in Chambersburg. "During the last few days the roads leading from Virginia . . . to this place have been black with 'contrabands,' making their way North . . . Some of them have passed through

Figure 4.3. George William Cook (*Howard University Record,* April 1916).

but many are still quartered among the negroes of the town—some of the houses being crowded almost to suffocation."[102]

Among the freedom-seekers who arrived in Chambersburg was seven-year-old George William Cook, once enslaved in Winchester. As enslaved people fled north on the morning of May 25, Cook, his mother Eliza and father Peyton, and six siblings dashed for the Keystone State. Although unclear what happened to the rest of his family, George found employment as a delivery boy—first delivering newspapers, then groceries. He ultimately went on to graduate as valedictorian of the Howard University class of 1881. He spent the next fifty-eight years working at Howard University in a variety of academic posts, including professor of commercial law and dean of the School of Commerce and Finance.[103]

While Cook and an undeterminable number of refugees from slavery escaped safely, hundreds did not. Stonewall Jackson's troops "overtook" some of them north of Winchester. Confederate artillerist George Neese explained, "As we came down the Martinsburg road we met refugees of the colored persuasion—men, women, and children . . . They had evidently started for the land of sweet freedom and glorious ease."[104] William Lyne Wilson, a Confederate cavalryman and a Shenandoah Valley native, wrote in his diary that after the battle ended he "constantly" saw Confederate "troopers marching back with prisoners . . . many negroes were also taken while attempting to escape with the Yankees."[105] While no evidence indicates that Confederates carried out the brutal attacks enslaved people and free blacks feared, Jackson did return some to their enslavers.[106] Others he locked up in local jails.[107]

In the case of Manuel, enslaved by Winchester's McDonald family, he made it safely out of Winchester but returned about one week after the First Battle of Winchester. Manuel fled the McDonald home on Amherst Street in early March when he learned that Cornelia McDonald intended to send him south with Jackson's army. Manuel escaped to Banks's army and quickly found employment as a teamster. During the retreat from Winchester Manuel drove a Union wagon, but at some point during the withdrawal he pondered not only the likelihood of making a successful escape, but wondered what would happen to the loved ones he left behind—his wife Catherine and two children. At some point during the retreat he abandoned his wagon and hid "in a field under a haystack." Once the threat of being captured by Confederates subsided, Manuel made his way to Winchester and hid in "a cottage" on Piccadilly Street. One week after the battle, someone informed Cornelia McDonald that Manuel returned to Winchester. When McDonald found him, she noted that he was "emaciated almost to a skeleton, and greatly frightened." Before they left the cottage for Hawthorne, the McDonald family home, Manuel told McDonald that he maintained little concern for himself, but fretted for "Catherine and her babies." McDonald noted that when Manuel arrived at Hawthorne he "seemed very repentant" about having fled in the first place.[108] During Manuel's conversation with McDonald he learned that Catherine and the children fled with Banks's army on the morning of the 25th. Manuel was heartbroken and asked McDonald to try to find them. Fortunately for Manuel, an unidentified male discovered Catherine and the children sitting along the roadside at some point between Winchester and Harpers Ferry in a state of utter exhaustion. According to McDonald's account of what transpired, Catherine had already made the decision to return to Winchester when she was picked up. McDonald recalled that Catherine turned back because she and her children had almost nothing to eat in days. Additionally, the horrifying scenes of other female refugees from slavery and their children collapsing from weakness, simply laying on the side of the "roadside with their babies to die" mortified Catherine.[109]

Manuel's and Catherine's story illustrates the complexity of life for enslaved people not only in Shenandoah Valley, but across the entire South.

They longed to be free, but understood that escaping only proved the first step on the path to freedom. Considerations for loved ones, coupled with concerns over providing long-term security, complicated decisions. Both took the initial step on the path to freedom by bolting from the McDonald household, but returned when they confronted the reality that they might never see their loved ones again and also realized they lacked the ability to sustain themselves.[110] While those who advocate a Lost Cause interpretation of the era might use stories such as Manuel's and Catherine's to perpetuate the myth of the happy slave, both Manuel and Catherine clearly, as Cornelia McDonald described, did not return out of affinity for their bondage or loyalty to the McDonalds. They came back out of allegiance to themselves, one another, and their children. Manuel and Catherine did not remain long at Hawthorne. Manuel, Catherine, and their two children fled Winchester during the first week of September 1862, when Union forces commanded by General Julius White evacuated the city and moved to Harpers Ferry to support the Union garrison there commanded by Colonel Dixon Miles. McDonald penned: "The next time the Federals occupied Winchester and later evacuated it, Manuel stole the family carriage and departed with their army, taking Catherine and the children with them."[111]

Manuel and Catherine were not the only refugees from slavery to return to Winchester in the first week of June. After Union forces entered Winchester on June 3, David Hunter Strother noted that as he rode south toward Martinsburg that day that the "road was alive with the fugitive population, now *en route* for home." Strother spoke to some of them, who informed him that they came back for reasons similar to those of Manuel and Catherine. "They had had a rough time since they crossed the river," Strother explained, "being for the most part without shelter, provisions, or money."[112]

For refugees from slavery who returned or for enslaved people who remained, the reappearance of Union forces in Winchester during the first week of June emboldened area African Americans. In addition to asserting that they were "perfectly free and . . . more disposed than ever before to avail themselves of their liberty," Winchester's John Peyton Clark observed that some enslaved people informed their enslavers that if they wished for them to remain, they would need to compensate them appropriately. "Some have gone so far as to demand wages from their masters upon condition of their remaining to work for them," Clark wrote in his journal.[113] While no evidence indicates that enslavers submitted to the requests for financial compensation, the fact that some enslaved people demanded money illustrates enslaved people's cognizance of how the constant state of flux in the

Valley—one that opened the door for an enslaved person to bolt at any moment—shifted the power dynamic between enslaver and enslaved.

As it had throughout the early part of spring, by the end of the season and throughout the summer of 1862, Winchester, with the continued presence of Union troops, again became a magnet for freedom-seekers. Reminiscent of scenes that unfolded in March 1862, John Peyton Clark noted a steady stream of enslaved people from surrounding areas entering Winchester. Whether these individuals came on their own accord or with assistance from Union soldiers, Clark seethed with anger at the "negro-stealing [that] has been progressing with fine success within the past three weeks." On August 12, Clark witnessed "a wagon drawn by four horses filled with negro women and children." Behind the wagon he saw "a large number of negro boys, women, and men." Some he identified as belonging to owners in Clarke County including George Burwell and John Page.[114]

Just as it had during Banks's tenure that spring, Winchester proved merely a stop on the path to freedom. The presence of Union soldiers coupled with the fresh memories of Confederates capturing fleeing refugees from slavery in the First Battle of Winchester's aftermath compelled some enslaved to seize this second opportunity. For example, thirteen individuals enslaved by Emma Cassandra Riely's aunt and sister viewed the Union presence in Winchester in June 1862 as their best opportunity to flee.[115] Those thirteen individuals were not alone in their flight. On June 25, Mary Greenhow Lee wrote that there "has been another stampede amongst the servants."[116]

Two days later, the long-awaited moment Frederick County's John Quincy Adams waited for arrived. Since the conflict began he begged his father to flee, but his father urged restraint, waiting to escape until he believed the entire family could do it successfully.[117] Adams, along with his father, mother, four brothers, and two sisters, ran away from the Calomese family. "On Saturday, June 27, 1862," Adams wrote, "we left old mistress, and young miss, and every other kind of miss." Adams and his family, like the lion's share of freedom-seekers who left the Valley in 1862, headed for Pennsylvania. They first went to Greencastle, where they remained for a few weeks. From there they journeyed further north to Chambersburg, next to Carlisle, and then Harrisburg. Evidence indicates that while the Adams family journeyed as far north as Elmira, New York, John Quincy returned to Harrisburg after the conflict.[118] While little is known about the fate of all of the family's members, John Quincy enjoyed great success after he settled in Harrisburg. He found employment as a coachman for a judge and eventually became an ordained minister in the A.M.E. Zion Church. Additionally, he became a voice for the rights of African Americans in Harrisburg. As a founding member of the Colored Protective League of Harrisburg, he fought to end segregation practices in the capital city's Grand Hotel. At the time of Adams's death in January 1917 a newspaper correspondent for the Harrisburg *Telegraph* lauded Adams as an "eloquent exponent of the doctrine of Christianity, and earnest believer in the future of the black race and the justice of the white man toward his deserving brother."[119]

While refugees from slavery such as the Adams family used the presence of federal troops to escape, other enslaved people believed the circumstances still not quite right. For those who remained, Union soldiers needed somewhere to house them. They commandeered the Union Hotel and abandoned buildings throughout the city. "The Union hotel is occupied by them, containing between two and three hundred . . . Many vacated tenements through-out town, of which there is a large number, have also been appropriated to their use," wrote a resident of Winchester.[120] As the numbers of freedom-seekers who reached Winchester rose each day, the frustration among the community's Confederate sympathizers increased. While some residents merely vented their frustrations quietly in diaries, others exhibited outward displays of that animosity. In mid-July a fifteen-year-old white boy shot some sort of projectile at "a negro on the street" with "a boy's blow gun."[121]

Tensions, however, did not only exist among Confederate sympathizers and refugees from slavery, but also among the refugees themselves. As space in Winchester became limited with the daily increasing numbers of freedom-seekers, disputes erupted as quarters became cramped. Near the end of July, three African American women got into some sort of quarrel with another female contraband. The situation escalated to the point where the three women dragged the unidentified woman from a house appropriated by Union soldiers to house refugees from slavery. Once in the street, one Winchester resident noted that three women struck the fourth one and tore the clothing from her body.[122] Near the end of August an argument broke out between a female refugee and several other African Americans quartered in the Union Hotel. During the tussle the children of one of the refugees had been "thrown over the stairs to the story below and . . . dreadfully injured." The fight so enraged one of the women involved that she determined to get back at the others by setting fire to the Union Hotel. Fortunately, Union soldiers who garrisoned Winchester discovered the attempt, doused the flames, and arrested the woman. Union soldiers took her "out to the camp and whipped" her as punishment for the attempted arson and injuries sustained by the unidentified child.[123]

Throughout 1862 the Valley's enslaved population navigated a complex, uncertain world. They not only had to determine the best moment to flee their enslavers, if they left at all, but also had to worry about being captured by Confederates and impressed into the Confederacy's service. Even if they evaded capture by Confederate soldiers, freedom-seekers still had to figure out how they would survive on their journey to points north. Additionally, if they fled to Union lines they had to deal with tensions between refugees with whom they shared living space. All of this, along with the incessant concern of being sold, compelled some of the Shenandoah's enslaved population to remain with their enslavers. Among those not enticed to leave at any point in 1862 was Sukey, enslaved by Frederick County's Barton family. Beyond all of the various concerns that confronted enslaved people throughout 1862, Sukey might have also decided to remain due to her child being ill. On December 7, 1862, three weeks after her "little baby" died, Sukey wrote a letter to Bolling Barton, the seventeen-year-old son of her enslaver who was a student at the Virginia Military Institute, wherein she expressed her despair and thanks for the aid her "white friends . . . mistress and master" offered during her difficult time. Sukey also used the letter to explain her allegiance. After referencing "our Confederate army," Sukey wrote Bolling that she "never was a Yankee."[124] While Sukey's words undoubtedly heartened the Barton family and superficially seemed to indicate a strong sense of devotion to the family and the cause they favored, her later actions clearly indicate that she penned what she did because she believed it beneficial to creating a stable environment for herself and her children. Approximately three months after Sukey's profession that she was "not a Yankee," she fled the Barton home south of Kernstown. On March 3, 1863, Randolph Barton wrote his brother Bolling simply, "Sukey has gone at last."[125]

While Sukey might have believed the likelihood of making a successful escape impossible in a year that brought with it so much uncertainty, other enslaved people who held similar beliefs became optimistic that freedom's prospects would improve following the public announcement of President Abraham Lincoln's preliminary Emancipation Proclamation. Less than one month after Lincoln announced his intent to free all those enslaved who resided in areas in rebellion against the United States on January 1, 1863, Union soldiers near Charles Town encountered "a solitary horseman, with a bucket on his arm, jogging soberly toward them." The enslaved male, identified as John, labored as a body servant for a Confederate officer from South Carolina who had given him a pass to go "anywhere between Winchester and Martinsburg in search of butter, etc., etc." Armed with the pass and news of "the proclamation," he fled to the nearest Union troops he could find, as he believed they would offer him "protection." Union soldiers questioned him about his knowledge of the Emancipation Proclamation and according to a newspaper correspondent who covered his escape, John clearly understood "that every slave is to be emancipated on and after the 1st day of January." When Union soldiers asked John, who also took the opportunity to profess his love for John Brown, about what enslaved people who were forced to labor for the Confederate war effort thought about the conflict, he told one: "Well, boss, they all wish the Yankee army would come."[126]

At the time Lincoln issued the preliminary Emancipation Proclamation only those enslaved such as John, who possessed passes which permitted mobility throughout portions of the Shenandoah Valley and allowed them to get close to Union troops in Jefferson County, could bolt for freedom. Unfortunately, for the Valley's enslaved population at the time Lincoln's initial pronouncement came, Confederates controlled most of the Shenandoah. When Union general Julius White evacuated Winchester and moved to Harpers Ferry in September, the door for Confederate control of the Valley opened. A significant Confederate presence remained until late November when Robert E. Lee began shifting the Army of Northern Virginia to Fredericksburg. The departure of the large majority of Confederate forces from the Valley, coupled with a greater Union presence, at least throughout the Valley's northern portion, really presented the first opportunity for enslaved people to assert themselves since the late summer.

Enslavers who did not record any indignant behavior from their slaves from early September through late November took notice of assertiveness among those whom they enslaved once the presence of Union forces increased. Winchester's Portia Baldwin Baker, who recorded no bold conduct among those she enslaved throughout the conflict up to this point, noted that some of her enslaved laborers started to act insolently by mid-December. For example, on December 30, Baker recorded that her enslaved female "Florence was stubborn and impertinent in the highest degree to-day."[127] Although one can never know precisely what caused Florence to act as she did, as she left no account, it is reasonable to surmise that since Baker did not previously report any similar behavior, that the presence of Union troops, as had been the case in other areas across the South, coupled with news of the Emancipation Proclamation, compelled Florence to finally assert herself.[128]

While the prospect of Lincoln's Emancipation Proclamation might have emboldened enslaved people such as Florence, the Union soldiers now mandated to enforce it wondered whether or not the edict was enforceable as Union armies suffered setbacks in Virginia that autumn, most notably at Fredericksburg. Even if it could be enforced, they questioned whether or not it would materially change the condition of lives for those emancipated by it. The Valley's David Hunter Strother wondered whether "the Federal Government" could afford "to invite the bitter and concentrated hostility of a whole section, when it has not shown itself able to repress the rebellion of a faction in that section?" Concerns about whether or not Union forces could support the Emancipation Proclamation with military success aside, Strother pondered, the day after the preliminary Emancipation Proclamation was announced, if "we mock the poor negro with offers of freedom before we have satisfactorily proved that we can defend our own?"[129]

For enslaved people, not only in the Shenandoah Valley, but all who lived and labored throughout the portions of the South where Lincoln's Emancipation Proclamation would take effect, the notion that on New Year's Day, 1863, with the stroke of Lincoln's pen, that they would be deemed "thenceforward and forever free" buoyed spirits.[130] However, after that initial excitement subsided, enslaved people realized that enjoying independence was contingent upon the same factors which it rested up to this point in the conflict—the ability to successfully escape to Union lines, the capability to secure basic necessities for survival, and continued Union presence in the region. As important as the signing of the Emancipation Proclamation was to bringing about slavery's eventual destruction, the process of acquiring one's freedom in 1863 in the Shenandoah Valley, as was the case elsewhere, continued to come as historians Ira Berlin, Marc Favreau, and Steven Miller succinctly argued, "slowly and unevenly."[131]

# 5

## "Freedom to Slaves!"

New Year's Day, 1863, the day President Abraham Lincoln declared free all enslaved people living in areas of rebellion against the government of the United States and opened the door for the recruitment of African Americans into the nation's army and navy, donned unseasonably warm in the Shenandoah Valley. As a bright sun burned in a cloudless sky, approximately 8,000 Union troops commanded by General Robert H. Milroy, an ardent abolitionist from Indiana, marched into Winchester from the west. As the long, blue-clad column neared the city's western boundary, officers in the rear of the column heard a raucous noise coming from the front. Concerned that it might be an attack, Colonel Joseph Warren Keifer, commander of the 110th Ohio Infantry, rode hastily to the front. When he arrived at the head of the division Keifer discovered General Milroy in a state of complete excitement, proclaiming to the troops that "this is Emancipation Day, when all slaves will be made free."[1] Before Milroy's command established camp on Winchester's west side he gathered his regiments and explained to them the importance of the day and the significance of the Emancipation Proclamation to the Union war effort and humanity. This was "the day President Lincoln will proclaim the freedom of four millions of human slaves," Milroy pronounced, "the most important event in the history of the world since Christ was born. Our boast that this is a land of liberty has been a flaunting lie. Henceforth it will be a veritable reality."[2]

Milroy's thoughts on New Year's Day, 1863, focused not only on the Emancipation Proclamation's significance, but also the Shenandoah Valley's important connections to slavery. Winchester was not only home to Senator James Mason, author of the 1850 Fugitive Slave Law, but also the home of Judge Richard Parker, the man who condemned John Brown to death. Shortly after his arrival in Winchester, the "Gray Eagle," as his men affectionately referred to him, wrote his wife Mary in Indiana that "the residence of the infamous scoundrel Mason who was with Slidele [*sic*] is here and Judge Parker who presided at the trial of old John Brown resides here."[3] Buoyed by the historical setting, Milroy added, "I am enforcing the proclamation of the President of the U.S., freeing the very slaves that old John [Brown] so insanely attempted to free . . . Plainly these events are directed and controlled by the Infinite Being who holds the nations of Earth in the hollow of his Hand."[4]

· During the first four days of Milroy's tenure in Winchester the area's enslaved population behaved as it had during prior Union occupations. Those who believed the time to flee was right left their enslavers, while others remained. Interestingly, Union soldiers such as William Hewitt, a soldier in the 12th West Virginia Infantry, were astonished that many of the area's African Americans had no knowledge about Lincoln's Emancipation Proclamation. "This was the day on which the President's Emancipation Proclamation was to take effect," Hewitt wrote, "but strange to say the colored people of Winchester seemed utterly ignorant of the fact that there was such a thing as any proclamation of freedom."[5]

Milroy undoubtedly desired to enforce the Emancipation Proclamation from the first minute of his occupation, but he had not yet received a copy of the final version and therefore did not know if the area he occupied was exempt from the Proclamation or not. While Milroy waited for final word, the region's enslavers, who had initially braced themselves for a large exodus of enslaved people, seemed confident as the days passed that the Emancipation Proclamation would not be enforced. Mary Greenhow Lee gloated in her diary on January 1, "The day has passed with less excitement than was anticipated—there was no further announcement of emancipation & we find from the papers Lincoln is afraid to carry out his plan."[6] Four days later another of Winchester's Confederate sympathizers, Laura Lee, wrote confidently, "Yesterday Lincoln's proclamation came in the papers, but thus far we have seen no effects of it."[7] The comments from Mary and Laura Lee proved premature.

On January 4, the day Winchester's civilians first read the Emancipation Proclamation, Milroy received his copy. Milroy pored over each word of the document and when it became clear that the area under Milroy's control was not exempt from it, Milroy promptly crafted a proclamation of his own, "Freedom to Slaves!" The following day, January 5, Milroy's soldiers began posting "Freedom to Slaves!" throughout Winchester and Frederick County. Cornelia McDonald noted one week later, "Lincoln's Proclamation flames at all the street corners."[8]

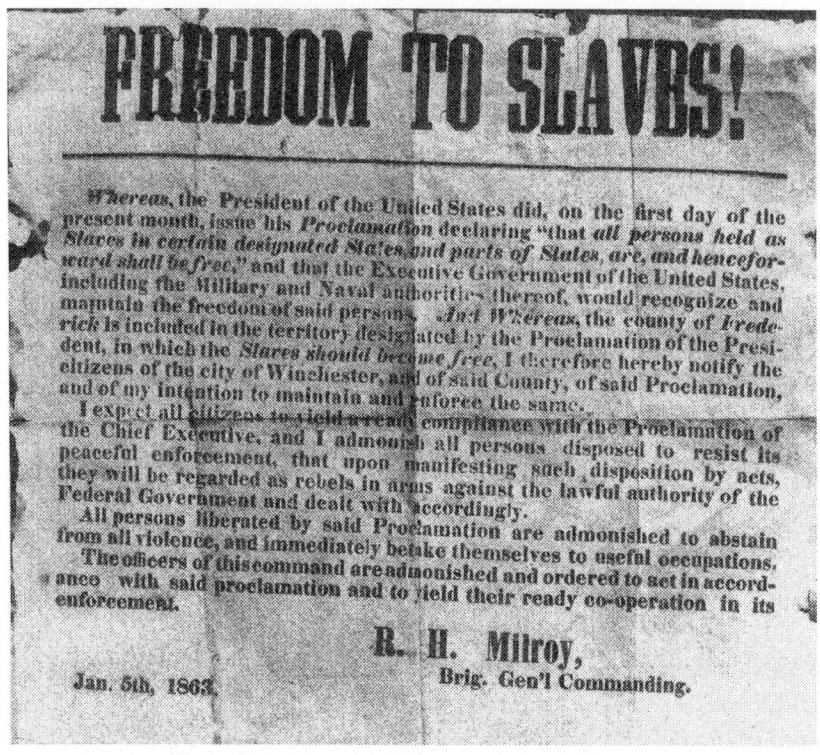

Figure 5.1. "Freedom to Slaves!" (Jasper County Public Library, Rensselaer, Indiana).

In addition to posting "Freedom to Slaves!" throughout Winchester's environs, Milroy's troops fanned out around area locales and went door-to-door, farm-to-farm announcing it. One of Milroy's subordinates, General Gustave Paul Cluseret, explained how the Gray Eagle's troops spread the word: "We . . . scattered throughout the country, from farm to farm, an order . . . notifying all slaves that they were free."[9]

Milroy's "Freedom to Slaves!" consisted of four key elements. First, Milroy opened with a basic statement that since "the county of Frederick is included in the territory designated by the Proclamation of the President, in which the slaves should become free," Milroy would do all in authority "to maintain and enforce" it.[10] Next, Milroy announced to area residents that he expected them to not in any way erect obstacles to emancipation. While the area's Confederate supporters certainly detested the Emancipation Proclamation, Milroy was also cognizant that some of the local Unionist civilians, as they had in other areas of the South, did not necessarily support the Emancipation Proclamation.[11] For example, Julia Chase, one of Winchester's staunchest Unionist supporters, detested the idea. "I can't reconcile it with his Inaugural when he said that he did not intend, or that Congress had any right, to interfere with slavery in any of the states," Chase wrote.[12] Alert to the challenges that civilians of all allegiances might present to slavery's annihilation, Milroy bluntly asserted in his decree, "I expect all citizens to yield a ready compliance with the Proclamation of the Chief Executive, and I admonish all persons disposed to resist its peaceful enforcement, that upon manifesting such disposition by acts, they will be regarded as rebels in arms against the lawful authority of the Federal Government and dealt with accordingly."[13] The threat of being "dealt with accordingly" usually meant arrest followed by exile.[14]

While Milroy recognized that civilians who harbored Confederate or Unionist sympathies might in some manner undermine emancipation's enforcement, that concern also extended to the men he commanded, troops who would ultimately be carrying out his plan to destroy slavery. Milroy's command included officers and enlisted men who did not support Lincoln's transformation of this conflict into one that would simultaneously reunite the nation and destroy slavery. Among his officer corps General Gustave Paul Cluseret, who commanded the van of Milroy's division that arrived in Winchester on Christmas Eve, 1862, was perhaps the most ardently opposed to implementing the Emancipation Proclamation. Cluseret, a native of France who came to the United States in 1862 to fight for the Union war effort, made it clear that "he did not come here to fight for negroes."[15] Private Thomas Crowl, 87th Pennsylvania Infantry, fumed about enforcing the Emancipation Proclamation in the Shenandoah Valley and angrily wrote his sister that "the war may go to hell for me, I never intend to stay here and risk my life for these damned niggers. This Nigrow freedom, is what is playing hell, this is a wrong thing, this will destroy our army we never enlisted to fight for Nigrows."[16] Similarly, Frederick W. Wild, an artillerist in the Baltimore Light Artillery, explained that he did not enlist "to free negroes, much less to make them masters over white men."[17] While Milroy could not have known what his troops wrote privately in letters to loved ones, he was certainly aware of the fallout that occurred throughout the Union Army following Lincoln's emancipation announcement in late September 1862, most notably reports of significant portions of some regiments signing petitions that threatened mutiny if Lincoln followed through on January 1, 1863. While Milroy's command did not contain any such regimental petitions, it did contain officers who publicly announced their disdain for the Emancipation Proclamation and promised that if required to enforce it, they would resign. For example, in the 110th Ohio Infantry, a regiment that contained a significant amount of Democrats, Captain William R. Moore threatened to resign his commission from the regiment rather than support any program that destroyed slavery and placed African Americans on an equal plane with whites.[18] In his attempt to preempt any discord in his ranks Milroy made it eminently clear to those who served in his division that they "are admonished and ordered to act in accordance with said proclamation and to yield ready co-operation in its enforcement."[19]

Finally, Milroy used "Freedom to Slaves!" to address those most profoundly impacted by it, the area's enslaved. Heeding Lincoln's instructions in the Emancipation Proclamation counseling the newly emancipated slaves "to abstain from all violence, unless in necessary self-defence, and . . . in all cases when allowed, they labor faithfully for reasonable wages," Milroy ordered that "all persons liberated by said Proclamation are admonished to abstain from all violence, and immediately betake themselves to useful occupations."[20] While evidence from white diarists indicates some destruction of private property by those emancipated, mainly the tearing down of wooden fences to be used as firewood, Milroy's directive seems to largely have been obeyed.[21] Mary Walls, an enslaver from Newtown, wrote that once Milroy started enforcing the Proclamation "it was perfectly surprising how well the Negroes did . . . after Lincoln's proclamation. We lived so near the border that they could have done a great deal of mischief if they had a notion."[22]

Although Walls seemed surprised, the lack of aggressive behavior among those freed by the Emancipation Proclamation should not be that shocking in retrospect. African Americans, not only in the Shenandoah Valley but elsewhere, as historian Aaron Sheehan-Dean concluded, understood the "experience of slave rebellions in the antebellum era and brutality with which they were repressed" and consequently believed widespread violence "counterproductive" to their ultimate goal of freedom.[23] In addition to understanding the uselessness of vengeful attacks, African Americans also comprehended that any sort of militant retribution required long-term material and financial support—things they did not possess. At times, access to everyday basic necessities proved difficult, let alone finding sources for firearms, ammunition, and other supplies required to sustain a successful insurrection.[24]

Although Milroy's enforcement of the Emancipation Proclamation never prompted violent behavior, anxieties existed not only in the Valley but among Virginia and Confederate authorities that it might lead to a bloody

Haitian-style insurrection.[25] When Alexander Boteler, a member of Virginia's House of Delegates, received a copy of Milroy's "Freedom to Slaves!" he immediately sent it to Governor John Letcher. Boteler informed the Commonwealth's chief executive: "I have just received [a] copy of a Proclamation 'Freedom to Slaves' recently issued by the notorious Milroy in the District which I have the honor to represent." Obviously aggravated and anxious about what Milroy's decree might lead to, he informed Letcher that "this man Milroy has announced his determination to enforce by arms on our devoted Valley the fiendish abolition policy which the infamous John Brown vainly attempted to inaugurate at Harpers Ferry and for which he received from . . . Virginia the punishment he so richly deserved."[26]

Letcher took immediate action by sending a message to the Virginia Senate and House of Delegates rebuking Milroy and Lincoln for their "brutal" proclamations, which Letcher believed "violated all principles of humanity." Letcher informed Virginia's legislature that Milroy was "in all respects a suitable tool, for the execution of so execrable a mark. He follows the lead of his master, and therefore promises to maintain the freedom of the slaves, urges a ready compliance with the Proclamation of Lincoln." In Letcher's eyes Milroy's emancipation edict violated "in the most positive manner, the provisions of our act of assembly, which declares if a free person advise or conspire with a slave to revolt or make insurrection, or with any person, to induce a slave to rebel or make insurrection he shall be punished with death."[27]

Active enforcement of emancipation might have caused Boteler and Letcher another concern: the Shenandoah Valley's counties might not be able to fill a quota of slaves in order to meet the demands of a proclamation Letcher issued in December 1862 that required every county in the Old Dominion to provide enslaved people to labor for Virginia's defense.[28] While an understandable concern for the counties closest to where Milroy operated—Frederick, Clarke, and Warren—it does not appear from extant statistical data that the Emancipation Proclamation or Milroy's "Freedom to Slaves!" had any significant impact on the ability of counties in the southern portion of the Shenandoah Valley to initially fill their quotas. In March 1863 Colonel S. Bassett French, who served as an aide in Letcher's administration, prepared a report that included the desired quotas and number of enslaved people actually impressed for three counties from the upper Shenandoah Valley—Augusta, Rockingham, and Rockbridge. French requested the three counties supply a total of 500 enslaved people to labor for the Confederacy. He required Augusta to supply 250, Rockingham 100, and

Rockbridge 150. Rockingham met its quota, while Augusta and Rockbridge came close. Augusta sent 231 of the 250 required, and Rockbridge fell eleven short of its requirement.[29]

Those 470 enslaved individuals impressed in early 1863 were sent to work on Richmond's defenses.[30] Despite the absence of accounts from those impressed from the Shenandoah Valley—a rarity from any part of the South—a sketch penned approximately three decades after the Civil War's end by Willis Carter illuminates the hardships impressed individuals confronted constructing Confederate fortifications around Richmond. Carter, who after the conflict moved to Augusta County and by the early 1880s worked as an educator and newspaper editor in Staunton, watched helplessly as his father Samuel Carter was taken by authorities from his enslaver, George Farrow, who lived in Albemarle County, just east of Augusta County in the foothills of the Blue Ridge Mountains. Eleven years old when his father was impressed, Carter wrote of that horrible moment: "Poor slaves were seized in every section, dragged brutally to different places, and forced under the scourge to build fortifications." As Carter reflected on his father's impressment decades later he thought the practice brutal on various levels. Not only did impressment place his father in an even more grueling labor environment, unimaginable considering the profusely documented difficulties enslaved individuals confronted laboring for enslavers, but it placed enslaved people in the unenviable position of building fortifications meant to defeat the very armies attempting to defeat the Confederacy and aid in slavery's destruction. Carter wrote that his father's labor and that of countless others worked "to build fortifications . . . to defeat if possible the men who sought to save the Union from the slavish disgrace that had already with its hideous crimes shocked the world from centre to circumference."[31] Additionally, Carter's account highlights another difficulty impressed individuals confronted: neglect.

Jaime Amanda Martinez's indispensable scholarship on impressment illuminates that enslaved individuals who labored on the construction of defenses confronted significant food shortages, inadequate housing, and insufficient medical care, despite promises from authorities they would receive proper treatment.[32] Carter's father became severely ill while constructing defenses around the Confederate capital, contracted pneumonia, and died. According to Carter's account it was "soon" after his father Samuel reached Richmond that "he had an attack of pneumonia which proved fatal."[33] The tragic end to Samuel Carter's life proved one of various reasons enslavers did not favor impressment.[34]

Entered according to Act of Congress in the year 1862, by M.B. Brady, in the
Clerk's office of the District Court of the District of Columbia

Figure 5.2. General Robert
H. Milroy (author's col-
lection).

Despite the ability of certain Shenandoah Valley counties to largely fulfill
their impressment quotas, Milroy's program of emancipation was viewed as
detrimental to stability throughout the region and prompted the Virginia
legislature to support Letcher's resolution, which branded Milroy an outlaw. On January 10 both houses of the Virginia legislature recommended
that Milroy be hung, as his actions called "for the severest measures of re-
pression."[35] The threat of death, coupled with a $100,000 reward for his
capture issued jointly by the Virginia and Confederate governments, concerned Milroy little. Guided by his Christian faith and belief that God would
shield him from all harm and that God had chosen him as an instrument to
eradicate slavery, Milroy did not worry about what might happen. Instead,
he focused his attention on destroying slavery in an Old-Testament style

scourge. Prepared to become a martyr for abolition's cause if necessary, Milroy penned his wife in biblical tone: "In ancient times the cry of a nation of slaves went up to a God out of Egypt and He hear them and sent Moses and Aaron to reason with the slave holders and try to get them to emancipate their slaves, but all arguments and reasoning . . . were received by the slave holders with scorn and ridicule." He continued his tirade that a "long bitter cry has went up to the same God from a nation of slaves in America. He has heard that cry for many years been sending good men to reason with the slave holders . . . but the slave holders have met all arguments. . . . with scorn." Unsympathetic with enslavers, Milroy believed that only brutal occupation, aggressive emancipation, and bloody conflict could adequately remove the blight slavery had placed on the United States' landscape. In forceful rhetoric, he explained to his wife in Indiana: "War, devastation, want, Misery, disease, terror and death are everywhere around them, but still they defy God and refuse to let their slaves go free . . . Hell deserving iniquity until like the Pharaoh and his host, they will overwhelm in total destruction."[36]

Once they learned of "Freedom to Slaves!" an undeterminable amount of enslaved people in and around Winchester fled their enslavers. The day after Milroy made his emancipation edict public, Colonel Joseph Warren Keifer observed refugees from slavery leaving. Lincoln's Proclamation, coupled with Milroy's announcement, "had the effect of causing those [enslaved people] within the lines of his command at once to leave their masters," Keifer noted. From Keifer's perspective some might have been motivated to leave out of fear that if they did not assert "their freedom" now under the Emancipation Proclamation, that they would have to remain slaves "for life."[37] Once enslaved people made the decision to leave their enslavers in January 1863 they "gathered up their little property with marvelous dispatch and presented themselves," one of Milroy's officers wrote.[38]

While evidence illustrates that some enslaved people boldly asserted their independence by fleeing at the first announcement of the Emancipation Proclamation, others perceived some level of risk in leaving. Once an enslaved person made it to Milroy's division in Winchester they knew that their freedom was secure; however, making it to Winchester sometimes presented challenges. Aside from concerns about securing foodstuffs and basic supplies for survival, freedom-seekers had to worry about being captured by Confederate troops who lurked throughout the Valley. In addition to bushwhackers and other irregulars, General William E. "Grumble" Jones commanded a contingent of Confederate cavalry that attempted to do all it could to disrupt Milroy's operations, including his enforcement of the Emancipation Proclamation. One month after Milroy announced "Freedom to Slaves!" Milroy learned that Jones was "gathering up the darkies . . . about ten miles" from Winchester. Although troopers from the 13th Pennsylvania Cavalry intercepted Jones's troopers and "rescued the negroes" on this occasion, there was no guarantee that Milroy could learn about every instance and rescue them every time.[39] Aside from the possibility of being captured by Confederates, enslaved people who decided to leave still ran the risk of being pursued by angry enslavers who refused to acknowledge Emancipation's reality. For instance, in mid-April 1863, a female enslaver, Jane Allen, tracked "a negro woman who had been her servant" all the way to Winchester in the hope of finding and reclaiming her.[40]

For those hesitant to leave out of concerns for personal safety, Milroy announced that any enslaved person who desired to leave their enslaver, but remained out of a fear of reprisals, could ask for assistance from Milroy's troops to be escorted from their enslavers to Union lines. Notes from enslaved individuals seeking help flooded Milroy's headquarters in Winchester on a daily basis. One Frederick County resident observed that enslaved people "send them [Milroy's soldiers] word that they wish to go to freedom and you know they are very accommodating and so they come out."[41] Each day Union detachments went out and assisted enslaved people flee their enslavers. Bettie Cadwallader, a white resident of Newtown, wrote that "they [Milroy's troops] come out to Newtown nearly evry [sic] day" to aid enslaved people.[42] Newtown's Steele family noted Milroy's "abolitionists" also coming to the community regularly. On February 2, a contingent of Union soldiers aided people enslaved by Dolph White in fleeing north to Winchester. Two weeks later the Steeles noted that Milroy's men "went to Tom Millers and Sam Hupes and took their negroes."[43] Sometimes the departures proved uneventful, but in some instances enslavers questioned the authority of Milroy's men. Among them was Clarke County's Kimball family. On February 24, 1863, a detachment of Milroy's men arrived to escort Fairinda and her child, enslaved by the Kimball family. Accompanied by a refugee from slavery, William (Fairinda's brother-in-law), the Union troops demanded her immediate release. Sigismunda Stribling Kimball challenged the request and demanded to see "written authority." Captain William Clagett, commanding the Union detachment, told Kimball that he did not have any "written authority," nor did he "require a special order for this occasion." Kimball insisted that Milroy had "no right to take them" as Fairinda and her child did not belong to Milroy, but the Kimballs. Clagett fumed and informed Kimball that they were human beings and did "not belong to anyone, the government has fixed that." Tired of arguing with Kimball, Clagett ordered four horses "hitched . . . to the [Kimball's] big wagon" and then loaded with "Fairinda and her child, then boxes, chests, [and] barrels of flour."[44]

As news of the aid Milroy's command offered enslaved people to escape reached the Confederacy's capital, reporters in Richmond started to embellish reports and suggested that Milroy forcibly removed enslaved people from enslavers. On February 10, Richmond's *Daily Dispatch* charged that Milroy "seduced . . . or coerced" enslaved people from "the service of their owners and carried [them] off." Four days later it continued in condemnation that "servants are persuaded off, and in many instances forced to leave their home."[45] While the *Dispatch* printed stories about Milroy making enslaved people leave whether they desired to do so or not, accounts from Valley residents, including whites who ardently supported the Confederate war effort, suggest that the Richmond reporters' accounts were inaccurate. On March 30, 1863, Anna Bell Cadwallader, a resident of Newtown whose brother served in a Confederate artillery battery, wrote her brother John that while so many of the area's enslaved people "have been flocking to Yankeedom by hundreds," others remained. She observed that Milroy's men left alone those who opted to stay. "The fact is the Yankees do not take any but what wishes to go."[46] The process of emancipation, even in the wake of the Emancipation Proclamation, in the Shenandoah Valley as it had elsewhere continued to be, as historian Kenneth Koons noted, "episodic and gradual."[47]

Regardless of when or under what circumstances enslaved people departed their enslavers it seemed, at least in the estimation of one of Milroy's subordinates, that those who bolted, either with or without assistance from Union troops, possessed little desire to remain in the Shenandoah Valley and instead wanted to "emigrate . . . north."[48] While many enslaved people who escaped to Milroy's command believed the North their "land of Promise," Milroy hoped those freed by the Emancipation Proclamation would view the Shenandoah Valley as the "land of Promise."[49] Milroy tried throughout his approximately half-year occupation of Winchester to convince African Americans to remain in the Shenandoah Valley and aid in the Union war effort in the region. "I try to persuade them to remain in V[irgini]a assuring them that they will remain free." Milroy's assurances carried little weight. Cognizant of the area's strategic importance to both sides, evinced by the incessant military activity in the area, the Shenandoah

Valley's African Americans, like those throughout all areas of the Confederacy frequently contested by both armies, knew that anything resembling freedom existed only as long as Union troops remained. Milroy wrote of various conversations he had with formerly enslaved individuals who expressed their desire to remain in the region, but only if they could receive assurances that Union troops would remain in the Valley in perpetuity and the Union army win the war. Unfortunately, Milroy could not offer such guarantees. "They say they would much rather remain among friends and neighbors with whom they were raised if the war was over and they could be assured that the Proclamation of Jan. 1st would be enforced, but considering the uncertainty of war and the certainty of slavery if the South should destroy the Union, they wish to make sure of their freedom while the way is open."[50]

Even though Milroy hoped these emancipated slaves would remain, he refused to stand in the way of their northward journey and used the transportation resources available to his division to move them "into P[ennylsvani]a and Ohio and . . . any place they are told . . . is a free state."[51] Almost on a daily basis hundreds of newly freed people boarded "empty trains" north of Winchester "going north . . . to carry these freed people from the land of their birth to where a slave condition could not overtake them."[52] When schedules allowed, either Milroy or members of his staff rode to the departure point north of Winchester, Stephenson's Depot, and wished them well. When Milroy ventured to the depot he gave each freedom-seeker an image of John Brown. "Most of them knew the story of John Brown," an Ohio officer explained, "and many of them had, in some way, been supplied with cheap wood-cut pictures of this early champion of their liberty." Colonel Keifer, who on occasion trekked to Stephenson's Depot to watch the trains depart, described the great exhibitions of joy these formerly enslaved individuals displayed as they boarded train cars and the locomotives steamed toward the Potomac River. Keifer clearly heard the commingling of "songs of freedom and the religious hymns peculiar to their race with the . . . cheerful music of the fiddle and banjo."[53] Occasionally, Keifer witnessed former enslavers coming to Stephenson's Depot to wish those they once enslaved well. "Pity was in some cases expressed. Tokens of remembrance were offered and accepted with emotion," Keifer explained.[54] While sometimes these freedom-seekers accepted whatever items a former enslaver presented them, Keifer also observed instances where formerly enslaved people refused anything their white enslavers offered. This act of rejection, Keifer believed, aside from making the decision to leave, became one of the freedom-seeker's first assertions of independence and repudiation "of a master's continuing authority over them."[55]

Although "every day," as Winchester's Cornelia McDonald noted, "there is a great exodus of negroes" for points north, not all who sought Milroy's assistance departed the Shenandoah Valley. Some decided to remain, work, and try to become self-sufficient. Among those who stayed and continued his labors repairing shoes and receiving wages from Winchester's whites was an unidentified African American male. Throughout her journal for 1863, thirteen-year-old Gettie Miller described various trips to "that colored mans" to take shoes for repair.[56] Others who remained found employment performing a variety of tasks for Milroy's division, including intelligence-gathering. Throughout his tenure in the Shenandoah Valley, Milroy used a variety of resources to spy on the area's Confederate civilians and collect information about Confederate forces in the area. Along with the use of secret detectives and Jessie Scouts (Union soldiers who dressed and portrayed themselves as Confederates), Milroy utilized formerly enslaved people for espionage activities. For freedom-seekers who fled to Milroy's lines and explained their desire to remain in the Shenandoah Valley, he enticed them to return to their enslavers and spy on them and their friends. Milroy gave them every assurance they were free and financially compensated them for their clandestine efforts. General Robert Schenck, commander of the Middle Department and Milroy's immediate superior, supported the practice and sent Milroy at least $500 "to prefer a system of espionage on the Rebs."[57]

By early February it became apparent to Confederate supporters that Milroy utilized formerly enslaved persons to spy on civilians. While some enslavers might have initially believed in January that enslaved people remained out of loyalty, within one month of Milroy's announcement that he would enforce the Emancipation Proclamation, it became clear that some worked as spies. On February 9, Mary Lee wrote simply that Milroy's use of African Americans for his "system of espionage is becoming more apparent."[58] On the same day as Lee's entry, Cornelia McDonald observed that Milroy used emancipated slaves "to enter houses and report what the women talk about or if the children play with Confederate flags, or shout for Jeff Davis."[59] In mid-April, Lee reported that "a servant of Dr. Neale's" accused Baldwin of secreting contraband items. As soon as Milroy received the report he immediately sent a detachment to confiscate the items.[60]

While emancipated slaves served a role in gathering information about local Confederate civilians, perhaps the most significant role they performed as spies was assisting Milroy break down the bands of Confederate irregulars, partisans, and cavalry who had plagued his operations since his arrival in the lower Shenandoah Valley. Although Milroy never silenced the cavalry forces of Confederate generals John Imboden or William "Grumble" Jones, an opportunity presented itself in the spring of 1863 to capture a Confederate guerilla referred to by Unionists as a "notorious murderer" and "heartless wretch," Captain Andrew Leopold (sometimes known as Lapole).[61] Throughout March and into April, Leopold wrought havoc on Unionist civilians and federal troops in the areas around Clarke and Jefferson Counties. One of Milroy's soldiers stationed east of Winchester in Berryville explained that "the pickets, outposts and reconnoitering parties were constantly annoyed and harassed by frequent attacks from guerilla bands, under command of Capt. Lapole."[62] In early April, Lieutenant David Powell, 12th West Virginia Infantry, served as the provost marshal in Berryville and became suspicious when an unidentified "negro man" came to his office and requested a permit so that he could "buy some sugar and coffee" from the "post Sutler." Instinct told Powell that this unidentified African American male desired to purchase coffee and sugar not for himself, but for someone else—perhaps a Confederate civilian who was attempting to skirt Milroy's directive prohibiting the sale of any goods to individuals who did not take an oath of allegiance to the United States.[63] Powell questioned the man and confirmed his intuition. The man, an enslaved person from Clarke County identified as Sam, had been sent by his enslaver, who was providing refuge for Leopold "and seven of his men."[64] Powell informed the man that any information he could provide that might lead to Leopold's capture would result in a $50 reward. After Powell communicated to Milroy that he possessed a good lead on Leopold's whereabouts, Milroy raised the reward to $80. The 12th West Virginia's William Hewitt noted that when presented with the offer the "negro at once acceded to the proposition and agreed to join the work of his capture."[65] So as not to arouse suspicion, Powell permitted Sam to purchase the items and return. However, Powell informed Sam that a contingent of the 1st New York Cavalry would venture to the west bank of the Shenandoah River opposite of where the enslaver's home stood. Once the sun went down Powell instructed Sam to "light three matches in succession" if Leopold and his men remained at the house. Sam did as Powell instructed. He lit the matches and directed the New Yorkers across the Shenandoah River to Leopold who, according to an officer in the 1st New York cavalry, "was in bed" at the time.[66] Without Sam's assistance, Leopold would have continued to harass Milroy's efforts in the region. After being taken to Winchester, Milroy then sent Leopold to Fort McHenry in

Baltimore, where he was tried for murder. Leopold was executed in May 1864.[67] While Sam played the most significant role in Leopold's capture and enjoyed financial reward, his involvement in seizing Leopold ultimately cost the slave his life. Determined to remain in the Shenandoah Valley and not seek refuge with Milroy's command, Sam "was literally shot to pieces" when Leopold's men discovered the role he played.[68]

Espionage proved not only a way for African Americans to assist the Union war effort and thus assume a role in assuring freedom's permanence, it also allowed them an opportunity to earn wages. However, for some the risk outweighed the reward and instead they determined to earn wages laboring for their former enslavers. When Milroy entered Winchester he announced that any emancipated slave who wished to remain with former enslavers possessed "the right to claim wages" from them and that federal troops would do all in their power to "protect their rights precisely as they will those of all other citizens."[69] This practice, not unique to the Valley, offered another means for formerly enslaved people to assert their freedom.[70] Among those who remained with his former enslaver in Winchester under the condition that he be paid was Remus, a man once enslaved by Dr. Robert Baldwin. Remus performed his assigned tasks, but when the moment came for Baldwin to financially compensate him, the enslaver refused. When Remus informed Union authorities that his employer had reneged, Milroy ordered a group of soldiers to escort Remus to Baldwin's home "to demand his wages." When Remus and Milroy's men showed up at Baldwin's home on the morning of June 9, Baldwin fumed and still refused. The Union soldiers tried to reason with Baldwin, but as one Winchester resident recalled, "the Dr. cursed Milroy, swore he would not pay a cent, sent him to the Devil &c. &c." Enraged by Baldwin's refusal to pay Remus, Milroy surrounded Baldwin's home the following day and offered an ultimatum—pay Remus the $40 in the next twenty minutes or be exiled with his entire family. Although Baldwin refused to pay Remus, Baldwin's friends quickly gathered the necessary funds and paid him. Undoubtedly pleased that Remus received the money owed him, Milroy still fumed that Baldwin was not the one who paid it. For Milroy this was about more than Remus receiving wages due. Milroy wanted former enslavers to recognize that African Americans now stood on an equal plane with whites. Determined to make his point that he expected white employers to not only pay individuals whom they once enslaved but to respect them, he banished Baldwin and his family from Winchester.[71]

Throughout his nearly half-year tenure in the northern Shenandoah Valley Milroy utilized African Americans to enforce this new social order, much to the dismay of those who supported the Confederacy. For example, a few days after Milroy issued "Freedom to Slaves!" several members of the McDonald family, after securing a pass from Union authorities, were stopped by Union pickets on Winchester's outskirts on suspicion that they carried documents addressed to Confederate officials. When Union pickets brought the McDonalds back to Winchester, Milroy ordered each person and their baggage searched for the letters and any other contraband. While in previous occupations the search would have been conducted by Union soldiers, this time the Gray Eagle directed an African American woman to do it. One of Winchester's Confederate sympathizers believed that having "a negro woman . . . examine their persons" was the "greatest indignity."[72]

Whenever an opportunity presented itself to show Confederate civilians that African Americans stood on an equal plane with whites or perhaps even usurped whites' status, Milroy seized it. In early February Milroy received a visit from Mary Baldwin, who begged and pleaded with him to permit her to purchase supplies for her family. As Milroy informed Baldwin that she could have whatever she desired if she took an oath of allegiance to the United States, a knock at his office door interrupted the conversation. When a staff officer opened the door and Milroy saw two African American women who wished to speak with him, he promptly ordered Baldwin to leave. Astonished that she had been kicked out, Baldwin seethed with anger and vented her frustration to Cornelia McDonald—someone whose enslaved people fled in 1862 and someone who believed that the only suitable place for African Americans was "on a cotton plantation."[73] Already angered by this point of Milroy's occupation with the way African Americans could "jostle and crowd ladies off the pavement into the gutter as may suit their convenience" and seemed to be "the only people who have any rights or liberty, and . . . In every instance [were] preferred to whites," McDonald proposed sending Milroy a "Valentine" of her own design that exhibited the disdain the community's white Confederate women possessed toward Milroy and those freed by his enforcement of the Emancipation Proclamation. McDonald painted a scene showing Milroy sitting down, pointing to the two African American women and telling them "Be seated ladies." As he welcomed them, McDonald showed Milroy then exclaiming to Baldwin, wearing a dress of red and white stripes emblematic of the Confederacy, "Out you d[amne]d Rebel." McDonald concluded the scene with Baldwin leaving and informing Milroy "Jackson will avenge us."[74]

Milroy's presence in the Shenandoah Valley during the first half of 1863 certainly created opportunities for African Americans and helped untold

Figure 5.3. Cornelia McDonald's "valentine," sent to General Robert H. Milroy on February 14, 1863, illustrates the difficulty Winchester's whites had with accepting African Americans as equals (Jasper County Public Library, Rensselaer, Indiana).

numbers flee bondage; however, not all of the Shenandoah Valley's enslaved population had the same access to freedom. Unlike General Banks's time in the Valley in 1862, when Union troops moved from Frederick County south to Rockingham County, Milroy's troops stayed largely confined to Frederick and Clarke Counties, with some brief incursions into Warren County. Milroy's lack of mobility throughout his time in the Shenandoah Valley made escape more difficult for enslaved people in the Valley's southern end. In fact, enslavers and slave traders in Augusta County scoffed at the Emancipation Proclamation and knew that without Union troops around to enforce it, it meant nothing. "The people of the South never felt that the institution of slavery was ever safe than at the present time," explained a correspondent for the *Staunton Spectator* on January 6. The *Spectator* proudly reported the results of some recent slave auctions that occurred where enslaved people sold between $1,015 for an eighty-five-year-old man deemed "defective," to $2,305 for a twenty-one-year-old male.[75] Throughout the first six months of Milroy's enforcement of the Emancipation Proclamation in the northern Shenandoah Valley the *Spectator* regularly advertised enslaved people for sale and notices from individuals looking to purchase. For instance, the *Spectator* ran John B. Smith's announcement calling for the "purchase [of] 50 Negroes."[76]

While Milroy's troops never ventured too far south in the Shenandoah Valley—which added an additional challenge to an already risky undertaking for enslaved people who wished to flee, for reasons mentioned previously in this chapter—it did not mean that enslaved individuals from the upper Valley did not attempt to escape and make their way to Milroy's command. Throughout Milroy's six months in the Shenandoah Valley enslavers and those who rented enslaved laborers from the Valley's southern counties regularly complained that their enslaved laborers fled, and the enslavers took out paid advertisements in newspapers in the southern Shenandoah Valley seeking their return. Most announcements merely offered the amount of the reward and a description of the enslaved person. For example, Thomas N. Burk of Rockbridge County promised a $600 reward for the capture of three enslaved males, Mark, Lewis, and Edward. Interestingly, of all the announcements published in the *Staunton Spectator* during the first half of 1863, Burk's is the only one that states they can be returned to him "either dead or alive—suggesting that Burk cared more about asserting dominance over those whom he enslaved rather than simply reclaiming valuable property from which he could reap reward.[77] Some advertisements during Milroy's occupation suggested that the refugees from slavery might attempt to move north and seek refuge with federal troops in Winchester. When S. F. Jordan announced a $750 reward for the capture of three enslaved laborers, Sandy, Jerry, and Bryant, who had run away from his Buena Vista Furnace in early May 1863, Jordan included a statement in the notice that he had "reason to believe they are trying to reach the enemy's lines down [north] the Valley."[78] In the middle of the month an official from Estaline Furnace in Augusta County promised a $200 reward for the apprehension of four rented enslaved laborers, John Fox, Phil, Bob, and Isaiah, who "may be trying to make their way to Yankee lines."[79] Several weeks prior, in late April, an Augusta County enslaver offered a reward for an enslaved female, Caroline, and her two children, Mary Adaline and Armistead. The enslaver suspected that they were "probably on their way to Winchester."[80]

Even though Milroy's command never ventured close to the Valley's southern reaches, evidence indicates that one of those who served in his command aided enslaved people from as far south as Augusta County flee. The Baptist chaplain of the 110th Ohio Infantry, James Augustus Harvey, reportedly "helped slaves run away" from Augusta enslavers. One month after Confederates captured Harvey at the Second Battle of Winchester a Staunton journalist charged Harvey with aiding Sarah Jenkins, a person enslaved by W. J. Shumate, on her journey north from Augusta County. The assistance Harvey provided prompted calls, after his capture in mid-June 1863, for him to be "handed over to state and civil authorities . . . to be prosecuted" for the role he played in aiding an undetermined amount of enslaved people escape. Harvey remained a prisoner until Confederate authorities released him in October 1863.[81]

Accounts such as those implicating Harvey or regular announcements from enslavers between early January into June 1863 do not fully reveal how many enslaved people ran away to Winchester from the upper Valley, but those bits of evidence provide some proof that despite being separated by more than a hundred miles from Milroy's force, depending on where they were enslaved, enslaved people in the upper Valley, a locale that remained more firmly in Confederate control than the lower Shenandoah Valley, believed that Milroy's aggressive enforcement of the Emancipation Proclamation presented an opportunity to flee. Whether in the four counties south of Winchester or situated more closely to Milroy's command, those enslaved in the Valley, as had enslaved people across the entire Confederacy, waited for the moment they believed most opportune. However, even for the most pragmatic enslaved person, arguably nothing made them reevaluate what constituted ideal circumstances to flee more than an impending battle.

By the second week of June anxieties among war planners in Washington, DC, increased as evidence indicated General Robert E. Lee's Army of Northern Virginia intended to use the Shenandoah Valley as an avenue of invasion into the North.[82] Although not concerned about being attacked and firm in the belief that his division could withstand an attack by a force three or perhaps even four times his size, Milroy tightened security and made preparations to evacuate ill Union soldiers during the first week of June.[83] How much enslaved people who remained with their enslavers during the first half of 1863 knew about the advance of the Army of Northern Virginia's Second Corps commanded by General Richard Ewell is unclear, but rumors of the Confederate approach might have compelled some of them to determine the time was now right to flee. Three days before Ewell's regiments entered the Shenandoah Valley at Chester Gap near Front Royal, a number of enslaved people from that community decided to bolt. Members of the Buck, Moffatt, and Kiger families reported those whom they enslaved had gone off during that time. In addition to taking themselves, enslaved people reportedly took various items from their former enslavers including "horses . . . their finest clothing and . . . various articles" with them.[84]

Three days later when Milroy ordered Colonel Andrew McReynolds's brigade from Berryville to Winchester, some enslaved people who remained with their enslavers did not want to again risk life in Confederate territory and attached themselves to the Union regiments marching west on the Berryville Pike. Frederick Wild, an officer in the Baltimore Light Artillery, noticed "a middle aged mulatto woman, loaded down with clothing, bedding, etc. leading a little girl about four years old," trailing the brigade as it left Berryville. As the column began the ten-mile march, Wild struck up a conversation with the unidentified woman and learned that her husband was once enslaved, but "had gone North some months before." Although she never explained why she did not go with her husband, she expressed her hope that she "would follow the Union soldiers and meet him." As McReynolds's brigade moved west, Wild pitied the woman who struggled to carry various belongings and the child who tired from the march. Wild offered to carry the "child in front of me on my horse." As McReynolds's brigade approached the Opequon Creek, just east of Winchester, a contingent of Confederates (Wild believed them cavalry) opened fire. The enslaved female with whom Wild became acquainted on the journey panicked. Fearing things might turn badly quickly, Wild heard the woman exclaim "Oh Lawdy God, what is gwine to become of me now?" Amid the shouts and fire, Wild also heard the Confederates shouting "Kill the nigger stealers!" Although the woman and child made it safely to Winchester, accounts of what happened to her after that do not exist. Nearly half a century after the melee Wild still remembered the woman and her child and wondered about their fate.[85]

The anxiety felt by the woman Wild encountered increased among African Americans as Ewell's command engaged Milroy's troops during the Second Battle of Winchester. That fear prompted some to flee to forts located northwest of Winchester that had been constructed or strengthened by Milroy's troops. According to an account by one Frederick County enslaver, enslaved people ran to Milroy's forts at the first sound of battle. They spared no time to even pack up some belongings, simply fleeing with only the clothes on their backs.[86] By the night of June 14, after having been engaged with elements of Ewell's command for two days, Milroy decided to evacuate Winchester for Harpers Ferry. For African Americans who had been in Winchester during Banks's retreat in late May 1862 it was déjà vu. As Milroy's regiments hastened north of Winchester, one of Ewell's divisions commanded by General Edward Johnson blocked Milroy's escape route near Stephenson's Depot, capturing more than half of the Union force. In addition to the more than 4,000 Union soldiers seized north of Winchester, Ewell's men apprehended hundreds of African Americans, both those freed by the Emancipation Proclamation and those born free. "*Many* Darkies were captured," during the retreat, Ann Cary Randolph Jones wrote to Lucy Parkhill three days after the battle.[87] Among those captured was Levi (Lee) Jenkins.

Born around 1824 as a free black, Jenkins worked as a blacksmith prior to the conflict's outbreak in his native Newtown. By the time Milroy occupied Winchester, Jenkins worked as part of Milroy's intelligence-gathering network.[88] Although born free, Jenkins's Confederate captors cared little about his legal status. To those from Ewell's corps who captured him the color of his skin labeled him as someone who could be seized and impressed into the Confederacy's service. Eight days after his capture, Confederate soldiers marched Jenkins and a column of several hundred African Americans south from Winchester on the Valley Pike. While Jenkins had never been enslaved, he witnessed its cruelty firsthand throughout his life. One could only imagine the thoughts that coursed through his mind as the column entered the community where he grew up, lived, and worked as a free person his entire life. As he undoubtedly contemplated a life of hard labor for the Confederacy, Jenkins might also have wondered what Confederates might do to him if they discovered his role of information-gathering for Union forces. Searching for a way to release himself from captivity and impending bondage, Jenkins made a drastic decision: when the mass of African Americans neared Newtown's southern boundary he broke ranks, ran to property owned by Thornton McLeod on the west side of the Valley Pike, and committed suicide by jumping head-first into McLeod's well. A member of Newtown's Steele family wrote that Jenkins "ran in the old house and into the yard and jumped into the well at the old McLeod house and killed himself."[89] Tragic as Jenkins's story is, his decision to kill himself was not unfortunately atypical. Jenkins's behavior is certainly similar to that of enslaved people throughout the institution's existence in North America. As historian Terri Snyder asserted, those who confronted slavery's realities and its physical or emotional toll considered suicide "an honorable escape from slavery."[90]

Not all of the African Americans captured by Ewell's troops north of Winchester were impressed into the Confederacy's service. Confederates returned some of them to their enslavers, among them several people enslaved by Frederick County's Jones family. While one of those enslaved by the Joneses, William Braxton, reportedly made it north, others who bolted with him did not fare so well. By June 18 three individuals enslaved by the Joneses—Mary, Sally, and Lavinia—had been returned to Vaucluse, located south of Winchester. Ann Cary Randolph Jones noted that when they came back, two of them, Mary and Lavinia, appeared to accept the outcome. However, Sally expressed her disdain for her servitude and her owners, and made it clear that she wished she would have succeeded and intimated that she might escape again if the right opportunity presented itself. In Ann Jones's estimation Sally was so "unhumbled" by the whole affair that she thought it prudent to do what any enslaver would do if they believed an enslaved prone to escape: sell them. "Sally I *think* ought to be sold," Ann Cary Randolph Jones explained several days after Milroy's defeat.[91]

Interestingly, one of those captured during the Union retreat and locked in the Winchester jail—Robert Discon, a free black—was ordered released by Confederate general Jubal Early when Early learned Discon "was a free man." Early's motivation for doing this remains unclear, as Confederate soldiers in the wake of Union demise at Winchester did not customarily discriminate between enslaved people and free blacks, as Lee Jenkins's circumstances illustrate. Although released by Early's order, once discharged from the Winchester jail Discon soon discovered that his status mattered little to others. A few days after his release he "was enticed to the stable of Mr. Levi Grim." Once inside, William H. Corbin, a master carpenter from Winchester, "handcuffed" Discon. Whether or not Corbin knew Discon is unclear, but Corbin certainly viewed this as a lucrative financial opportunity. Within days Corbin carried Discon to Richmond, where he sold him for $2,400 "to a Mr. Wilson of Georgia." Although it is unclear what happened to Discon once Wilson purchased him, Discon's case further illustrates that the free status of African Americans meant nothing.[92]

Those of the Shenandoah Valley's African Americans not captured on June 15 and who moved north into Pennsylvania still confronted the prospect of being seized by Confederates as the Army of Northern Virginia pushed north to the Potomac River and the Keystone State. After Milroy's defeat Rachel Cormany, a resident of Chambersburg, Pennsylvania, observed that "contrabands" who sought refuge with Milroy's command streamed into town "as fast as they could on all and any kind of horses, their eyes fairly protruding with fear."[93] Just as Ewell's men did north of Winchester, they did not differentiate between free blacks and enslaved people as they pushed into southern Pennsylvania. They kidnapped hundreds of African Americans and sent them south.[94] Chambersburg's Amos Stouffer noted four days after Milroy's defeat that Ewell's men were "scouring the country in every direction about Waynesboro, Greencastle, Mercersburg [and] Finkstown for horses and cattle and Negroes."[95]

Among those who fell captive were enslaved people who had fled the Shenandoah Valley several months prior to Milroy's defeat and carved out a new life in southern Pennsylvania. For instance, in March 1863 Milroy's troops assisted a sizable family of enslaved people "consisting of a mother with three grown up sons and three grown up daughters with a son in law and a daughter in law and seven grandchildren" flee their owners in White Post, located in Clarke County. This contingent of sixteen newly emancipated slaves "established themselves in Green Castle[,] P[ennsylvani]a." The adults secured jobs and finally "began to feel that the shackles had fall[en] off." However, as one Union officer wrote in 1865, when "Gen[era]l Lee's rascals . . . came into Penn[sylvania]," they quickly discovered that even though living in a free state their freedom still proved uncertain. Although unclear exactly at what moment in the aftermath of the Second Battle of Winchester it occurred, a group of "Sec[essionist] raiders headed by a Mr. Meade" arrived in "Greencastle with wagons . . . to get plunder and hunt up niggers." Unmercifully, they ripped one of the women who had fallen ill "from her bed." The horrific scene frightened two of the children, Maria and Lucy, and prompted them to flee. However, both were caught. While not clear how many of the sixteen enslaved people who ventured north in March 1863 were captured, surviving evidence indicates that at least three had been "put into the wagon and driven off" south back to their enslaver in Clarke County.[96]

One week after the Second Battle of Winchester, just as Joseph Howland Coit, an Episcopal clergymen and professor at the College of St. James located six miles south of Hagerstown, Maryland, was sitting down for his afternoon tea, a man who identified himself as "Sever" from Winchester showed up at Coit's residence in search of a person enslaved by his father who fled north during Milroy's retreat. Coit knew nothing about these freedom-seekers and explained as much, but Sever cared little. After Coit could not produce the individuals Sever sought, Sever took Coit's African American cook and her two children. Helpless and fearful of what Sever might do should he attempt to prevent their kidnapping, Coit did nothing to stop the man from Winchester. "It was a sad sight," Coit confided to his diary.[97] Unfortunately for African Americans who either retreated north · after the Second Battle of Winchester or who lived in the path of the Army of Northern Virginia's advance that June, it was not uncommon for either

Confederate soldiers or civilian slave hunters to kidnap African Americans and send them south.

Union defeat at Winchester in mid-June 1863 marked the end of arguably the best opportunity the Shenandoah Valley's enslaved population—particularly those in its northern reaches—had to escape slavery up to that point in the conflict. In the months that followed Milroy's loss the Shenandoah Valley became a revolving door, as Union and Confederate forces came and went frequently throughout the remainder of the year and into the early months of 1864.[98] Although the remaining months of 1863 proved unstable and did not present ideal conditions for enslaved people to escape, instances of enslaved people in various places throughout the Shenandoah Valley fleeing bondage do exist, albeit infrequently. While there is no way to precisely determine exactly how many enslaved people fled enslavers during the summer and autumn of 1863, an examination of surviving newspaper advertisements seeking the return of refugees from slavery for that time frame offers some insight. The *Staunton Spectator*, a weekly newspaper, published announcements in its August, September, November, and December issues from enslavers seeking the return of enslaved people who bolted. All of the notices, which offered rewards ranging from $100 to $500, were for enslaved males between the ages of eighteen and forty. While most notices merely posted the date the enslaved person fled, along with their description, one suggested a possible destination. On December 15, 1863, William S. McChesney, a Staunton enslaver, appealed for the return of two enslaved males, an eighteen-year-old male, Jesse, and a thirty-year-old male, Wilson. McChesney believed that Wilson might venture north to Jefferson County and unite with his wife, who was enslaved by the Hensel family in Shepherdstown.[99]

While the desire to be reunited with his wife might have motivated Wilson to flee, Andrew, an enslaved man from Rockbridge County, opted for escape when he confronted physical punishment. Shortly before Christmas, Andrew's enslavers, the Chandler family, suspected he stole a "*whole hog.*" Lucy Chandler, who intimated the family had confronted "more troubles" recently with their enslaved laborers, explained that they wished to make an example out of Andrew. Escorted to the ice house, his enslaver ripped off his shirt and bound his hands. Fortunately for Andrew, his owner forgot the whip. When his enslaver went to the house to get one Andrew seized the opportunity, untied himself, and fled into "the woods." Search parties attempted to locate him, but to no avail. Although records for most of the documented escapes during the final months of 1863 do not reveal whether or not those attempts succeeded or failed, Andrew's attempt failed—though the failure came not as a result of his enslaver finding him, but of Andrew returning himself. Why he returned is unknown; however, like other enslaved people who returned to their enslavers at various points in the conflict, he might have done so out of concerns about leaving loved ones behind or wondered how he would survive.[100]

Clipped announcements from unidentifiable Shenandoah Valley newspapers in the collections of the Harrisonburg-Rockingham Historical Society also reveal that despite the unsettled nature of the conflict in the Shenandoah Valley in the months after Union defeat at the Second Battle of Winchester, some enslaved people still attempted escape, although not nearly as frequently as they had during the first half of 1863. For instance, in late September 1863 John Bowman announced the escape of an enslaved man identified as Jason. Undoubtedly bitter over Jason's departure, Bowman only offered a "one cent reward" for "his apprehension" and "without thanks."[101] Two months later Thomas Walker offered a $200 reward for the seizure of his twenty-seven-year-old enslaved man Albert.[102]

Extant notices for refugees from slavery for the latter half of 1863 reveal not only that enslaved people continued to flee from bondage, but suggest that it was something undertaken mostly by young men during this uncertain time. Although women and children fled enslavers at various moments up to Union defeat at Winchester in 1863, the lack of a constant Union troop presence made flight much more difficult for women. Since colonial times, fleeing bondage had proved more difficult for women for a variety of reasons. Historians have contended that in addition to an enslaved female not possessing the requisite physical stamina to reach a destination, those who had children seemed less likely to leave, as they made flight more difficult. Beyond that, scholars have contended that females travelling alone or with children aroused greater suspicion than men, as it was not uncommon for enslaved males to be sent out by enslavers for various errands.[103]

Although evidence indicates that enslaved females seemed reluctant to flee during this period where the military situation seemed in constant flux, it also reveals that they were attuned to the area's rapidly changing military situation and at the hint of Union troops being nearby they at least considered escape. On August 17, 1863, a contingent of Union cavalry entered Winchester for a brief period that morning. For Emily, a female enslaved by Mary Greenhow Lee, this seemed a likely moment to flee. According to Laura Lee, Emily "got into a passion" and expressed her dissatisfaction with her enslavement. Emily left the house and approached the Union cavalrymen and asked if they could take her with them. Whether the Union soldiers refused, or at some point during the exchange Emily thought about those she would leave behind (two enslaved people about whom she cared deeply, Sarah and Jim Will) is unknown, but Emily ultimately returned to the Lee home. Perhaps Emily even considered what she would do once she entered Union lines, where she would go from there, and how she would support herself.[104]

Emily's considerations typified the difficulties the Valley's enslaved population confronted throughout a year that began optimistically and concluded with so much uncertainty. Events of 1863 continued to illustrate to enslaved people and free blacks alike that anything remotely resembling freedom or security was always contingent on which army controlled the Valley. As the Confederate invasion of Pennsylvania made eminently clear, not even escape to a free state guaranteed liberty. As 1864 dawned and the conflict in the Valley entered what would become its bloodiest and most destructive year, the Shenandoah's African Americans would have to continue to navigate a complex environment where they balanced their quest for freedom and survival with their desire for Union victory and slavery's ultimate destruction.

# 6

## "This Causes Great Excitement"

Despite the military instability that continued to plague the Shenandoah Valley as 1864 dawned, the Valley's enslaved population continued to seek opportunities to claim their freedom. Although it occurred more sporadically as compared to the spring of 1862 or the first half of 1863, examples exist of enslaved people fleeing enslavers in those unpredictable early months of 1864. For instance, in January 1864 an enslaver from Rockingham County promised a $100 reward for the capture of two enslaved men, Isaac and Oliver.[1] While uncertainty exists as to the precise factors that compelled these two seventeen-year-olds to flee, little doubt remains as to why Henry, an enslaved male from Augusta County, escaped his bondage at Elizabeth Furnace in early March. A mid-March advertisement that appeared in the *Staunton Spectator* and offered a $25 reward for Henry's apprehension contended that rather than fleeing north, he went to Staunton to be with his wife. Whether Henry made it successfully to Staunton, reunited with his wife, and then escaped from the Valley or not is unclear, but repeated notices for his capture appeared in the *Spectator* throughout the remainder of March and into April.[2]

Although surviving evidence indicates, as noted in the previous chapter, that enslaved females seemed less likely to leave enslavers during this prolonged period of instability, a few cases of enslaved females bolting from their enslavers exist. On February 2, James Brown offered a $50 reward for apprehension of his twenty-year-old "negro girl Mary Ann."[3] Slightly more than a month later George Harnsberger noted that his thirty-three-year-old enslaved female "KIT ranaway from [his] residence near Waynesboro."[4]

Equally sporadic at that same time were reports of enslaved people who remained, but attempted to assert themselves in some way. A little more than a week before Harnsberger posted a $100 reward for Kit's capture, a resident of Rockbridge County noted that two barns had been burned. Although not officially confirmed, Lucy Maria Chandler believed both acts of arson perpetrated by the area's enslaved.[5] In addition to a handful of acts of incendiarism, Lucy Chandler recorded an unusual amount of belligerence from her enslaved female Rachel in early March. After Chandler relocated Rachel's bedroom to a less desirable part of the house, Chandler explained that Rachel "got very angry . . . [because] I wanted to fix up the room and my room for company. And she cut up high because I moved her out." Now fully expecting that "Miss Rachel will leave me," Chandler noted that she might consider selling Rachel before she fled and "buy a good girl."[6]

Less than one month after Chandler reported various behaviors of enslaved people in the Valley's southern end, something occurred in the Shenandoah's northern counties that neither its African American inhabitants or white residents could have ever fathomed would be witnessed in the Shenandoah Valley—a regiment of United States Colored Troops (USCT) coursing through various lower Shenandoah Valley communities seeking able-bodied African Americans to fill the ranks of the 19th USCT.

Organized in mid-December 1863, the 19th USCT's ranks were initially filled with men from Maryland's Eastern Shore. Three months after the regiment first gathered at Benedict, Maryland, it still needed recruits to bring the regiment to full strength. On March 22, 1864, Lieutenant Colonel Joseph G. Perkins received permission to take a portion of the unit to Harpers Ferry and begin recruiting in the northern Shenandoah Valley.[7]

After the 19th USCT "arrived at Harpers Ferry with much difficulty," it procured "a four-mule baggage wagon" and began its journey to Winchester. As Perkins's command marched on the Berryville Pike on the morning of April 3, it came under fire at a point, according to Captain James H. Rickard, one of the 19th's white officers, "halfway between" Berryville and Winchester. Initially the regiment's officers concluded that they had been "intercepted by a rebel force."[8] Lieutenant Colonel Perkins, who, according to one of the regiment's officers, "seemed bent on making some kind of demonstration with his regiment of colored men," formed his men in "a rocky piece of woods" on the north side of the Berryville Pike. After the 19th formed and returned fire, Perkins sent one of his white officers to investigate the identity of the Confederate unit who ambushed them. While the troops who opened fire on the 19th USCT were, according to one of the regiment's white officers, "dressed in gray" they were not Confederate soldiers, but rather believed to be a contingent of Jessie Scouts—Union soldiers who dressed as Confederates and gathered intelligence oftentimes by infiltrating Confederate ranks. After the brief melee, Captain Rickard recorded that the scouts did not open fire accidentally, but instead did so in an effort to test the mettle of this green regiment of African Americans. "It was found that a company of scouts, dressed in gray," Rickard explained, "had opened fire on our men to see how they would stand." Although appalled to learn why this group of scouts opened fire on the 19th USCT, Rickard seemed pleased that the troops "did not flinch."[9]

Nearly four decades after the event, Lieutenant William Beach of the First New York Lincoln Cavalry wrote briefly about the incident in his regimental history and offered a slightly different account of the event's sequence. Beach noted that the 19th USCT did indeed exchange fire with scouts from the First New York, but they were not dressed in Confederate uniforms. Additionally, Beach claimed that the 19th USCT opened fire first after one if its officers, presumably Perkins, stopped the four scouts whom he supposed were from John Singleton Mosby's command dressed in Union uniforms.[10] Regardless of which account presented the most accurate portrayal of events, there is no denying that white Union soldiers fired on the 19th USCT.

The brief melee ended when the First New York's Captain Frank Martindale sent a messenger "with a handkerchief on a sabre" to find Perkins. After the incident Perkins fumed that the situation had escalated to this point. Perkins berated the scouts for not properly identifying themselves and shooting at his men. During the course of Perkins's rebuking of the scouts, Captain Martindale approached Perkins and told him that if he did not stop incessantly badgering his men, Martindale would turn his New Yorkers on Perkins and then "kill every nigger you have here." Perkins believed it best to back off and continue to Winchester.

Although unclear who fired first, the "friendly fire" incident resulted in one casualty, the 19th's Private Benjamin Curtis. A formerly enslaved man from St. Mary's County, Maryland, Curtis enlisted in the regiment on January 11, 1864. One of the New Yorker's bullets struck Curtis in the forehead, above his left eye. Miraculously, Curtis survived the wound, although his left eye suffered severe damage and he lost sight in it. "One colored man was struck on the forehead by a Minnie ball," a member of the 19th USCT later recalled, "and a piece of his skull as large as a silver dollar knocked out." Perhaps even more remarkable than Private Curtis surviving the injury is that he returned to the regiment in November 1864 and was eventually promoted to corporal.[11]

Curiously, the incident on the Berryville Pike received no mention in official reports, nor does it appear any disciplinary action was taken. Captain Rickard's account was published in 1894 and a discussion of it in the regimental history of the 1st New York Lincoln Cavalry was published in 1902, and Curtis's compiled service record offers the only documentation of the incident. The fact that the confrontation received no mention or no disciplinary action was taken against the soldier who wounded Curtis (believed to be Ed Goubleman) or Captain Martindale, who threatened to kill all of the men in the 19th USCT, reveals the difficulties African American soldiers and the white officers who commanded them confronted from white Union soldiers.[12] Sadly, this does not appear to be unique.[13] White commanders of USCT regiments throughout the South reported acts of injustice perpetrated against them by white enlisted men and officers, with little repercussion. As Ira Berlin concluded "remedies came slowly and imperfectly," when complaints were levied against white troops for discriminatory practices "leaving many" African American soldiers and those who commanded them "broken both in spirit and in body."[14]

When Perkins's command entered Winchester on the afternoon of April 3, the community's white inhabitants seemed aghast. From the moment President Lincoln signed the Emancipation Proclamation and opened the door for African American military service, rumors that USCT regiments would enter the Valley were commonplace and struck fear into the hearts and minds of those who supported the Confederate war effort.[15] Now, more than one year after Lincoln issued the Proclamation, one of the area's Confederate civilians' worst fears materialized. As the 19th entered Winchester, an astonished Mary Greenhow Lee observed to her "inexpressible horror, a party of negro infantry." Beyond shocked, Lee explained that she "was near fainting & more unnerved than by any sight I have seen since the war . . . there is nothing I have dreaded so much during the war . . . as being where negro troops were garrisoned . . . I feel perfectly unprepared for the emergency."[16] Another of Winchester's white inhabitants explained that the sight of the 19th USCT entering town and setting up camp in front of the Market House was something that area Confederate sympathizers "had been for some time dreading." To Laura Lee it proved "a most revolting spectacle."[17] Whether in Winchester or elsewhere in the Confederacy where USCTs appeared, the sight of African American soldiers in Union blue unnerved those who supported the Confederacy because it signaled a dramatic shift in the South's racial hierarchy and, as historian Andrew Lang contended, signified "a society undergoing rapid transformation."[18]

In addition to documenting anxieties about being in a locale where African Americans held sway over them, one of Winchester's Confederate civilians offered commentary on whether or not African Americans possessed the general qualities necessary for soldiering. Believing African Americans incapable of making decent soldiers—a perspective not unique to either North or South—Laura Lee wrote that "expecting such creatures to fight" was sheer "madness and folly."[19] Lee's words not only offer insight into how a white woman who lived in a household that utilized enslaved labor viewed African Americans as Union soldiers, but also offers a lens through which to examine how some of the Valley's Confederate civilians might have ultimately felt about arming African Americans to fight for the Confederacy. The Confederate government grappled with this issue, as historian Kevin Levin noted, "stretching back to the very beginning of the war."[20] While calls for utilizing African Americans as soldiers gained no traction in the conflict's first three years, because it undermined white racial superiority, discussions intensified in early 1864 when Confederate president Jefferson Davis considered a proposal from Confederate general Patrick Cleburne to utilize enslaved individuals as Confederate soldiers. Davis struck down the proposal and issued a directive forbidding further discussion of Cleburne's plan.[21] Considerations of whether or not to arm African Americans did not die in January 1864. Historians such as Kevin Levin and Bruce Levine have shown that the debate intensified throughout 1864, as Union armies pressured the Confederacy on multiple fronts.[22] Although Laura Lee never specifically recorded her thoughts on the merits of utilizing African Americans as soldiers in the Confederate army, it is reasonable to surmise from her thoughts on the 19th USCT's recruiting mission that she believed African Americans unsuitable to soldier in any army.

News spread quickly among the community's African Americans that Lieutenant Colonel Perkins sought recruits to fill the regiment's ranks. There seemed to be little enthusiasm among not only Winchester's African American population to join the 19th, but those in various communities throughout the lower Shenandoah Valley where the 19th recruited. One of Winchester's white inhabitants noted that when area African Americans learned that Perkins intended "to conscript all the Negro men here," they began "hiding."[23] Similarly, James Hooff, a resident of Jefferson County, noted that the area "servants" were "running from the . . . regiment."[24] When an elderly enslaved person from Jefferson County, Aunt Peggy, learned of the 19th USCT's mission she feared that her two grandsons might be taken from her. She quickly gathered some food and directed the two boys to hide in the woods.[25] With area African Americans hiding and elderly family members assisting in concealing men of military age, the 19th USCT's recruiting mission proved an impossible task. Captain Rickard noted simply of the difficulty in recruiting in the northern Shenandoah Valley: "The negroes had become scared and kept out of sight."[26]

When the 19th USCT returned to Baltimore after about a week of recruiting in the Valley, Captain Rickard believed the "regiment returned . . . without any recruits." In actuality the 19th gained two recruits during its visit to the Valley—Henry Woodbury from Charles Town and John W. Douglass, an eighteen-year-old farmer who hailed from Martinsburg.[27] The lack of enthusiasm to join the 19th's ranks did not sit well with white Union troops in the area. From the perspective of the 1st New York Cavalry's James H. Stevenson, it seemed not only cowardly but reprehensible that more African Americans did not join the 19th USCT and more actively support the Union war effort. "The negroes in the Valley took to the Blue Ridge to escape . . . which didn't look very patriotic," Stevenson wrote, "to say nothing of ingratitude."[28]

Although the 19th's spring recruiting mission yielded only two recruits, Woodbury and Douglass were not the only two African Americans with Valley connections to serve in the regiment. On August 24, 1864, John Able, a Rockingham County native, enlisted in the regiment at Frederick, Maryland.[29] Two days earlier fellow Rockingham native Henry Harrison enlisted in the regiment at Frederick. While Able enlisted voluntarily, Harrison's enlistment records indicate that he enlisted as a substitute for James H. Percy, a native of Allegany County, Maryland. While Able survived his military service, Harrison did not. He died on October 4, 1865, at the "post hospital" in Brownsville, Texas, from complications of diarrhea.[30]

The lack of enthusiasm displayed by African Americans in the lower Shenandoah Valley during the 19th USCT's recruiting mission was not unusual. Various efforts to recruit African Americans throughout the South during the conflict fared similarly. For instance, during a recruiting drive in Louisiana, appeals to join the United States Colored Troops met with a "lukewarm" reception.[31] In an early 1864 recruiting effort in Alabama, James T. Ayers, a white Kentuckian who eventually enjoyed some success in recruiting for the 17th USCT, discovered significant reluctance among African Americans to join.[32]

While white Union soldiers such as Stevenson might have interpreted reluctance as cowardice and pro-Confederates might have viewed African Americans' disinclination to enlist as a sign of support for the Confederate war effort, scholarship has clearly shown that the decision for African

Americans in the South to enlist in USCT regiments was plagued with myriad considerations. Among the chief concerns for African Americans was what would happen to family members left behind.

Additionally, potential recruits had to consider the discrimination they might confront from white troops. How quickly news spread of the incident on the Berryville Pike on the morning of April 3 is unknown, but the fact that white Union troops opened fire on the 19th USCT proved one episode in a litany of moments throughout the conflict where white Union soldiers showed a complete lack of respect for African American troops. Furthermore, African Americans who considered enlistment also needed to confront the harsh reality of being grossly mistreated and murdered should they fall into the hands of Confederate soldiers.[33] While the horrors of Fort Pillow (April 12, 1864) or Poison Spring, Arkansas (April 18) had not yet taken place, various instances underscored the brutality African Americans could encounter should they fall captive to Confederate troops. For example, on June 7, 1863, in the aftermath of the fighting at Milliken's Bend, reports surfaced that Confederate soldiers had beaten African American troops and executed two.[34]

The lack of unwillingness to join the 19th USCT in April 1864, however, does not mean that African American men with connections to the Shenandoah Valley did not enlist in USCT regiments. More than 600 African Americans who came from the Shenandoah served in USCT units during the conflict. While not clear at what point these individuals left the Shenandoah Valley, an examination of compiled service records for identifiable African Americans with links to the region reveals that 30 percent enlisted prior to the 19th's recruiting mission, with the bulk enlisting in a USCT regiment at some point after early April 1864.[35] Among those who enlisted prior to the 19th's recruiting mission was Edward Hall. Born in Jefferson County in 1827, Hall was brought to Winchester as a slave at the age of seven. In the final weeks of 1863, that most unsettled period in the lower Shenandoah Valley, Hall left his wife Ellen and ten-year-old son Charles, ventured to Maryland, and enlisted in Colonel Delavan Bates's 30th USCT.[36] Hall officially mustered into the regiment on March 31, 1864. As part of General Edward Ferrero's division of the Ninth Corps, Hall and the 30th USCT fought in some of the fiercest engagements of the Civil War's final year, including the Battle of the Crater on July 30, 1864, and assaults against one of the Confederacy's last strongholds along the Atlantic Coast near Wilmington, North Carolina—Fort Fisher. Although injured when a hay bale fell on him while unloading a ship at Morehead City, Hall, who rose to the

Figure 6.1. Tombstone marking Sergeant Edward Hall's grave in Winchester's Orrick Cemetery (photo by Jessica N. Kronenwetter).

rank of sergeant, survived the conflict.[37] After mustering out of the 30th USCT in December 1865, Hall reunited with his family in Winchester. He remained in Winchester where he worked as a gardener and day laborer until his death in 1915.[38]

Sergeant Hall counted himself among the approximately 88 percent of African Americans from the Shenandoah Valley who survived the conflict. The remaining 12 percent offered the ultimate sacrifice—Jesse Scott among them. Born in Staunton, Virginia, Scott was twenty-six years old at the time of his enlistment in the 43rd USCT in March 1864. On July 30, 1864, Private Scott suffered a severe wound at the Battle of the Crater. Evacuated from the battlefield, Scott was sent to the *Connecticut*, a hospital ship anchored near Norfolk, Virginia. He succumbed to his wound on August 15, 1864.[39] Others, such as Private William Bird, perished not from battlefield wounds but from illness. Twenty-eight years old at the time he mustered into the 25th USCT in January 1864, the Rockingham County native did not even have an opportunity to fight. Sick with bronchitis, Bird was sent to Summit Point Hospital in Philadelphia, where he developed pneumonia. He died on March 22, 1864.[40] The service and sacrifice of individuals such as Hall, Scott, and Bird counter the 1st New York Cavalry's James Stevenson's perspective that the Valley's African Americans proved ungrateful cowards.

The distrust that gripped the lower Shenandoah Valley's African Americans at the time of the 19th USCT's recruiting mission continued into May, as 9,000 Union troops commanded by General Franz Sigel marched south from Martinsburg toward Winchester.[41] While the city's African Americans, according to a veteran in the 34th Massachusetts Infantry, were the only ones who came out of doors and "greeted our progress," uncertainty about what all of it meant seemed to loom large in the estimation of Sigel's men. Staff officer David Hunter Strother, who had experienced the Valley's African Americans flocking to Union lines in 1861 and 1862, did not see that same behavior among African Americans who lived in the Shenandoah Valley's northern reaches on this occasion. Strother wrote that "the Negroes were all afraid to go with us, the reverses of the Federal troops having made them timid."[42]

Although African Americans in the lower Valley might have behaved diffidently, news of Sigel's advance might have compelled enslaved people in other parts of the Valley to flee. During the first four months of 1864 announcements seeking enslaved people who bolted appeared in Valley newspapers, but their frequency intensified with the spring campaign. For instance, between January and early April 1864, the *Staunton Spectator* ran advertisements for a total of eight enslaved people who escaped enslavers in Rockingham and Augusta County.[43] At the end of April, the *Spectator* printed notices seeking the return of nine enslaved people who bolted from Elizabeth Furnace in Shenandoah County. In May, the *Spectator* printed advertisements from enslavers seeking the return of six enslaved people, young and old, male and female, from Augusta to Jefferson County.[44]

Sigel only penetrated as far south as New Market, where, after suffering defeat on May 15, he moved north to Middletown. Aggravated with Sigel's conduct, General Ulysses S. Grant promptly removed Sigel from command. Six days after New Market, Sigel's replacement, the abolitionist-minded General David Hunter, arrived at Belle Grove mansion and took command.[45]

Five days later, Hunter's Army of the Shenandoah marched south. For the first time in two years, federal forces penetrated into the Shenandoah Valley's southern counties. As Hunter moved south, destroying property and carrying out Grant's directive to live off the land as much as possible, some enslavers attempted to secret enslaved people and livestock in the mountains.[46] As Hunter's command moved south his men "saw a great deal of smoke" in the mountains "and were told it came from the camps of the refugees who were hiding from us with their Negroes and cattle."[47] While some enslavers might have thought this the best option to safeguard those whom they enslaved, enslaved people viewed this as their best opportunity to flee. One of Hunter's staff officers recorded that large numbers of enslaved people seized "the first opportunity" to bolt to Union troops from their enslaver's mountain camps. Once these freedom-seekers reached Hunter's army they shared all sorts of information with Union troops, including the location of various mountain hideouts. Perhaps most significantly, these refugees from slavery directed Hunter's "foragers" to the location of stockpiles of food-stuffs and livestock that kept Hunter's troops fed as they marched south.[48]

As Hunter's column moved south the numbers of African Americans who trailed his army grew. Edgar Peirce, 14th Pennsylvania Cavalry, explained that "a great many darkeys followed us."[49] David Hunter Strother echoed that "Negroes . . . [are] coming in continually."[50] While neither Peirce nor Strother ever estimated the amount of African Americans who flocked to Hunter's army as it moved south, the 123rd Ohio Infantry's Charles M. Keyes surmised that "several hundred negroes came through with us."[51] While various veterans of Hunter's army believed the enslaved people who sought refuge proved useful for the information they provided or the roles they filled as camp servants, some of Hunter's men resented what they believed to be preferential treatment on Hunter's part toward the African American refugees. A Pennsylvania cavalryman griped about African Americans being loaded into wagons and allowed to ride while some "white soldiers dragged themselves along."[52] David Hunter Strother, however, countered this notion that Hunter offered favored treatment to African Americans. Strother observed an elderly African American woman, about seventy-five years old in his opinion, who walked "striding along on foot with wonderful endurance and zeal."[53] Although no records exist to fully substantiate, it is reasonable to surmise that Hunter reserved the wagons for freedom-seekers afflicted with some sort of malady. Doctors who examined some refugees from slavery noted their deplorable physical condition. A number had backs "terribly scarred with the lash from the neck to the waist," while another "contraband" had a visible shoe imprint on his body from his enslaver stomping on him.[54]

Near the end of the first week of June, Hunter's command approached the strategically important city of Staunton.[55] Although instances existed, as noted previously in this study, of enslaved people from Staunton and its immediate environs escaping their enslavement prior to June 1864, Hunter's entrance on June 6 marked the first moment that Union troops occupied the city. That Union presence, as it had in places like Charles Town and

Winchester earlier in the conflict, emboldened the area's enslaved population and prompted greater numbers to believe attaining freedom a reality. On the day Hunter entered Staunton, resident Joseph Waddell wrote · simply, "Quite a number of negroes ran off."[56] Among the first enslaved people to greet Hunter's army as it entered Staunton were those who labored at the Western Lunatic Asylum. A *New York Tribune* correspondent attached to Hunter's army was among the first to interact with them. As Hunter's "advanced guard" marched into Staunton the correspondent noted how the Union troops were "hailed by a number of colored people, servants belonging to the Asylum who had congregated outside of the main entrance on the roadside to welcome the 'Yankees.'" The scene of Hunter's troops marching into Staunton, coupled with enslaved people welcoming Hunter's command, unnerved the institution's superintendent, Dr. Francis Stribling. Beyond concern over losing his labor force, Stribling fretted that the institution's enslaved laborers would reveal the whereabouts of stockpiles of supplies hidden in the building and intended for use by Confederate soldiers. Dr. Stribling instructed the enslaved laborers to not look into the "brutal eyes of the Yankees." He even threatened to lock them up in "cells if they did not immediately comply with his commands." At this moment the correspondent for the *Tribune* intervened and informed the contingent of enslaved people that "they were now free, and at liberty to either go or stay, just as they pleased."[57] "This announcement was received with great joy," the journalist explained. After this pronouncement these now formerly enslaved people informed Union soldiers about the location of Confederate supplies throughout the asylum. They also alerted Hunter's troops to the location of significant amounts of currency. Based on the information, Hunter's men searched the complex and "discovered Government property to the value of $300,000, consisting principally of Rebel uniforms ready-made, and cloth of the army pattern."[58]

Over the next few days Hunter carried out his task of destroying militarily significant targets in Staunton, including the jail and structures that supported the Virginia Central Railroad's operations.[59] Interestingly, Hunter did not target all buildings in Staunton that supported the Confederacy's military operations. Among the places not destroyed were the quartermaster's, commissary, and ordnance buildings. Although Hunter spared them because they were privately owned, he allowed the community's African Americans—and anyone else who wanted—the opportunity to loot the various stores.[60] One of Hunter's staff officers observed that "a mixed mob of Federal soldiers, Negroes . . . mulatto women, children . . . were engaged in plundering the stores and depots."[61]

After four days in Staunton, Hunter departed and continued his expedition southward. As Hunter's army aimed for Lexington, forty miles away, the area's enslaved population continued to flock to his army. Just as had been the case with Hunter's brief occupation of Staunton, this was the first time Union troops pushed this far south in the Shenandoah Valley, giving African Americans in those southern counties the best opportunity that presented itself thus far in the conflict to flee. As Hunter's men moved into the Valley's southern reaches by mid-June, Private William Stark, 34th Massachusetts Infantry, observed: "The negroes have had no chance to escape until now." Although to Stark it seemed that the number of enslaved people who sought refuge with Hunter's army amounted to "an army of them . . . old men and women, children and babies all going for freedom," not all fled.[62] While Union armies usually presented the greatest occasion for enslaved people to escape, those who fled still had to weigh their yearning for freedom against their desire for survival. While Hunter's troops provided short-term protection, they afforded no long-term stability. Just as had been the case during various Union occupations in the lower Shenandoah Valley during the conflict's first three years, when some enslaved people remained while others bolted, enslavers in the southern Valley interpreted an enslaved person's desire to stay put during Hunter's incursion as a sign of loyalty. Joseph Waddell, who as noted earlier boasted that few enslaved people resided in the Valley, watched as "large numbers of negroes went off with the Yankees," but gloated that those whom he enslaved remained.[63] "They could not have behaved better, and I really feel thankful to them," Waddell confided to his diary on the day Hunter occupied Staunton.[64]

Those African Americans who ventured south with Hunter's army ended up moving all the way to Lynchburg, Virginia. After Confederate general Jubal Early's army forced Hunter from Lynchburg on June 18, Hunter's army, and the African Americans who sought Hunter's protection, retreated into West Virginia. How many from the Valley might have fallen into Confederate hands or how many collapsed on the long journey is unknown. However, by mid-July a newspaper correspondent in Wheeling, West Virginia, recorded that "contrabands" who had refuged themselves with Hunter arrived in Wheeling near the end of the second week of July.[65] When the refugees from slavery arrived they were quartered in the Athenaeum. Initially built for "theatrical purposes," the Athenaeum transitioned to a prison during the

Civil War.[66] After examination by doctors, those formerly enslaved males deemed physically able were "mustered into the service of the United States." It is not entirely clear if "the gang of fifty" men willingly volunteered or were mustered into USCT regiments, or utilized by the federal government as teamsters, laborers, and so on. Before being sent off to their assigned tasks "the contrabands . . . were paraded" through Wheeling's streets. The scene, according to a newspaper correspondent, "created a great deal of merriment among the people."[67]

For enslaved people who remained in the Valley there was little merriment, as Early's army, once it forced Hunter from Lynchburg, cleared the Shenandoah Valley of any remaining Union troops as he pushed north into Maryland and then east toward the outskirts of Washington, DC. The events that transpired in the Shenandoah Valley in the spring and early summer of 1864 tremendously unnerved General Grant. By the end of July, Grant realized that the only way to hammer Lee's Army of Northern Virginia into submission in front of Petersburg and throw open the gates to the Confederate capital was to first seize control of the Shenandoah Valley. Throughout the conflict the Valley had been a place of incessant disaster for Union forces and had been utilized by Confederates as an avenue of invasion into the North, and also a point from which they could threaten Washington. From Banks and Milroy, to Sigel and Hunter, control of the Valley proved elusive. On August 6, 1864, Grant aimed to change the war's strategic course in the Shenandoah Valley by appointing thirty-three-year-old General Philip Sheridan (known as "Little Phil") as commander of the largest Union army ever assembled in the region, the Army of the Shenandoah. As Sheridan organized his command at Harpers Ferry he received clear instructions from both President Lincoln and Grant to not bring on an engagement with Early unless Sheridan could be assured of victory. Aware of the adverse impact defeat would have not only on Union operations in Virginia, but the negative backlash another military setback in the Shenandoah would have on Lincoln's chances to win reelection in November, Sheridan opted for a pragmatic approach in dealing with Early during the first month at the Army of the Shenandoah's helm. "I knew that I was strong, yet, in consequence of the injunctions of General Grant, I deemed it necessary to be very cautious, and the fact that the Presidential election was impending made me doubly so."[68]

Until mid-September, Sheridan's and Early's commands maneuvered between Harpers Ferry and Fisher's Hill, located just south of Strasburg. Sometimes various elements of their armies clashed, but nothing of significance occurred. Although Lincoln might have been appreciative that

Sheridan proceeded cautiously as originally instructed, the president also surmised that a lack of any significant activity from the largest Union force to ever set foot in the Shenandoah Valley might also prove detrimental to his chances for reelection. On September 12, Lincoln wired Grant: "Could we not pick up a regiment here and there, to the number of say ten thousand men, and quietly, but suddenly concentrate them at Sheridan's camp and enable him to make a strike?"[69] Grant concurred, and the following day notified Sheridan that he wished to meet with him on the 17th in Charles Town. Aware that the meeting could result in being handed a plan he had no desire to implement—or worse, being removed from command—Sheridan determined to gather as much information as he could about the strength and disposition of Early's troops so that he could go to Charles Town with a strategy.

As Sheridan lamented his dilemma with his longtime friend and commander of the army's Eighth Corps, General George Crook, Sheridan concluded that he needed an informant behind Confederate lines in Winchester. Crook, familiar with the area's pro-Unionist sympathizers, recommended a twenty-four-year-old Quaker teacher in Winchester, Rebecca Wright.[70] Throughout the previous several months Crook had interacted with Wright, having eaten dinner at her house on various occasions. Although Crook seemed "convinced" of Wright's "loyalty and high character," he wondered, if confronted with the opportunity to provide intelligence to aid the Union war effort, whether she would as "she was under constant surveillance" by Winchester's Confederate civilians.[71] Sheridan, however, hoped that loyalty to the Union would outweigh any concerns Wright harbored.

Satisfied with Crook's recommendation and hopeful Wright would assist, Sheridan next needed someone to go between the Union lines around Berryville and Early's position in Winchester. Sheridan preferred someone who would not arouse suspicion. Fortunately for Sheridan, a few days before Sheridan lamented his trouble to Crook, Major Henry K. Young, commander of Sheridan's scouts, informed Sheridan about an African American man from nearby Millwood, Tom Laws, who might prove beneficial to Sheridan's efforts in gathering intelligence about Early's army.

Enslaved from the moment of his birth on January 7, 1817, at the time of the Civil War, Laws was enslaved by Richard Byrd in Clarke County.[72] Until this point in the conflict there is little evidence that Laws did anything to aid the Union war effort, but now the forty-seven-year-old Laws quickly found himself thrust into one of the Civil War's most significant moments in the Shenandoah Valley. During the second week of September, Laws and his wife Mary, enslaved by Philip Burwell, were approached by two of Young's scouts, who learned that Laws could pass in and out of Winchester as he pleased. Thirty years after Sheridan's 1864 Shenandoah Campaign, Laws explained in a letter to James Taylor, an artist correspondent attached to Sheridan's army, that he "could go to Winchester any time" he chose as his "master lived there." Additionally, Laws possessed a permit signed by Confederate authorities that allowed him to enter Winchester three times per week to sell vegetables to the local inhabitants.[73]

Having someone who could freely move in and out of Winchester intrigued Sheridan tremendously. The fact that Laws was African American proved an added bonus. Despite the important efforts of African Americans in intelligence-gathering for Union forces since the early part of the conflict, many Confederates did not see African Americans as a threat when it came to spying.[74] In his recent study of espionage activities supporting the Union war effort Douglas Waller concluded that "most" Confederates "did not believe blacks were mentally capable of disclosing much military information." This gross miscalculation of African Americans' intelligence oftentimes prompted Confederate soldiers to rarely challenge individuals such as Laws as to the intent of their business in a particular community.[75] Despite the advantages of utilizing Laws as a messenger, Sheridan still wondered if Laws was reliable and could be trusted if asked to be part of the effort to gather intelligence about Early's command. When Sheridan pressed Major Young about Laws's trustworthiness Young unequivocally stated that Laws could perform any task handed to him. "The scouts had sounded this man," Sheridan recalled of his exchange with Young, "and finding him both loyal and shrewd, suggested that he might be useful."[76]

With a potential informant behind Confederate lines in Winchester, access to Laws, and the pressure to develop a plan before his meeting with Grant in Charles Town, Sheridan requested Young's scouts bring Laws to him. When Laws and Sheridan met, one of the first questions Little Phil asked was whether or not he knew Rebecca Wright. Although Laws informed Sheridan he did not, he assured him that he "had a great many acquaintances in Winchester" and could find her.[77] After questioning Laws, Sheridan seemed convinced of Laws's "fidelity" and asked if he would "carry a letter to" Wright. Without hesitation, Laws agreed.[78] He carried the note, which asked if Wright could "inform" Sheridan "of the position of Early's forces, the number of divisions in his army, and the strength or any or all of them, and his probably or reported intentions," in his mouth. Sheridan wrote the note carefully on a piece of tissue paper, "compressed it into a small pellet," and wrapped it in tin foil.[79] While Sheridan felt confident in Laws's ability to pass in and out of Winchester inconspicuously, carrying the message in this manner offered another layer of security. If for some reason Confederate pickets stopped and questioned Laws, he could simply swallow the note.[80]

Around noon on September 16, Laws arrived at Wright's home on North Loudoun Street. When Laws knocked on the door, Wright was working at her desk. When Wright opened the door she found Laws, who appeared to her "an intelligent well-dressed man."[81] Seeing that Wright appeared somewhat startled, he removed the note from his mouth, handed it to her, and informed her that Sheridan needed her help. Wright initially informed Laws that she "did not have anything to do with the rebels and knew nothing about them."[82] Laws could have left it at that, but he persisted. The more Laws spoke the clearer it became to Wright of the "earnestness" of his mission. Laws informed Wright that he would return at 3:00 p.m. and collect any information she might wish to pass along to Sheridan.[83]

After Laws left, Wright weighed the hazards and benefits of aiding Sheridan. The first thought that coursed through Wright's mind was what would happen to her and her family should Winchester's overwhelmingly Confederate majority discover her clandestine activity. Conflicted, Wright sought the advice of her mother Rachel, as "the thought of the great danger" simply "overpowered" Rebecca Wright.[84] While Rachel advised her daughter that assisting Sheridan carried great risk, she also explained that people everywhere made great sacrifices for the Union's preservation. "Men are dying for their country, and thy life and my life may be needed too," Rachel explained. After the conversation Rachel advised her daughter to go to her room and pray for God's guidance.[85]

No one can know for certain what thoughts coursed through Rebecca Wright's mind as she contemplated her decision, but it is reasonable to surmise that at some point during her deliberation she reflected on the treatment Confederate soldiers had accorded her family at various moments during the conflict. During the war Confederates searched the Wright home, as they did other Unionists, for evidence of any material support for the Union war effort. Wright might also have considered the treatment her father Amos received in March 1862. As Stonewall Jackson prepared to evacuate Winchester in early March 1862, he arrested scores of Unionist males. Amos Wright, branded as a "radical" by Confederates, was among those seized by Jackson. Although Rebecca Wright never discussed her father's fate as motivation to aid Sheridan, a correspondent for the *Cincinnati*

*Daily Gazette* theorized in 1873 that Amos's treatment served as the catalyst. "Her father was imprisoned by the rebels. It was owing to this circumstance that Miss Wright became so embittered that she made every effort to communicate with the Federal troops," the *Gazette* explained.[86]

After weighing all in the balance, Wright opted to provide Sheridan with the information she possessed. Two days before Laws arrived at Wright's home, an unidentified convalescent Confederate officer visited Wright. According to a postwar letter penned to Charles Coffin, Wright explained that the officer boarded at a home next door to the Wright house and became enamored with her as she worked in the family garden. Unaware of her role in intelligence-gathering for Sheridan, Wright made small talk with the Confederate. Wright recalled, "I asked questions, never thinking of using the information."[87] During the conversation the officer innocently divulged information that ultimately proved useful. He informed Wright that due to the lack of activity from Sheridan over the course of the previous month, a division of Confederate infantry and artillery battalion had departed the Shenandoah Valley to join the Army of Northern Virginia in the trenches around Petersburg.

When Laws returned, according to Wright, they did not speak. Wright "silently gave" Laws a message, written on tissue paper, wadded and carried in the same manner as the note Sheridan penned to Wright, which stated that General Joseph Kershaw's infantry division and Major Wilfred Cutshaw's artillery battalion had left the Shenandoah Valley to join the Army of Northern Virginia near Petersburg.[88] "I have no communication whatever with rebels, but will tell you what I know," Wright wrote to Sheridan. She continued, "The division of General Kershaw, and Cutshaw's artillery . . . have been sent away, and no more are expected, as they cannot be spared from Richmond. I do not know how the troops are situated, but the force is much smaller than is represented."[89] Sheridan utilized the information Wright supplied via Laws to formulate a plan. Three days after Laws ventured to Winchester, Sheridan attacked and defeated Early's army at the Third Battle of Winchester.[90]

Although undoubtedly pleased with the battle's result, both Wright and Laws hoped that their role in intelligence-gathering for Sheridan would remain clandestine. Wright's role was eventually discovered in early 1867. On January 19, 1867, Sheridan sent General James Forsyth to Winchester to deliver a gift and note of appreciation to Wright. In the note, Sheridan explained the value "of the great service" Wright "rendered the Union cause" in divulging information through Laws.[91] Sheridan also gifted Wright an "elegant gold watch . . . brooch . . . of gold, beautifully wrought into a gaunt-let, and set with pearls."[92] At the time Wright received these items a reporter from the *Baltimore Sun* was boarding at the Wright home and began to pry into the reason for Forsyth's visit. Rebecca's sister Hannah, who sympathized with the Confederacy, revealed that the gift came from Sheridan.[93] By February 20, 1867, all of Winchester knew about Wright's gift and her connection in intelligence-gathering.[94] Wright recalled that when the story broke, "most of the community were wild with indignation."[95] Once people learned of her role, Rebecca and her family were "socially castrated by the people of Winchester."[96] The environment became so hostile that Wright and her family left Winchester for Philadelphia. Forced from Winchester and confronting financial ruin, Wright turned to Sheridan for aid. Along with assistance from General Ulysses S. Grant, Wright received an appointment as a clerk in the United States Treasury Department on July 6, 1868. She held that post until her death in May 1914.[97]

Throughout the whole affair Wright remained tight-lipped about Laws's role. The part Thomas Laws played remained mostly quiet for the remainder of his life. He died on April 16, 1896. In the aftermath of Laws's death, Confederate veteran John Worsham attempted to uncover the identity of the man who had carried the messages. Worsham, who was in the process of gathering material for his memoirs, *One of Jackson's Foot Cavalry,* in the early twentieth century, reached out to Confederate veteran Samuel J. C. Moore, who lived in Berryville, to see if he had any knowledge of who carried the information to Wright. In his postwar reminiscence published in 1912, Worsham included a letter from Moore stipulating that Moore employed Laws as a gardener and inquired in 1869 as to whether or not Laws "was the bearer of the letter" to Wright. According to Moore, Laws seemed extremely hesitant "to talk about it" at first. This was justifiably so, considering that once area residents learned of Rebecca Wright's involvement they boycotted her boarding house, spat on her, cursed her, and forced her out of Winchester. However, after Moore assured Laws that he "would not harm him," Laws spoke "freely" about his role.[98] Moore appears to have kept good on his promise of bringing Laws no harm or leaking the information.

Twenty-one years before Worsham published his recollections a group of veterans from the Union army's Sixth Corps, after dedicating a monument in the Winchester National Cemetery to the memory of General David A. Russell, killed at the Third Battle of Winchester, attempted to find "the colored man that carried the despatch [sic]." A veteran of the 23rd Pennsylvania Infantry explained that they discovered it was Laws, found him, and took

Figure 6.2. Grave of Thomas Laws in Milton Valley Cemetery, Josephine City, Berryville, Virginia (photo by author).

him to Washington, DC, where he met with Rebecca Wright, "who took him to the War Department and took affidavit of identity which is now on file." Now seventy-four years old, someone in the War Department offered Laws "a position . . . for the balance of his life," but Laws demurred, noting that he was "living with his grandchildren" in Clarke County "and doing well and contented."[99]

While Laws arguably proved the most significant African American to support Union intelligence-gathering operations, as his role helped launch the Union campaign that finally wrested the Shenandoah Valley from Confederate control, countless others—free and enslaved, young and old, male and female—rendered important service to the Union war effort even after

Sheridan's Army of the Shenandoah secured victory in the Valley at Cedar Creek on October 19, 1864. Although Cedar Creek ended major campaigning in the Shenandoah Valley, fighting did not instantaneously cease in mid-October. Bands of Confederate partisans and irregulars still posed problems for Sheridan's army.

Throughout the final months of 1864 African Americans, as they had throughout the conflict, proved useful allies in reporting the activities of Colonel John Singleton Mosby's Rangers.[100] For example, in mid-November a young African American boy, about nine or ten years old, alerted Captain Richard Blazer, who commanded a contingent of scouts in Sheridan's command, of the approach of a portion of Mosby's partisans.[101] Henry Pancake, one of Blazer's scouts, wrote that soon after crossing the Shenandoah River at Jackson's Ford in Jefferson County and stopping to cook some breakfast, "a colored boy came up and said about 300 of Mosby's Guerillas had crossed the ford and taken position in the woods, half way between the ford and Cabletown, and were watching us." According to Pancake the unidentified boy "had been sent by a Union woman near the ford to apprise us." Whether the young boy was enslaved or not is unknown, but the information he provided proved reliable. Pancake noted that Blazer ordered him and Lieutenant Thomas Coles to investigate. As the two climbed "the hill and got a good view of the rebs," Pancake recalled that "all the intelligence given by the colored boy" had been "confirmed."[102] Historian Darl Stephenson, the foremost expert on Blazer's Scouts, concluded that after the young boy provided information to Union scouts he more than likely remained with Blazer's men, "fully expecting the Scouts to be victorious." However, outnumbered by more than two-to-one, Mosby's command bested Blazer's scouts. Unable to escape, Mosby's men seized the young boy. According to Blazer, who was captured during the fight at Kabletown, the Confederate partisans hung the boy and left him on the field amidst the other members of Blazer's men killed in the fight. Based on Stephenson's research and Winchester National Cemetery burial records, it is highly likely that this unknown African American boy murdered at Kabletown on November 18, 1864 is buried in grave 2001 in the cemetery's Ohio section, along with seven other members of Blazer's command killed there.[103]

The actions of Laws, the unknown boy at Kabletown, and countless other unidentifiable African Americans who supplied information to Union troops during the autumn of 1864, referenced by Union soldiers in diaries and letters, not only reveals a willingness among enslaved and free blacks to support the Union war effort and assume an active role in slavery's destruction, but shows that for the first time since mid-1863, the lower Shenandoah Valley's African Americans believed the situation more stable with the presence of such a substantial Union force and possessed no reservations about supporting Union operations. The uncertainty and distrust that existed among the lower Valley's African Americans in late 1863 and throughout the spring and early summer of 1864 seemed to dissipate. Scenes reminiscent of Banks's and Milroy's tenures once again appeared in the lower Valley as the Army of the Shenandoah gained a stronger grasp in the region. For example, on the night of September 17, just two days before Sheridan's victory at the Third Battle of Winchester, an undetermined number of African Americans rushed into Sheridan's camp near Berryville seeking protection. The sound of individuals rapidly approaching the camp in the darkness, offering no pronouncement of their identity, startled the Union pickets. Unaware of who approached, the pickets opened fire, but ceased when they discovered the group's identity. Fortunately, the pickets inflicted no injuries. A trooper from the 18th Pennsylvania Cavalry noted of the episode: "During the night we are called to arms by our camp guard firing into a squad of negro refugees approaching camp without warning."[104]

While Sheridan's campaign coursed throughout the Shenandoah Valley that autumn, untold numbers of African Americans sought refuge with the Army of the Shenandoah. All eleven people enslaved by Joseph and Abigail

Figure 6.3. African Americans following Union general Philip H. Sheridan's Army of the Shenandoah in the autumn of 1864 (George T. Stevens, *Three Years in the Sixth Corps*, 1866).

"WASHERWOMEN" IN THE ARMY OF THE SHENANDOAH.— A LAUNDRY ESTABLISHMENT.
From a Sketch by Joseph Becker.

Figure 6.4. Laundering clothes was among the various tasks African Americans performed for the Army of the Shenandoah in the autumn of 1864 (*The Soldier in Our Civil War*, 1890).

Coffman left the Coffman's home in Rockingham County and sought protection with Sheridan's command. Two of Coffman's enslaved laborers, perhaps as a final act of defiance, alerted Union troops to where the family hid all of its livestock.[105] Similarly, Justice Peter Roller's enslaved male, Bill, fled with Sheridan's army.[106] One account from Page County noted that "many . . . slaves had departed with the Northern horde." Surgeon George Stevens, 77th New York Infantry, wrote that as the Union army started its retrograde movement north from Augusta County in late September, during the "Burning," that "negroes who sought freedom from their ancient bondage . . . followed." Pulled in "one of the huge Virginia wagons," the African American refugees formed part of the "Sixth corps hospital train" as the army moved north. Stevens reported that some of Sheridan's "soldiers manifested great interest in this curious load of refugees, and freely divided with them their hard tack and coffee."[107]

As the numbers of African American refugees grew during Sheridan's campaign of destruction in the Valley between late September and early October, he utilized the labor of some of them to destroy the railroad at various points.[108] Staunton's Joseph Waddell, undoubtedly bitter that two of his enslaved laborers, Moses and Stephen, fled and were "impressed . . . into their (Union) service," wrote that Sheridan's troops took "all the negro men . . . down the Railroad to destroy the track and bridges."[109] The Army of the Shenandoah not only utilized the labor of young African American males, but employed countless others who performed various labor tasks and camp chores for the Army of the Shenandoah.[110]

However, as had been the case at other points in the conflict, not all enslaved peoples believed it prudent to flee to Union troops. While in hindsight Sheridan's victories proved the final crushing blow for the Confederate war effort in the Shenandoah Valley, at the time no one knew the ultimate consequences of those successes. While two individuals enslaved by Joseph Waddell left with Sheridan's army, another of his enslaved laborers, Wright, stayed put.[111] In Rockingham County four individuals enslaved by David and Susan Coiner bolted by the fall of 1864, but two remained.[112]

In addition to concerns about leaving behind family or friends and concerns about survival in a new place, one thing that might have made some remain with enslavers is fear of mistreatment by Union soldiers. While accounts such as those by Surgeon Stevens noted that federal troops sympathized with and attempted to assist African Americans, sharing their rations with them and so on, examples do exist during Sheridan's tenure in the Shenandoah of Union soldiers taking what meager possessions enslaved people owned from them. An examination of Southern Claims Commission records reveals that Union troops did not discriminate between loyalty or race during the campaign—all was fair game.

Polly Blackwell, a free black woman from Rockingham County who saved and eventually purchased her husband, filed a claim with the Southern Claims Commission seeking $865 for damages done to her property during Sheridan's campaign. Blackwell noted that Sheridan's men killed all of her hogs and took whatever property they "pleased." In her written statement Blackwell stated that she attempted to convince Sheridan's troops to cease, but they noted that this was revenge for "the burning of Chambersburg." The Union soldiers who desolated her property in one week also charged that she "was hiding property of rebels." She attempted to convince them otherwise, but all of her entreaties fell on deaf ears. Worse than the damage and pilfering Blackwell endured, the federal government refused her claim, noting that the testimony she provided was "vague" and that she did not provide specific evidence that the items taken were utilized by Sheridan's army.[113]

Even when loyalty was not called into question, some African Americans found themselves stripped of their property by Union troops. Savery Iverson, an enslaved man from Clarke County, testified to commissioners that he "contributed to the Union cause and taken them to barns to stay at night and attended them when sick and have answered questions and given them what information I could . . . I always did all I could for the Union." Despite Iverson's many efforts throughout the conflict he reported that Sheridan's troops seized what little items he possessed.[114] Another African American from Clarke County, Taylor Thornton, had $33.50 worth of pork and flour taken by Union troops.[115] Frederick County's Meshack Johnson, labeled as "a colored man . . . loyal [and] . . . often rendered good service to the United States by giving information as to the whereabouts of the Rebel soldiers," had his two horses taken by Sheridan's command in August 1864.[116] While Iverson, Thornton, and Johnson had various pieces of property seized, Milford Jones, a free black who lived near Stephenson's Depot north of Winchester, had his entire log house razed by Sheridan's troops during the winter of 1864–65 to be used in the construction of log huts.[117]

Additionally, at least one instance of physical violence against an African American girl exists during the Army of the Shenandoah's tenure in the Valley. Shortly after the Battle of Cedar Creek, ten-year-old Serena Spencer, the daughter of Abe Spencer, a free black potter from Middletown, had been sent on an errand when three Union soldiers attacked and attempted to rape her north of Middletown near John Miller's farm. Spencer's daughter fought back.[118] "I give that tallest feller all that was comin' to him," she noted in a postwar interview. She continued: "Every time he got near enough I'd rake with my finger-nails right down his face . . . he knocked me down, and then I used my feet as well as my hands." While her efforts fended off one attacker, another soldier attempted to smother her mouth, but she "bit him awful." A third soldier attempted to choke her and had it not been for the intervention of John Miller, a white resident of Middletown, Serena believed she would have been killed. She noted that Miller "was comin' out of his gate ridin' his horse [and] he saw that some one was havin' trouble with the soldiers. So he galloped full speed to where we was fightin. He knew me well and my parents, and when he saw who it was he hollered: 'Let go of that child! Let go of that child!'" Miller took the three soldiers to Sheridan's headquarters at Belle Grove where punishment was doled out—their heads were shaved and then they were tied up by their thumbs.[119] Light sentences, such as the one pronounced upon the three Union soldiers for the attack and attempted rape of Serena Spencer, unfortunately proved commonplace.[120]

When Clifton Johnson interviewed Spencer in the early 1900s about her wartime experiences she not only vividly recounted that horrific moment and other thoughts about the final battle of Sheridan's 1864 Shenandoah Campaign, but told Johnson that life proved nearly impossible during the conflict. As Serena's attack illustrates, African Americans had to be extremely careful about who they trusted. "We never knew what was goin' to happen . . . I tell you it was time through hyar [sic] when the North and South was fightin," Serena informed Johnson.[121] Whether aware of Serena's horrific moment or not, another African American female from Middletown echoed that every enslaved or free black person in the community, throughout the war, was more "or less uneasy and fearful . . . those was pitiful times—pitiful times."[122]

The uneasiness the Shenandoah Valley's African Americans felt throughout the conflict's four years subsided with news of Lee's surrender at Appomattox. They no longer had to navigate a complex world of being in Union territory one day, Confederate the next, and in no-man's land another. Confederate surrender also marked the end of enslaved people determining the best time to flee and weighing the consequences of escape not only for themselves, but family and friends who might have been left behind. Union military success also, as historian Elizabeth Varon noted, "marked the demise of slavery."[123] Considering all that the war's end meant, a formerly enslaved person from the Middletown area explained simply that she "was glad when" she "heard that the war was over."[124]

Although understandably glad of all that Union success brought with it, the Valley's African Americans, as they had elsewhere, quickly realized that although Union triumph marked slavery's Constitutional death and eliminated wartime challenges, the postwar era brought a whole new set of trials. The Civil War's end proved not a conclusion, but merely marked the beginning of the next chapter in the campaign to realize freedom's totality.

# 7

John Brown's "Soul Is Still Marching On"

Shortly after the Civil War's end John Trowbridge, a prolific author and contributor to the *Atlantic Monthly*, conceived an idea for a book about the conflict's impact on Southern landscapes, communities, and populations.[1] During the research sojourn for his book *The South: A Tour of Its Battle-fields and Ruined Cities*, Trowbridge visited eight Southern states. When Trowbridge arrived in the Shenandoah Valley in 1865 he seemed aghast at the war's aggregate effect on the Valley. "We passed through a region of country stamped all over by the devastating hell of war. For miles not a fence or cultivated field was visible," he wrote.[2] Although Trowbridge wanted his book to provide a record of how "the great contest of arms just closed" impacted "the country . . . [and] its inhabitants," he hoped the book might also capture how defeated Confederates felt about the most significant change brought by Union victory—slavery's destruction. Without any "fictitious coloring . . . spoiled by embellishment," he wanted to offer a "correct impression . . . of the still greater contest of principles not yet terminated."[3]

In places such as Georgia, Trowbridge encountered open hostility to emancipation and African Americans.[4] However, when Trowbridge visited the Shenandoah Valley, he believed a radical transformation was under way. During his time in the lower Valley he witnessed interactions that made it appear as though those who once supported the Confederacy regarded African Americans as citizens. He wrote, "The humble freedman . . . mothers and daughters of the despised race . . . [were] now citizens . . . free to come and go."[5]

Although to Trowbridge it appeared that the Shenandoah Valley's African Americans enjoyed the privileges of "citizens" even before ratification of the Constitutional amendments that granted those rights, whether he truly observed this or created it, what he wrote stood in stark contrast to the reality. In the conflict's aftermath, Watkins James, who served as assistant United States assessor in the lower Valley counties of Frederick, Shenandoah, and Warren, believed that a significant number of former Confederates in that portion of the Valley harbored greater animosity toward African Americans than they did prior to the war's outbreak. James observed: "Their feelings . . . towards the freedmen, are more hostile to-day than they were at the close of the rebellion . . . there is an animosity between the rebels and the negroes which would never be settled."[6]

Staunton resident William J. Dews, a music professor, echoed James's perspective. Unable to accept emancipation's reality, Dews explained to members of the Joint Committee on Reconstruction on February 14, 1866, that "generally speaking, they [former Confederates] do not recognize it [slavery's abolition]" and were "very bitter" toward African Americans.[7] Thomas Ashby, a Front Royal resident who supported the Confederacy, seemed more than ready to accept Union victory, but could not stomach the prospect of African American citizenship. "The people of the South . . . fought bravely for their Constitutional rights and had submitted this question to the arbitration of arms. The contest had been decided against them, and they [former Confederates] were prepared to accept this decision," Ashby wrote. But the notion of placing "a servile race" on the same political footing as whites seemed unconscionable.[8] Unequivocally, Ashby believed that African Americans were "a race totally unfit for the duties of citizenship."[9] In a manner similarly blunt to Ashby, Augusta County resident John B. Baldwin believed African Americans "are generally inferior to the white race."[10] All of these accounts illustrate that it was not one but various factors that contributed to the hostility former Confederates harbored toward African Americans. Unable to comprehend African Americans as social and political equals, no longer being able to benefit from enslaved labor, or the fact that individuals enslaved prior to the conflict were now free and thus offered an incessant reminder of the Confederacy's failure all proved reasons some former Confederates seethed with anger toward African Americans.

The anger former enslavers in the Shenandoah Valley felt in the wake of Union victory prompted some to brutalize individuals once enslaved in unprecedented ways. A formerly enslaved person from Augusta County remembered that when some "masters . . . found out they couldn't keep their slaves," they "began to treat them about as bad as could be." Some newly freed people attempted to reason with their former enslavers in an effort to convince them not to take out their frustrations over Confederate defeat and slavery's abolition on them. One male ex-slave who resided "in the vicinity of Staunton" explained to his former enslaver "that I didn't think we colored folks ought to be blamed for what wasn't our fault, for we didn't make the war, and neither did we declare ourselves free." One person within earshot of these remarks became so enraged over these "saucy" remarks that he pulled out a revolver, and as the African American man remembered, "put a pistol to my head, and was going to shoot me." Fortunately, the African American man "got away from him."[11]

As so many former Confederates teemed with resentment over the prospect of African American equality in the Civil War's wake and some threatened violence against the newly freed people, the region's African Americans searched for stability. While all African Americans knew they were technically free, they struggled to find a way to realize all that freedom entailed. One formerly enslaved person likened the reaction of freed people to freedom to that of a bird: we "were like a bird let out of cage. You know how a bird that has been long in a cage will act when the door is opened; he makes a curious fluttering for a little while. It was just so with the colored people . . . They didn't know at first what to do."[12]

While few, if any, of the Shenandoah Valley's African Americans possessed the answer as to how they would realize freedom's full potential, some believed that leaving the region offered arguably the best opportunity. "It is quite natural that the freedmen should desire to leave the scenes of their late bondage and humiliation, and *seek* homes among those who have always sympathized with them and who are prepared to receive them with open arms and open doors," wrote a correspondent for the *Staunton Spectator* in the summer of 1865. Somewhat sympathetically, the journalist wrote that African Americans who remained in "the land of their birth" would encounter "prejudices of generations . . . It will be many long years before their social condition, in the South, can be materially changed."[13]

Whether the Shenandoah Valley's African Americans decided to remain or leave, they understood that seeking the protection of Union soldiers proved a key element to enjoying any of freedom's benefits. As news spread throughout the region of Confederate defeat, freed people were drawn to Union troops like metal to a magnet.[14] On May 1, 1865, for instance, a resident of Staunton wrote that "Negroes are flocking to the Yankee camp" of the 22nd New York Cavalry.[15] When throngs of formerly enslaved people entered the Union camp, the regiment's officers warned that while they "were not at liberty to send them home" the cavalrymen did not have the means to support them, nor could they provide them with transportation to other areas. One Staunton resident wrote, "The officers have told everybody that they did not want the negroes to go off with them, and would furnish them neither transportation nor rations."[16] Despite that warning, freed people from the area around Staunton flocked to the 22nd New York's camp. As the troopers moved north to Winchester on May 2, 1865, scores of freed people from Augusta County clung to the cavalrymen. "The Federal troops started early this morning down the Valley. Many negroes, men, women and children accompanied them," observed a Staunton resident.[17]

Among those who sought the protection of federal troops to journey safely from his former Augusta County enslaver to Harpers Ferry that spring was an unidentified African American male. Once he arrived at Harpers Ferry the man quickly found employment as a waiter at a hotel.[18] While some freed people who journeyed to Harpers Ferry found employment there, others quickly learned that Harpers Ferry proved to be a gateway out of the Shenandoah Valley and to a potentially improved life at some location in the North. In fact, Harpers Ferry became so overcrowded that federal officials there established an employment office. It was not, however, created for the purpose of finding suitable occupations for African Americans in the area, but in northern locations, specifically New York, Rhode Island, and Ohio.[19]

Interestingly, not all of the Shenandoah Valley's freed people journeyed north; some went south. In a letter dated March 20, 1870, Shenandoah County resident Carrie Bushong wrote simply, "the Negroes are going south."[20] While Bushong's letter offers no insight into why area African Americans might have gone south, it is not unreasonable to surmise that some might have done so to relocate family members from whom slavery separated them. Others might have ventured south in search of opportunity, particularly the chance to own land as a result of the Southern Homestead Act.[21] Regardless of where they went or what motivated them to leave, census data reveals that the Valley's African American population did decrease by the time of Bushong's letter. Between 1860 and 1870 the Shenandoah Valley's African American population shrank approximately 13 percent (approximately 3,700 individuals).[22]

While federal officials could not concern themselves with the fate of those who departed the Valley, they fretted for the security of those who remained and searched for answers as to how best support the freed people. On June 9, 1865, General Isaac Duval penned a note to General Alfred T. A. Torbert, the overall commander of federal troops in the Shenandoah Valley, seeking advice on how to provide for the "relief" of the region's African Americans. "The condition of the Negro families in this vicinity is in my opinion becoming alarming. Large families of women and small children are . . . now roaming over the country . . . destitute and almost naked . . . I deem this a matter of vast importance to the community at large and earnestly recommend immediate action."[23]

Unnerved by Duval's grim assessment, Torbert looked to the Bureau of Refugees, Freedmen, and Abandoned Lands (popularly known as the Freedmen's Bureau), commanded by General Oliver O. Howard, for guidance. Established in March 1865, Howard knew the Bureau's charge a Herculean one. The legislation that created the Bureau demanded it oversee "the supervision and management of all abandoned lands, and the control of all subjects relating to refugees and freedmen from Rebel States." The Bureau's duties ran the gamut, from helping freed people find employment, reuniting families, providing "freedmen . . . tracts of land, within insurrectionary States," offering access to education, and providing life's basic necessities.[24] The responsibility of making certain the Bureau upheld its responsibilities in the Old Dominion rested upon the able shoulders of Colonel Orlando Brown, who organized Virginia into ten administrative districts. The Shenandoah Valley initially comprised the state's Sixth District. Since 1863 Brown had served as general superintendent of Negro affairs in the area around Norfolk, so he comprehended the myriad challenges formerly enslaved people confronted.[25] He believed that having a stable living environment proved a crucial first step on the pathway to stability and freedom. Hence when Torbert's letter of concern reached Brown's desk in Richmond in June 1865 he advised Torbert to make certain freed people had a place to live, even if it meant living with former enslavers for the time being. Brown explained to Torbert, "You will not allow the colored people to be turned out of doors. Call upon the military [to] prevent this." Additionally, Brown instructed Torbert to make note of any local authorities who have "taken action against the interest of the negroes report it at once to this office."[26]

As news spread of Brown's directive some of the Valley's former enslavers expressed resentment, as the war had left them so destitute that they did not possess the resources necessary to care for people they once enslaved and their families. One Shenandoah Valley newspaper lamented that for some former enslavers keeping freed people proved "a burden . . . This [is] regarded as a great injustice, as the citizens have scarcely enough to support themselves." After speaking with some residents in the lower Valley the correspondent noted that the Freedmen's Bureau's edict demanding that "the colored people" should not "be turned out of doors" limited area whites' "rights of freedom." Even former enslavers who possessed the financial wherewithal to pay freed people to labor for them complained just two months after Lee's surrender at Appomattox that "the able-bodied negroes have all left, those only remain who are not able to do any work." Former enslavers believed that they, not the Freedmen's Bureau, should determine who they employed. One journalist believed that former enslavers "should have the privilege to employ such labor as should be most advantageous to them."[27]

Of course not all former enslavers abhorred the prospect of employing ex-slaves; instances exist in the Shenandoah Valley when freed people appealed to remain with former enslavers and they assented. For example, several months after the Confederacy's collapse, George, once enslaved by Newtown's Walls family, appeared at the home of Dr. William and Mary Walls and appealed to them for employment. Mary Walls wrote, "After the war, George came back . . . all dressed up in a fine black suit and a high silk hat. I hardly recognized him." Like so many freed people, George returned to his former enslaver not because he enjoyed his bondage, but because as historian Chandra Manning has argued, freed people had nothing and former enslavers had everything.[28] Initially, Walls informed George that the family could not hire him. Already employing their formerly enslaved male Henry, Mary Walls explained bluntly "that we could not afford to hire him." After some additional prodding by George, Mary acquiesced and agreed to hire George as the Walls's cook. George labored for the family "for about a year." Mrs. Walls ultimately fired George because during his time as a body servant for Dr. Walls, who had served in the Confederate army as a surgeon, George "had learned so many bad habits." Among the behaviors he developed was stealing food. While George referred to it as "foraging like [he] used to do in the army," his theft of food from neighbors mortified Mrs. Walls.[29]

In Front Royal, "Uncle Lewis," once enslaved by the Ashby family, decided to remain with his former enslaver. Aged and infirm, Lewis knew he was in no condition to realize freedom's potential. He died "a few weeks after the conflict." While the Ashbys interpreted Lewis's desire to remain as an indication of gratitude for his enslavement, he did so out of faithfulness to himself in his final days, rather than loyalty to his former enslaver.[30] Others formerly enslaved by the Ashbys remained for a few years after the Civil War, but only long enough to save sufficient money to provide for their independence. For example, Susan lived and worked for the Ashbys for three years after the conflict before she departed. During the time she labored for her former enslavers she saved the wages she earned as a housekeeper and the additional income she received "taking in washing and doing light work" for others in Front Royal. Eventually, Susan accumulated enough wealth "to buy a neat little house in Front Royal" and according to one member of the Ashby family, "she lived in comfort until she died."[31]

While records indicate that Susan eventually left her former enslaver without any difficulty, some ex-enslavers in the Shenandoah did all they could to make the transition from slavery to freedom as miserable as possible. For example, when Emma Morris, once enslaved by John S. Lupton, decided to leave, Lupton and his wife refused to permit Emma "to take away a night gown or drawers and the skirt" Lupton's wife had given her. Emma refused to accept the Lupton's unreasonable request and asked Freedmen's Bureau officials to intervene. Once Bureau agents in Winchester reviewed the case, they ordered the Luptons "to cause to be delivered to Emma Morris the night gown and the two prs. of drawers."[32]

In addition to turning to the Freedmen's Bureau to secure basic property, African Americans also looked to Bureau officials for help in finding suitable employment. Although a report filed in the House of Representatives in May 1866 stated that African Americans in the Shenandoah Valley received an average pay of $12 per month, the wages formerly enslaved people earned varied tremendously throughout the region.[33] A survey of all contracts negotiated at the Freedmen's Bureau office in Winchester for 1866 shows that monthly wages ranged from $3 per month, the salary Caroline Thompson received as a house servant for Robert Conrad, to $15 per month, the wage paid Thomas Leitz by the Barton family for work as a farm laborer at Springdale.[34] Some employers even offered less than what Caroline Thompson received. When Calvin Hall signed his contract on May 12, 1866, to labor as a "house servant" for Miss Mannie McCole in Frederick County, he was promised an annual salary of $2 (approximately 17 cents per month) and the assurance that McCole would "furnish" Hall with "proper and suitable quarters, all summer and winter clothing and shoes."[35] Some received not even the slightest pittance and instead worked for a share of the crop they helped cultivate. For instance, when Jasco Thompson signed his labor contract with Clarke County resident Patrick Tracy, Thompson received no wages but instead was promised "to receive one-third of crops." Tracy also agreed to provide Thompson a "house and garden patch."[36] In Augusta County, William F. Snapp agreed to not only let the formerly enslaved George Washington take one-third of the crop as compensation, but agreed to "furnish the necessary horses and feed for the same, ploughs, harness, and farming implements generally." Additionally, Snapp permitted Washington to keep "one fourth part of all the wood so cut and hauled" to Staunton.[37]

The terms of Thompson's and Washington's contract proved typical of crop-sharing agreements in the war's aftermath.[38] What proved unusual was that they received those terms in the Shenandoah Valley. Although prevalent in the war's aftermath throughout various parts of the South, and oftentimes preferred by freed people, few agreements negotiated in the Shenandoah Valley, at least in the first three years following the conflict's end, offered a share of the crop as compensation in lieu of wages.[39] In addition to Thompson's agreement, administered by Bureau officials in Winchester, an examination of all labor contracts administered by the Staunton office of the Freedmen's Bureau office between 1865 and 1868 reveals that only about 3 percent of labor contracts offered during that period offered a "share of crop" as compensation.[40] In fact, white employers throughout the Shenandoah so rarely used it that in the autumn of 1868 a journalist for the *Staunton Vindicator* urged it be considered, since it seemed so successful in South Carolina. "Among the various styles of contracts with the freedmen none seem to work better," the journalist wrote of sharecropping. The *Vindicator* continued, "The farmer furnishes plow animals and farm implements, and keeps all under his own care and control . . . Those who have tried this plan says it works to the satisfaction of both parties, and give to the laborer who behave himself a permanent home and an interest in the place he cultivates."[41]

Despite the popularity of compensating African Americans in areas beyond the Valley with a "share of the crop" instead of wages, the practice never seemed to take hold in the Shenandoah. Perhaps, as historian Kenneth Koons has posited, the practice never gained traction in the Valley (even by the early 1880s) because white farmers did not believe African Americans capable of managing all that such an agreement entailed.[42] Additionally, white employers in the Valley might have preferred paying wages instead of a crop-sharing system, as white employers believed offering a regular wage allowed them to exert more control over their African American employees. This sentiment, as historian Eric Foner argued, was not unique to the Shenandoah Valley and existed elsewhere. "Planters resisted sharecropping as a threat to their overall authority" and "insisted sharecroppers were wage laborers, who must obey the orders of their employer," Foner concluded.[43]

Sharecropping's unpopularity certainly did not result from an unwillingness of the Valley's African Americans to work on farms after the conflict. An examination of all labor contracts negotiated at the Freedmen's Bureau office in Staunton from 1865 to 1868 reveals that 55 percent of freed people worked as "farm laborer" or "farm hand" for wages. Although the wages earned ranged from $5 to $15 per month, it appears that the Valley's African

Americans preferred real wages to working for a share of the crop, a sentiment expressed by freed people in other parts of Virginia, particularly west of the Blue Ridge Mountains.[44]

Some of the Valley's African Americans, however, did not have a choice as to how they were compensated for their labor. African American children, either orphaned or unable to be cared for by parents, sometimes found themselves indentured to white employers as a result of agreements negotiated by Freedmen's Bureau officials. Concerned that African American orphans or minors might be exploited by whites under current apprenticeship laws in former slaveholding states, General Howard issued a circular on October 4, 1865, stating that Bureau officials would act as guardians for these children and execute indentures with white employers "for the apprenticing of orphan minor children of Freedmen."[45] Although well intentioned, these indentures, even more so than some labor contracts negotiated by the Freedmen's Bureau that offered little compensation, most closely resembled slavery. In Winchester, for example, one month after Howard issued his directive, Freedmen's Bureau official William McKenzie approved an apprenticeship indenture for a fifteen-year-old African American boy identified as Robert. The agreement bound Robert to Jordan Pifer for a "full term of six years."[46] The indenture promised Robert a rudimentary education to learn how "to read and write" and an annual stipend of $10, which would increase $5 per year "for the duration of his apprenticeship." The contract offered him no freedom and demanded loyalty required in the enslaved–enslaver relationship. The indenture ordered that Robert "shall serve his master faithfully honestly and industriously, his secrets kept and his lawful commands everywhere readily obeyed." It also required Robert to be available to Pifer at all times. The contract commanded, "He shall not be absent from said master[']s service day or night."[47]

White employers not only held a clear advantage over their black employees in what at times seemed a reinvention of slavery, but sometimes attempted to shirk what little responsibility they possessed and refused to pay the paltry sums owed their workers. On a regular basis Freedmen's Bureau officials in the Shenandoah Valley received complaints from African American laborers that their white employers refused to pay them. Complaints about lack of payment for wages dominated the docket of Freedmen's Bureau agents, with more than half the complaints filed by African Americans pertaining to wages.[48] Among those who filed a complaint was the formerly enslaved David Jefferson, who charged his former enslaver, Robert McCampbell, with nonpayment for services rendered. Jefferson accused McCampbell of breaking his promise "to pay him wages from the first part of January till the fifteenth of April." McCampbell swore under oath to Bureau officials in Woodstock "that he did promise to pay him wages for the time stated and that he intended to pay him, but that he did not have the money." The Freedmen's Bureau agents cared little and ordered McCampbell to compensate Jefferson "$42 for time and of half month service of $12 per month."[49]

While McCampbell tried to justify not paying his employee on the basis that he lacked sufficient funds, other white employers such as George Rodgers refused to pay a portion of freed person Aaron Green's wage due to Green's inability to work for six weeks while he recovered from an injury to his leg. Despite being injured "by a log falling on his leg" while laboring for his employer, Rodgers withheld $9 from Green, contending that he "retained" the money "as compensation for boarding Green six weeks while disabled."[50] The Freedmen's Bureau ruled in Green's favor and ordered Rodgers to fully compensate him.[51]

As freed people sought employment and fair labor conditions, there appeared to be a concerted effort among some ex-enslavers in various locales to keep formerly enslaved individuals in as close a state of slavery as possible. For instance, E. C. Clarkhurst, an official from the US Treasury Department who visited Rockbridge County in the first week of August 1865, could not fathom the animosity that existed among former enslavers toward those they once enslaved. "I understand that the Planters have held meetings and determined not to hire any negro formerly owned by them who leaves," Clarkhurst explained to Captain William Stover How, the superintendent of the Freedmen's Bureau in the Valley's Sixth District, "or applies, for work elsewhere. In other words they are determined to hold them, without remuneration, as formerly."[52]

The desire of some former enslavers in the Shenandoah Valley to not employ African Americans increased in the week's leading up to and in the aftermath of the election for delegates to Virginia's constitutional convention on October 22, 1867—the first election in which African American men could vote in Virginia courtesy of section 5 of the Military Reconstruction Act enacted by Congress in March 1867 which permitted "male citizens . . . twenty-one years old and upward, of whatever race, color or previous condition . . . the qualifications" to vote.[53] Those who formerly supported the Confederacy feared that if African Americans participated in the election that Virginia would certainly be governed by a new state constitution that not only included provisions for African American suffrage and public schools funded partially by a poll tax on the Commonwealth's male citizens, but threatened to disenfranchise white citizens loyal to the Confederate war effort.[54] In an effort to suppress African American political involvement, white employers threatened to terminate employment or not rehire them if the convention vote did not turn out in favor of maintaining the status quo. For instance, Captain Eleazur H. Ripley, the Freedmen's Bureau agent in charge of Warren, Page, and Clarke Counties, reported that one month after the election, which resulted in the election of sixty-eight Republican delegates, twenty-four of whom were African American, to only thirty-six Democrats, that a number "of the whites" in the counties under his control "have told the freedmen if they did not vote with them *against* a new constitution they would turn them off or would not employ them anymore."[55] Similarly, Thomas Jackson, the Freedmen's Bureau agent in Augusta County, reported: "Since the election there has been a most outrageous attempt to deter freedmen from voting . . . contracts have not been so frequent the last half of this month."[56]

The threats seemed to have little impact on the region's African Americans. In late November 1867 Captain Ripley believed that the "threats will have no weight with the freedmen."[57] Ripley believed that the region's African Americans remained "still determined to adhere to the Republican Party" despite the efforts of their "employers . . . exerting every power in their hands to compel them to vote with them against the new Constitution."[58] He also thought that the need for labor throughout the Valley would mute threats that if African Americans voted "for the new constitution they will be driven from their work."[59] From Ripley's perspective he supposed it more of a ploy on the part of white employers "to reduce wages for the coming year" than to control Virginia politics.[60]

Although Ripley remained confident that white employers in the Shenandoah Valley would not carry out their threats of terminating or not rehiring African Americans in the wake of the 1867 election, his counterpart Thomas Jackson in the upper Shenandoah Valley was not so certain. Fearful of what might happen, Jackson implored African Americans in the area around Staunton to stop attending political events and voicing their concerns. Jackson believed that the energy African Americans exerted at these meetings not only deepened divisions between African Americans and white employers, but distracted African American laborers from their work, thus giving employers an excuse to either reduce wages or terminate employment.[61] The moment of truth arrived with the start of the new year, the time when white employers renewed contracts. At least in the three counties under

Ripley's control, there appeared no decline in the number of labor contracts offered. In his first report for the new year of 1868 Ripley happily informed his superiors in Richmond that "the freedmen have been making contracts for the coming year and at about the same pay as they received last year."[62] Two months later, Ripley noted after a tour of the area under his control that "the freedmen [are] doing very well and all well satisfied with their contracts for the present year."[63]

Whether truly satisfied or resigned to their fate, some Freedmen's Bureau officials recognized that the contractual system they helped perpetuate clearly favored white employers and consequently did little to adequately ameliorate conditions for African Americans. At the end of April 1867, Captain T. A. McDonnell, a Bureau official charged with control of operations in Frederick and Clarke Counties, lamented to Orlando Brown that while the "general condition of the freedpeople in both counties is steadily improving," wages remained "low . . . throughout the Valley." Convinced that former enslavers "are determined to keep the former [slaves] in the most abject poverty and convince them that their former slavery was preferable to their present starvation prices for labor."[64] After two years of operations in the Shenandoah Valley this official believed only one thing could save the region's African Americans from their current state and thrust open the gates to a life of true freedom—education. "His [formerly enslaved individuals] thirst for education will soon however relieve him from the thralldom under which he has so long and patiently suffered and enable him to demand and obtain a fair remuneration for a fair day[']s toil," the official explained to Brown.[65]

The region's African Americans also understood the value of education. By the end of 1865 the Freedmen's Bureau, with support from the American Missionary Association, the Old School Presbyterian Church of Pittsburgh, and the New England Baptist Society, established nine schools throughout the Shenandoah Valley between Lexington and Harpers Ferry.[66] By the end of the year those nine schools enrolled 1,403 students. Staunton boasted the largest school with 385 students, and Harrisonburg the smallest with twenty-five.[67]

As the various benevolent Christian organizations deployed teachers to the Valley to take control of the nine schools the teachers wondered, like all educators meeting students for the first time, what level of excitement for learning their students possessed. When Sarah Jane Foster, a native of Maine, arrived at her school in Martinsburg, West Virginia, in the autumn of 1865 the enthusiasm for education among the area's African Americans inspired her. The freed people "are eager to learn, and some even come in several miles from the country," Foster wrote.[68] Foster, who taught both day and night school, believed that the adult students she taught at night had a far better grasp of how education opened the door to opportunity than younger students. While Foster complained that some of the students in her day school, the majority of whom were under age eighteen, "are disposed to be inattentive to their books, but no more so than any children," the older students who attended her night school comprehended "the importance of the time." Those students, who ranged in age from twenty to sixty-two, were "a pleasure to teach," Foster explained.[69]

Foster not only found her adult students delightful, but also offered the opportunity to some of her best to teach lessons. Student John Brown ranked among Foster's superlative adult pupils. On various occasions Brown taught "map lesson[s]." Brown's ability to grasp material and present it to students cogently caught the attention of more than Foster. Reverend Nathan Cook Brackett, a Freewill Baptist minister who served as superintendent of education for Freedmen's Schools throughout the Shenandoah Valley, also believed Brown possessed great potential. Brackett encouraged Brown to journey to Lewiston, Maine, for additional schooling, but Brown refused. Although flattered by the offer Brown supposed "it his cross" to remain in the Valley "and stand or fall with those of his color."[70]

Teachers throughout the Valley not only taught the region's African Americans the basics of education, but also stressed the value of living a moral life. Particularly among her students younger than eighteen, Foster noted "slight falsehoods continually told." While Foster attributed this to their upbringing in slavery, telling lies in order "to avoid punishment or blame," she abhorred it and instructed her students to stop. Foster "endeavored to impress upon" her students that "lying [was] one of the worst vices." Freedmen's teachers also instructed students on the value of temperance.[71] The message of temperance taught in Freedmen's Schools certainly took hold among some freed people in the Shenandoah Valley. In Page and Warren Counties, for example, African Americans organized "the Union Relief Association." The association counted among its most important tasks taking "steps to prevent intemperance and break up this habit of drinking . . . so prevalent when they were slaves."[72]

As eager as Foster found her adult students to learn, seemingly a majority of whites throughout the region were equally determined to block any educational opportunity for African Americans in the Shenandoah Valley. Monthly Freedmen's Bureau reports reveal that whites throughout the region largely opposed the establishment of schools. For example, a report filed by a Freedmen's Bureau agent in April 1868 noted that the idea of schools for African Americans was "very much opposed . . . throughout the division."[73] A few months later in June, the animosity remained unchanged. "Bitterly opposed to it," one Freedmen's Bureau official noted.

While Valley inhabitants opposed to education oftentimes kept their animus against it to themselves or verbally professed their disapproval to Freedmen's Bureau officials, others displayed their dissatisfaction in more dramatic fashion. When Reverend Brackett announced his intention to open a school for African Americans in Charles Town approximately one year after the Civil War ended, a mob threatened him. Only the intervention of a Confederate veteran, whom Brackett had saved from death after the Battle of Cedar Creek in October 1864, rescued Brackett from harm.[74]

Those who opposed the establishment of schools resisted in other ways. For instance, those who owned real estate that the Freedmen's Bureau tried to rent for use as schools simply offered properties at exorbitant rates, making it financially unfeasible for the Bureau to enter into a lease agreement. When Freedmen's Bureau officials tried to purchase vacant lots to build schools the owners oftentimes refused to sell. In the spring of 1868 one official lamented: "With the exception of the buildings now occupied I find it impossible to hire for school purposes and parties even refuse to sell land if schools . . . for freedpeople are erected upon them."[75]

Some area whites showed their disdain for Freedmen's Schools by violently lashing out against teachers—threatening bodily harm and even death if they continued to teach. Just months after the Civil War ended the teacher assigned to the school in Woodstock by the American Missionary Association, presumably Rev. D. A. Mills, confided to the town's postmaster Mr. Ives that he could not cope with the incessant threats he received. Ives discouraged Mills from relinquishing his teaching position and instead urged him to "take six or seven of the young men home with him to protect him."[76] Some of Woodstock's angry citizens posted a note on the front door of the postmaster's house "blaming him for boarding this man who was teaching the colored school." When notes and verbal threats failed to budge Mills, some of the locals "took to snow-balling the teacher."[77]

Further south in Luray, a contingent of approximately twenty individuals took more drastic measures to convince Mr. G. Hammond, another teacher dispatched by the American Missionary Association to the Shenandoah Valley, to quit.[78] After refusing to relinquish his teaching position after receiving an anonymous note "that he must leave or take the consequences,"

Hammond was snatched from his bed in the middle of the night, placed in a boat, and taken to the middle of the Shenandoah River. After being "held under the water some time" the mob "threatened, if he did not leave the county in three days, he would be shot dead."[79] Unfortunately, the historical record is silent on Hammond's ultimate fate.

Other cases exist where groups of angry whites barged into schoolrooms and threatened those inside. In Martinsburg, Sarah Jane Foster's night class was interrupted in January 1866 when angry residents busted down the door and "disturbed" Foster's teaching.[80] Toward the end of January another of her class sessions "was disturbed" by a band of "intruders." Two of Foster's older students chased after them, caught two and turned them over to a Freedmen's Bureau official in Martinsburg, Captain J. H. McKenzie.[81]

While some used direct threats to dissuade teachers from teaching, others threatened local inhabitants who in some way supported the teachers. For example, Sarah Jane Foster was so badly slandered by a "mob" and incessantly harassed in Martinsburg and "pointed out as a 'nigger teacher'" that the woman from whom she rented a room, Mrs. Hoke, refused to board her any longer.[82]

Despite the difficulties teachers confronted in the Shenandoah Valley there seemed to be a quiet defiance among them to remain, no matter how significant the threat. Perhaps taking to heart General Howard's thoughts that Freedmen's Bureau teachers should "not [be] afraid of outrage . . . [and] not afraid to die," teachers in the Valley stood firm.[83] After being regularly harassed and having her schoolroom broken into on multiple occasions, Sarah Foster seemed convinced more than ever to remain. In early February 1866 she confided to her diary: "I must try and be patient. I cannot name my trials for no one sympathizes with them. I know that God is at work here and am not going to cast off his children for ignorance and mistakes."[84]

Regardless of the obstacles Freedmen's schools confronted throughout the Shenandoah Valley and the resolve of some area inhabitants to terrorize teachers and students, the Freedmen's Bureau, various Christian organizations, the minority of area whites who supported education for freed people, and area African Americans worked tirelessly to expand the number of schools throughout the region. By the end of 1868 the number of Freedmen's schools throughout the region grew to forty-two. However, as the quantity of schools increased the responsibility of teaching no longer exclusively rested with northern teachers who journeyed south, but with locals.[85] For example, of the six teachers responsible for Winchester's eight schools, at least two were local—James Washington, a literate free black blacksmith prior to the Civil War, and Sarah Percival.[86] Percival, who was, as one Freedmen's Bureau official noted, "born and has always lived in this town," refused to accept money for the use of her home on Braddock Street as a school. Additionally, she rejected wages as compensation for the hours she spent teaching her eighteen students. She taught, recalled one official, out of "the desire to see the [freed] people educated."[87]

In Harrisonburg, John Scanlon, an Irish immigrant who journeyed to the United States in 1843 and was the owner of the Virginia House Hotel, offered the use of a room in his home as a school free of charge. Labeled as no "defender of slavery and opposed to it as cruel practice," Scanlon also agreed to board the teacher when everyone else refused. Those actions, coupled with his desire to get "a white female to teach in [the] colored school," created such an outrage that locals boycotted his business. His desire to aid African Americans in their pursuit of a better life financially ruined him.[88]

In some locales, such as Jefferson County, where many whites regarded African Americans "with the basest contempt," freed people assumed the responsibility of establishing schools. For example, in Shepherdstown, the community's African Americans took the lead in building a school. After securing a lot, the community's African Americans pledged $200 to build the structure.[89]

Despite their best efforts to improve their lot and realize a life in freedom—along with assistance from the Freedmen's Bureau, various northerners who journeyed south after the Civil War, and a contingent of sympathetic local whites—the Shenandoah Valley's African Americans confronted rampant hatred and numerous obstacles in the war's aftermath. Complaints flooded Freedmen's Bureau offices throughout the region of criminal acts perpetrated against area African Americans by whites for which appropriate penalties from local authorities were not assessed. For instance, on January 18, 1868, two white men, Charles Chamberlain and Frederick Boyer, shot an African American man, Charles Barbour, in the back in Newtown. After Barbour fell off his horse, Chamberlain and Boyer stole it. The local court issued a warrant for the arrest of the two men; however, local officials "abandoned" any effort to locate them after a haphazard search. A report filed with the Freedmen's Bureau in late February 1868 noted that the two men remained "at large" with no indication that local officials desired "any further efforts to arrest" them.[90]

Further south in Lexington, Bureau officials received a complaint from Lizzie Harper, an African American woman who accused a student, identified in the report as "Misver," of rape. According to the report, not only did civil authorities not investigate the case, the community's mayor, J. M. Ruff, "allowed and assisted at the escape of [the] student . . . who attempted rape of an aggravated character upon the person of Lizzie Harper."[91]

Two months before Harper's case, Bureau officials in Winchester received a complaint that a female African American, Sarah Brown, had been attacked by a white man, John Ross. According to the report Ross, "while intoxicated went on premises of Sarah and kicked her in [the] breast and abdomen." Although the case went to trial in Frederick County and the court ruled against him, the punishment he received did not match the heinousness of his crime. The court simply ordered the "defendant to pay costs and give bond." The records do not indicate that Ross served any jail time for assaulting Brown.[92]

No African Americans were immune from violence, mistreatment, and injustice, including young children. Less than one year after the Civil War's end a group of teenage boys ganged up on an African American boy, approximately eight or nine years of age, in the Shenandoah County community of Edinburg. An adult who witnessed the bullying at the town's post office recalled, "There was a little black boy there between eight and nine years of age, and there were some four white boys teasing him, knocking off his hat, pulling him, and calling him 'Freedmen's Bureau' & c." Watkins James, among those who witnessed the scene, intervened, stopped the harassment, and demanded to know the identity of the children's parents. His entreaty fell on deaf ears as "not . . . one" white adult present offered up the parents' identity. The harassment that James witnessed proved the rule rather than the exception, as "one old gentleman" confessed that this sort of behavior among the community's white teenagers toward younger African American children "occurred every night."[93]

This sort of boorish behavior against African American children was not limited to Shenandoah County. Further south in Rockbridge County the son of Judge John W. Brockenbrough "assaulted a little negro for singing patriotic songs in the street."[94] Although never punished by the local courts, Brockenbrough's son, who according to Freedmen's Bureau records frequently attacked African Americans, apparently met his match in Caesar Griffin, an African American male. In the spring of 1868 Griffin shot the judge's son and wounded him. The court, although it found Griffin guilty, acknowledged that he shot Brockebrough's son "in self defense." Griffin received "two years imprisonment in the Penitentiary."[95]

Three years later in Frederick County, A. Latham, a white male, assaulted a young African American girl, the daughter of Lucy Forge Fletcher. The local prosecutor charged Latham with "entering" Fletcher's home "and beating [the] child with stick, also shaking by hair of head." After the court ruled against the plaintiff and ordered her to pay "for $1.00 costs," Fletcher petitioned Captain T. A. McDonnell for assistance. McDonnell and other Freedmen's Bureau officials believed the case should be reheard in a "Mil.[itary] Court," but county magistrate S. R. Atwell intervened and recommended against it. Letters from Atwell and other "communications of the Citizens of Winchester" prompted Bureau officials at the state level to not pursue any further action in the case.[96]

While a survey of records "Relating to Murders and Outrages" reveals that courts frequently turned a blind eye to crimes committed against African Americans or doled out penalties that did not match the crime, at least one example exists where authorities rectified injustice. In the spring of 1868 a Rockbridge County court sentenced John Burns, an African American, to sixteen years in prison "for burglary with attempt to commit rape on a [white] daughter of R. J. Echols." When Douglas Frazar brought the case to the attention of Freedmen's Bureau officials he contended, and Bureau officials concurred, that the "evidence show[ed] no proof of guilt." In fact, the report filed with the Bureau suggested that friends of Echols's daughter contrived the story "to clear her from guilt in the eyes of the community." After Orlando Brown reviewed the proceedings at his office in Richmond he recommended Burns "receive a full and immediate pardon." Virginia's governor Henry Wells, a former Union army officer, agreed to the pardon.[97]

As African Americans searched for justice and ways to realize freedom in the Civil War's aftermath, some in the Shenandoah Valley believed that the best way to ensure freedom was the establishment of distinctly African American communities. Shortly after the war's end African Americans established the community of Douglass Grove, situated three miles southeast of Martinsburg in Berkeley County—one of four African Americans communities in the county.[98]

Further south in Rockingham County a portion of Hill Top Farm, once owned by one of Harrisonburg's most prominent slaveholding families, the Grays, was reestablished as a community for African Americans known as "Africa" or "Newtown" in 1869.[99] That same year, northeast of Harrisonburg, another group of freed people, with assistance from a white couple, William Carpenter and his wife Hannah (members of the Brethren Church), carved out the community of "Little Africa" (eventually and more popularly referred to as "Zenda").[100] In the northern part of the Shenandoah Valley, African Americans gathered in a community to the east of present-day Stephens City known as "Freetown."[101]

In 1870 former enslaver Ellen McCormick, owner of Clermont Farm in Clarke County, sold thirty-one acres of the property, in an effort to avert financial ruin following the death of her husband Edward, to a group of twenty-four African Americans. Josephine Williams, an enslaved woman who had once labored for the McCormicks, was among those who purchased the land. As African American families laid out streets and constructed houses in what would become known as Josephine City, some of Berryville's white inhabitants seemed uncertain as to what having a distinctly African American community would mean for Berryville. The *Clarke Courier* wondered in October 1870 "how such a settlement will affect the interest of this community." The correspondent freely admitted that the "introduction of so large a number" of African Americans into so small a space, "is a natural cause of some uneasiness."[102] Although some whites appeared anxious about what the establishment of Josephine City might mean to them, they recognized how the establishment of that community provided freed people with a sense of purpose and self-respect. Former Confederate Samuel Moore noted that the freed people who settled "Josephine City" enjoyed "the greatest pleasure . . . to own their own homes . . . they lived happily from day to day."[103]

Additionally, the Valley's African Americans established churches as a means of asserting and protecting their freedom. Typical of what occurred throughout the South, Shenandoah Valley African Americans pooled resources and organized fundraisers to support the construction of churches. For instance in Staunton, African Americans held multiple fundraisers in the closing weeks of 1865 and opening days of 1866 to "purchase the old Market House which will be refitted as a church."[104] Valley newspapers in the immediate years following the Civil War are filled with notices of intentions to erect churches in Staunton, Natural Bridge, Mt. Sidney, and Harrisonburg.[105] In Newtown, the formerly enslaved Rev. Robert Orrick, regarded as "one of the wealthiest and best-known colored men of the South," donated materials necessary to rebuild the community's African American Methodist church that had been destroyed in the autumn of 1864 when Sheridan's army razed it to repurpose the building's materials to construct winter quarters.[106] Churches, places W.E.B. DuBois hailed as "the first dis-

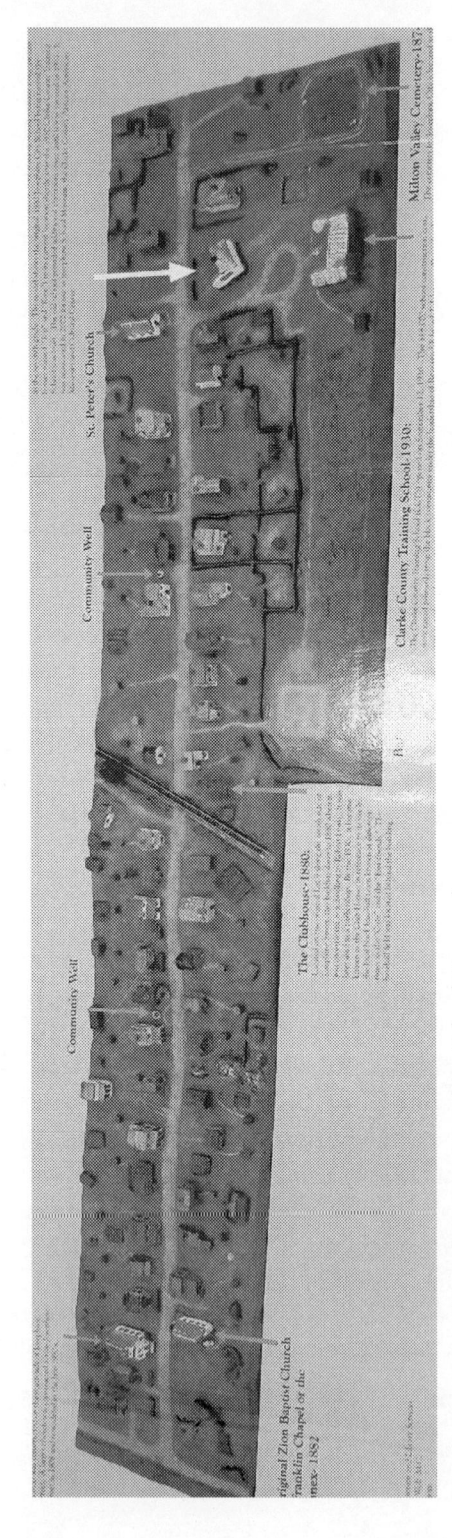

Figure 71. Model of Josephine City (Josephine School Museum).

tinctively Negro American social institutions," not only provided refuge and independence from whites, but served as a venue for African Americans to freely discuss issues relevant to their pursuit of freedom.[107]

The overall effort of the Shenandoah Valley's Africans to ameliorate their condition inspired a reporter for *The National Anti-Slavery Standard* who visited the Valley in March 1869. Undoubtedly an admirer of John Brown, the reporter believed that in the Shenandoah Valley Brown's "'soul is march[ing] on' in the freedmen schools . . . that soul is still 'marching on,' no longer in war and emancipation, but in the elevation and Christianizing of the colored race."[108]

John Brown's soul marched on in the Valley in another important way by 1869—political activism. In addition to approximately 90 percent of the region's African American males registering to vote and casting ballots in earlier elections, by 1869 a contingent of the Valley's African Americans attempted to exercise their right to remove an official from office they believed no longer suitable to his post: Judge Richard Parker, remembered by area African Americans as the man who sentenced John Brown to death in the autumn of 1859.[109] In February 1869 a contingent of "negroes and carpet-baggers about Winchester, who were clamorous for his [Parker's] removal," petitioned Massachusetts senator Charles Sumner to assist. Despite Sumner's efforts and "chronic growl[ing]" on the Senate floor against "this atrocious Virginia Judge," Parker survived the motion.[110]

Unable to remove Parker from his post in early 1869, African American males in the Valley now turned their energies toward the state gubernatorial election slated for July that year, when incumbent Henry Wells squared off with Gilbert Walker. Despite both candidates being northerners, the candidate of the "True Republican" party, Walker, seemed more palatable to white Democrats than Wells. The New York native Walker, as historian Richard Lowe astutely observed, represented "the party of slaveholders and secessionists," while the incumbent exemplified "freedom and justice."[111]

In the weeks leading up to the election, newspapers throughout the Shenandoah Valley tried to rally white voters to Walker's standard. White voters of Rockingham County appeared "in a blaze of excitement in regard to the coming election," reported one correspondent. To its south, white inhabitants of Augusta County mobilized to vote for Walker. The editors of the *Staunton Spectator and Vindicator*—which urged white voters "To the polls! To the polls!"—made it eminently clear to its white readers what this election's outcome meant. Less than three weeks prior to the vote it warned that if Wells won, African Americans in the Valley and across the

Old Dominion would receive more rights, hold more offices, and use their authority to punish former enslavers. "Negro constables and policemen would come down with their official batons on the white race. Negro magistrates would try their late masters for imaginary offenses," the newspaper noted apprehensively.[112] It warned further that any tax revenue collected by African American officials would not be used to benefit whites, but African Americans exclusively. One reporter opined that African American officials would "apply your taxes to build school-houses for his children." Simply, the newspaper's editors wanted its readers to consider if "they [were] willing to be under the dominance of an inferior race?" With the caveat that "times will be hard, far harder than any you have seen yet," if Wells won and African Americans filled more state and local offices, the editors urged area whites to cast a ballot for Walker and that if they refused to support him, "you will repent . . . and your repentance will come when it is too late to remedy your monstrous mistake."[113] The *Spectator and Vindicator* even appealed to the memory of Stonewall Jackson to galvanize support for Walker among the region's whites. "It would appear strange if the 'Stonewall' county should prove recreant to a sacred duty enjoined by every consideration of patriotism."[114]

Aware of how the election's outcome could alter any gains they enjoyed in the region, the Shenandoah Valley's African Americans mobilized. One correspondent covering the election in the Valley noted that the region's "negroes have splendidly organized [and] banded together."[115] Those efforts proved futile in the end. Despite high voter turnout among African Americans, a greater voter turnout among whites in a region and state that boasted more whites than African Americans meant victory for Walker.[116]

Gilbert Walker won every county in Virginia's Shenandoah Valley. His margin of victory, while close in the statewide election, was a landslide in the Valley, with Walker receiving 14,332 votes. Wells mustered only 4,651 in the region.[117] After the election one Valley newspaper reported that Walker's victory saved the region's whites from "the stupid negro."[118] Throughout the Valley and the Old Dominion whites, who opposed African American equality, believed that Walker's political triumph over Wells had set them "free."[119]

Walker's political success, Virginia's readmission into the Union in January 1870, and the withdrawal of federal troops from the Commonwealth thereafter marked the beginning of the end for African Americans to enjoy many of the profits freedom offered in the Civil War's aftermath. In the decades that followed, the situation for the region's African Americans appeared to observers to remain stagnant. A resident of Warren County wrote that while "slavery has been abolished in the sense of property interest, the negro is in all those personal characteristics as much a slave to-day as he was before the Civil War. He still struggles in poverty . . . [and] are as degraded as any laboring class can become."[120]

Despite an erosion of their freedom and a tectonic shift back to conservatism following the 1870 election, this was not an entirely new situation.[121] As they had during wartime, African Americans persisted and asserted their freedom in various ways, among them public commemorations of emancipation.

While African American celebrations of slavery's destruction in Virginia predated the Civil War's end, the practice did not appear with any regularity in the Shenandoah Valley until the summer of 1869, when approximately 2,000 individuals gathered in Shepherdstown in early September to commemorate slavery's end.[122] During the celebration, which included a parade with individuals carrying banners festooned with images of President Abraham Lincoln and General Ulysses S. Grant, along with games, dancing, and food, attendees listened to remarks intended to inspire and encourage African Americans.[123] In a manner typical of addresses delivered at emancipation celebrations throughout the South, one of the speakers at the Shepherdstown celebration, W. U. Saunders, gave thanks to God, "an all-wise Providence [who] had worked their liberation through war and bloodshed." Saunders's remarks went beyond expressing gratitude for slavery's destruction; it challenged the ideology of the Lost Cause by promoting the Emancipation Cause. After noting that slavery had sent "our nation . . . reeling and teetering toward destruction," Saunders reminded those present that African Americans shouldered their fair burden in the war's outcome and that they did not, as this study has shown, passively wait for emancipation to come to them. "The sacrifices of that war were shared by the colored men, that when rebel hands dared violate that flag, the 'Black Boys in Blue' answered to a Nation's call, and by his aid was that flag preserved." Furthermore, as undoubtedly a challenge to former Confederates who attempted to make life difficult for African Americans in the postwar era, Saunders reminded those present that the Civil War's outcome guaranteed "equal privileges to all men."[124]

The following month African Americans from the vicinity of Charles Town commemorated emancipation in a similar fashion. Among the speakers was the formerly enslaved W. W. Grimes. In a somewhat similar vein to Saunders, Grimes believed that God, "a kind and merciful Benefactor," played an important role in slavery's abolition.[125] Grimes also emphasized the importance of hard work and respectful cooperation with whites, a theme historian William Blair concluded to be typical across the South. "Unless we go industrious we cannot progress. We should be very cautious and obedient to the white race of people," Grimes stated.[126]

In the ensuing decades the Shenandoah Valley's African Americans held emancipation celebrations at various locations and on various dates. Like other locales throughout the South, the first quarter-century after Union victory experienced a variety of dates for emancipation celebrations. While dates marking the moment Union troops entered Richmond, Lee's surrender at Appomattox, or Lincoln signing the final Emancipation Proclamation proved popular, so too did the date of Lincoln's announcement of the preliminary Emancipation Proclamation on September 22.[127] Analysis of newspapers from Charles Town to Staunton between war's end and 1890 reveals that dates closest to the anniversary of the preliminary Emancipation Proclamation proved most popular in the Valley.[128] Surviving evidence examined during the twenty-five years after the Civil War also shows that Emancipation celebrations did not occur on an annual basis in all locations. While hazards of attack, such as that which occurred in Hampton, Virginia, in April 1866 when former Confederates attacked African Americans who celebrated freedom on the first anniversary of Lee's surrender at Appomattox, might have prompted various communities to forego celebration in a particular year, financial considerations and competing celebrations figured into the decision-making too.[129] African Americans in Charles Town planned a celebration in late September 1869, but abandoned the idea after events had already been held in Shepherdstown, Martinsburg, and Winchester. Charles Town's African Americans opted to cancel its festivities due to these nearby events and "the scarcity of money."[130]

When celebrations did move forward they usually occurred without violence, but were not entirely immune to threats. For instance, the celebration slated to occur in Harrisonburg on September 22, 1878, was supposed to feature Frederick Douglass. However, a reporter for the *Shenandoah Herald* reported that Douglass opted not to attend after an unidentified African American minister from Harrisonburg sent Douglass "a telegram . . . advising him that it would be unsafe for him to come." The minister's suspicion might have indeed been correct, as on the morning of the celebration the "minister's house was discovered to be in flames." A reporter from Woodstock, Virginia, who covered the story surmised that the minister's house was committed to flames "in retaliation for his officious meddling" with issues related to race relations in Harrisonburg.[131]

Threats of violence, however, proved only one mode of attacking Emancipation celebrations. As historian William Blair noted, those who once supported the Confederacy diminished the value and necessity of such events.[132] A visitor to Shepherdstown in the summer of 1877, identified simply as "E," understood African Americans' impulse to celebrate emancipation but believed it more useful to spend the time working. "I had my doubts as to the expediency of keeping this day as an anniversary. They can better show that they are free by being industrious, saving and educating themselves and their children," "E" wrote.[133]

Some newspaper correspondents attempted to lessen the significance of Emancipation celebrations by reporting low turnout among African Americans, thus suggesting their ambivalence toward it. A correspondent in Shepherdstown recorded that despite the weather being "very favorable" for the celebration that took place in late September 1873, "the attendance was small."[134] While attendance numbers do not exist for this particular event, coverage of celebrations in other locales report robust attendance. For example, a reporter in Charles Town recorded African American attendance at "about 2,000" during an Emancipation celebration four years earlier in that locale.[135] If attendance in Shepherdstown was indeed "small," it might signify less about African American indifference to the celebration and more about racial tension in Shepherdstown and how secure African Americans might have felt attending the event in 1873.

While Emancipation celebrations proved a means for African Americans to commemorate freedom, discuss freedom's meaning and how to realize it, and challenge the Lost Cause version of Civil War history, one thing irked African American leaders about Emancipation celebrations: the lack of consistency as to when it was commemorated. Following the dedication of the equestrian statue to General Robert E. Lee on May 29, 1890, Richmond's George R. Williams, an African American Union veteran who vehemently opposed the monument, determined the time had come for all African Americans to converge on Richmond to determine a national day to celebrate emancipation and challenge the burgeoning Lost Cause mythology and white reconciliationist narrative of the war that threatened to write out slavery's centrality to the conflict and the critical role African Americans played in the Union war effort. Williams and his organizers settled on a three-day stretch in October 1890 for this "Grand National Celebration" of slavery's destruction and to discuss the selection of one-day to commemorate emancipation nationwide.[136]

As planning got under way for the event in Richmond, newspapers in the Shenandoah Valley reported on the preparations. The *Shenandoah Herald*, a paper based in Woodstock, noted that "colored people from all part of the country will assemble in Richmond in large numbers on the 15th, 16th, and 17th of Oct. to participate in the great jubilee attending the celebration of the twenty-seventh anniversary of the emancipation proclamation."[137]

While Williams and his staff readied for the event in Richmond, communities elected delegates to represent them in the debates that would take place on the celebration's final day, October 17, to "establish a National Thanksgiving Day for Freedom." Among those who represented the interests of the Shenandoah Valley's African Americans was Willis Carter. Once enslaved, Carter had risen to prominence in Augusta County as an educator, leader, and newspaper editor.[138] After opening ceremonies on the 15th and a parade the following day, the delegates devoted the final day to debating the date emancipation should be commemorated nationwide. After considering all possible dates, the convention determined January 1 the most appropriate. The *Staunton Spectator*, which offered little coverage of events in Richmond, published a brief notice reporting that "the negroes . . . decided to adopt the 1st day of January, that one which Lincoln signed the proclamation, as the day they would, in future throughout the country, celebrate their emancipation from slavery."[139] Although the group reached consensus in Richmond, January 1 was never observed as a national holiday. Additionally, as historian William Blair has concluded, African Americans continued to celebrate slavery's end on dates that suited them in their localities.[140] That certainly proved the case in the Shenandoah Valley. For example, African Americans in Berryville celebrated the fortieth anniversary of emancipation in mid-October 1903.[141]

While Emancipation celebrations challenged the Lost Cause version of Civil War history, so too did African American involvement in Memorial Day ceremonies. Following in the tradition of Decoration Day, first observed by African Americans on May 1, 1865, in Charleston, South Carolina, the Valley's African Americans honored the Union dead buried in the national cemeteries in Winchester and Staunton. The action of "the colored population" strewing "flowers and evergreens over the graves of Union soldiers" interred in those graveyards proved a significant act and "countered the Lost Cause," as historians Robert Heinrich and Deborah Hardin concluded.[142]

Memorial Day, however, served not merely to honor those—including

African Americans buried in those cemeteries—who aided in bringing about Confederate defeat and slavery's end, but it was also an opportunity to verbally challenge the Lost Cause. Arguably the most significant of these Memorial Day moments occurred on May 30, 1881, when Frederick Douglass addressed a large gathering at Storer College in Harpers Ferry, an all–African American institution established in 1867. Douglass's remarks, which he freely admitted had been previously "delivered in many parts of the North," extolled John Brown's virtues. Aware that individuals such as Edward Pollard, one of the architects of the Lost Cause, labeled Brown with such adjectives as "fanatical" and "assassin," Douglass hoped to change that paradigm.[143] In his address Douglass characterized Brown as a "true martyr and hero . . . a just man."[144] Although Douglass's comments probably did little to alter former Confederates' perceptions of Brown, his remarks could be viewed as an attempt to beat proponents of the Lost Cause at their own game. Just as former Confederates viewed their efforts during the war—including all of those reprehensible things perpetrated against African Americans during the conflict—as heroic, Douglass believed Brown's efforts to bring "freedom to the slaves" to be gallant.[145]

Commemorations, either Emancipation celebrations or Memorial Days, offered opportunities for the Shenandoah Valley's African Americans, just as they had elsewhere, to gather, remember the important roles African Americans played in the Union's restoration and slavery's destruction, challenge the Lost Cause version of the conflict, and maintain hope. They were not, however, the exclusive tools through which the Valley's African Americans sustained faith that they could attain freedom's rewards after 1870. Individual persistence, which manifested itself in personal success, also kept optimism afloat.

When Rev. Robert Orrick, once enslaved, who had amassed significant wealth in the decades after the conflict as a result of business ventures and utilized his affluence to support other African Americans, died in 1902, African Americans looked to him as an example of what unflinching individual resolve might achieve. Reflecting on his life, one noted that Orrick "was an example which it would be well for the younger members of his race to emulate."[146]

Caroline Jenkins, whose story as noted in the introduction partially inspired this study, and her husband, Abraham, purchased a log cabin and the lot on which it stood from Sarah Willey in 1872. Situated at the corner of Church and First streets in Middletown, Virginia, this cabin, once in a state of disrepair, now lovingly restored by its current owner, offers not only

Figure 7.2. Caroline Jenkins's tombstone (photo by author).

a tangible link to the experience of the Shenandoah Valley's African Americans during the Civil War era, but serves as a monument to a realized hope of two people once enslaved: property ownership. The couple lived in the humble abode for the remainder of their lives. Abraham died in 1883 and "Aunt Caroline," as she was affectionately known, passed away in 1907.[147] Upon their deaths both were buried in the Mount Zion African American Cemetery in Middletown.

Possessing the financial wherewithal to purchase this property proved a remarkable feat for any African American in the Shenandoah Valley in the early 1870s; in the 1870 census only four of Middletown's 119 African American inhabitants owned real estate.[148] In the southern end of the Valley only four of Staunton's 1,377 African Americans were reported to own property when census officials collected data in the summer of 1870.[149] In Winchester only sixty-four of the community's 1,300 African Americans owned property at the time of the 1870 census.[150]

While no evidence exists that notes how property ownership among a small percentage of African Americans by the early 1870s might have inspired hope, it showed that however brutal and impossible life was, the Valley's African Americans, bolstered by hope, continued to persevere.

# Conclusion

More than a decade ago the distinguished historian Nell Irvin Painter committed to paper what I have always taught my students—that the interpretation of the past is fluid. New evidence surfaces, and historians ask different questions with each generation. "Historical narratives change over time," Painter wrote. "What we want to know about the past at one point in time differs from what we wanted to know at an earlier point."[1] The earliest chroniclers of the Shenandoah Valley's Civil War–era history cared little about African American history. They purposefully ignored it or mispresented it to promulgate the Lost Cause narrative. Of course, these earliest chroniclers were not alone. Ignoring the African American experience proved the norm across the nation for a century after the Civil War's end. American history prior to the Civil Rights era of the 1960s, as Painter rightly points out, "was largely the story of white people" because it was not until a century after the Civil War and slavery's destruction that African Americans were, as Painter noted, "seen as truly American people."[2]

As shocking as Painter's statement might seem, it is even more striking that in the Shenandoah Valley, an area that experienced the Civil War incessantly and proved significant to both the Union and Confederate armies, efforts at examining aspects of the African American experience during the Civil War era have been particularly slow in coming. The handful of historians mentioned in this book's introduction, along with sites such as Harpers Ferry National Historical Park, Cedar Creek and Belle Grove National Historical Park, Josephine Community Museum, and Belle Grove Plantation, have started to peel back the layers exposing the lives, tragedies, and triumphs that African Americans at their sites endured during the United States' most tumultuous period.

Throughout this study evidence reveals that when examined as individuals the lives of enslaved people in the Shenandoah Valley and free blacks differed little from other parts of the South. Furthermore, stringing together evidence solidified that emancipation in the Shenandoah Valley came not at one sweeping moment, but at various points throughout the conflict. For some enslaved people emancipation came and in an instant disappeared—a reminder of freedom's fragility. Additionally, the Valley's African Americans, as they had throughout the South, did not sit passively and watch the conflict pass them by, but rather assumed an active role in resisting the Confederate war effort and supporting the Union in a multitude of ways including soldier, spy, laborer, and teamster. This study also serves as a reminder of the challenges white Union soldiers, at various points during the war, posed to African Americans. However, despite all they endured, whether in the years leading up to the conflict, during the war, or in its aftermath, the Valley's African Americans persisted, buoyed by hope that one day freedom's rewards would be attained.

As much as this volume reveals about the complexities of life for the Valley's African Americans during the Civil War era, discussions I have had with African Americans who have offered assistance with this project—who shared stories from their own lives—demonstrate that hatred and ignorance sadly still exist.

While this book examines much through a broad array of primary materials, one of the central themes that courses throughout is that of hope. To some, hope is the denial of historic reality. However, as James H. Cone, regarded as "the father of Black theology," argued, "hope accepts history, but believes that the historical is in motion, moving toward a divine fulfillment . . . It is the belief that . . . reality is not fixed, but is moving in the direction of human liberation." Sustaining hope, Cone maintained, meant that African Americans "looked beyond the condition of servitude and perceived that the real meaning of their existence was still to come."[3]

My hope is that this volume not only deepens understanding of the Shenandoah Valley's African American experience, but that it inspires and teaches broader lessons. It is my aspiration that the Civil War–era experiences of the Shenandoah Valley's African Americans examined in this book teach the power of hope, the value of persistence, encourage people to approach history with an open mind, and that in the end, however long it might take, history will always arc toward truth.

# NOTES

**Introduction**

1. Ayers, *In the Presence of Mine Enemies*, xviii.
2. Rhea, *Carrying the Flag*, 3.
3. Ayers, *In the Presence of Mine Enemies*, 26.
4. Waddell, *Annals of Augusta County Virginia*, 245; Simmons and Sorrells, "Slave Hire," 169.
5. Wayland, *The German Element of the Shenandoah Valley*, 179.
6. Davis, *The Shenandoah*, 94.
7. Brundage, "Shifting Attitudes Towards Slavery," 333–335. It is important to note that at this time Rockbridge County did not exist; it was part of Augusta County.
8. Davis, *The Shenandoah*, 129.
9. Hale, *Four Valiant Years*, 192.
10. Tanner, *Stonewall in the Valley*, 25.
11. Population of Virginia in 1840, accessed June 1, 2018, http://www.virginiaplaces. org/population/pop1840numbers.html; Population of Virginia in 1850, accessed June 1, 2018, http://www.virginiaplaces.org/population/pop1850numbers.html; Population of Virginia in 1860, accessed June 1, 2018, http://www.virginiaplaces.org/population/ pop1860numbers.html.
12. Adams, *Narrative of the Life*, 9.
13. Ibid., 27.
14. Ibid., 28.
15. Stowe, *Uncle Tom's Cabin*, 191.
16. Mahon, *The Shenandoah Valley*, 6.
17. Koons, "'The Colored Laborers,'" 239–240.
18. Longenecker, *Shenandoah Religion*, 121.
19. For further examination of hiring practices in the Valley see Simmons and Sorrells, "Slave Hire," 169–193; Noyalas, *Two Peoples*, 7–9.
20. Longenecker, *Shenandoah Religion*, 121.
21. Sheehan-Dean, *The Calculus of Violence*, 136.
22. For an examination of how some historians have downplayed the reaction of African Americans in the Shenandoah Valley to John Brown's Raid on Harpers Ferry see Link, *Roots of Secession*, 184; Quarles, *Allies for Freedom*, 102–104.

23. This number is derived from Shenandoah Valley Battlefields Foundation, *Shenandoah Valley Battlefields National Historic District*, i.

24. Adams, *Narrative of the Life*, 39.

## Chapter 1. "In the Land of Bondage"

1. Denkler, *Sustaining Identity*, 37.

2. Hofstra, *The Planting of New Virginia*, 221; Zambone, *Daniel Morgan*, 8–9.

3. Hofstra, *The Planting of New Virginia*, 221.

4. For further discussion of the demand for hemp as a factor in the increased importance of slavery in the Shenadoah Valley see Mitchell, *Commercialism and Frontier*, 166–167.

5. Brundage, "Shifting Attitudes," 333–335.

6. *Richmond Enquirer*, August 22, 1845; statistical data for the Shenandoah Valley from 1790 to 1860 is derived from the following: "Population of Virginia in 1790," accessed June 1, 2019, http://www.virginiaplaces.org/population/pop1790numbers.html; "Population of Virginia in 1800," accessed June 1, 2019, http://www.virginiaplaces.org/population/pop1800numbers.html; "Population of Virginia in 1810," accessed June 1, 2019, http://www.virginiaplaces.org/population/pop1810numbers.html; "Population of Virginia in 1820," accessed June 1, 2019, http://www.virginiaplaces.org/population/pop1820numbers.html; "Population of Virginia in 1830," accessed June 1, 2019, http://www.virginiaplaces.org/population/pop1830numbers.html; "Population of Virginia in 1840," accessed June 1, 2019, http://www.virginiaplaces.org/population/pop1840numbers.html; "Population of Virginia in 1850," accessed June 1, 2019, http://www.virginiaplaces.org/population/pop1850numbers.html; "Population of Virginia in 1860," accessed June 1, 2019, http://www.virginiaplaces.org/population/pop1860numbers.html.

7. "Population of Virginia-1830," "Population of Virginia-1840," Population of Virginia-1850," "Population of Virginia-1860." For additional discussion of fears that gripped whites in the aftermath of Nat Turner's Revolt see Breen, *The Land Shall be Deluged in Blood*, 105–106.

8. Noyalas, *Two Peoples*, 12–13.

9. Frederick County Will Book, 22: 502, WFCJJC.

10. Whitman, *The Price of Freedom*, 109.

11. Denkler, *Sustaining Identity*, 35, 38.

12. Simmons and Sorrells, "Slave Hire," 170; Hofstra, *The Planting of New Virginia*, 222.

13. Simmons and Sorrells, "Slave Hire," 171.

14. Hiring agreement between Thornton McLeod and Joseph Long, December 28, 1850, Joseph Long Papers, NHC.

15. Simmons and Sorrells, "Slave Hire," 174.

16. Noyalas, *Two Peoples*, 7.

17. Simmons and Sorrells, "Slave Hire," 173.

18. Ibid.

19. Ballard, *Dismissing the Peculiar Institution*, 6.

20. Simmons and Sorrells, "Slave Hire," 173; *Staunton Spectator*, January 14, 1857.

21. For an example of this beyond the Shenandoah Valley see Zaborney, *Slaves for Hire*, 39.

22. *Winchester Republican*, January 23, 1857.

23. This figure is based off the prices stated in the *Staunton Spectator*, January 14, 1857.

24. Simmons and Sorrells, "Slave Hire," 171.

25. Hiring agreement between Thornton McLeod and Joseph Long, December 28, 1850, Joseph Long Papers, NHC.

26. Savitt, *Medicine and Slavery*, 187–188.

27. Davis, *The Shenandoah*, 94.

28. Savitt, *Medicine and Slavery*, 187.

29. Simmons and Sorrells, "Slaves for Hire," 177.

30. Greer, "Cather and Enslaved Life in the Northern Shenandoah Valley," 3–4.

31. Ibid.

32. Adams, *Narrative of the Life*, 9.

33. Veney, *The Narrative of Bethany Veney*, 7.

34. Perdue et al., *Weevils in the Wheat*, 346. For further discussion on the limitations and issues with WPA interviews see Silber, *This War Ain't Over*, 81–85.

35. Perdue et al., *Weevils in the Wheat*, 346.

36. Adams, *Narrative of the Life*, 9.

37. Veney, *The Narrative of Bethany Veney*, 10.

38. Ibid., 34.

39. Perdue et al., *Weevils in the Wheat*, 243.

40. Veney, *The Narrative of Bethany Veney*, 10–11.

41. Ibid., 11.

42. Savitt, *Medicine and Slavery*, 251.

43. *American Slavery as It Is*, 178.

44. Ibid., 74.

45. Ibid., 178.

46. Ibid., 65.

47. Ibid., 89; Dunaway, *Slavery in the American Mountain South*, 165. For further discussion of use of this type of device see Berlin et al., *Remembering Slavery*, 146; Willis and Krauthamer, *Envisioning Emancipation*, 56.

48. Carr quoted in Ballard, *Dismissing the Peculiar Institution*, 15.

49. Zigler, *History of the Brethren in Virginia*, 77.

50. Adams, *Narrative of the Life*, 20.

51. Miller, "Slave Trader, Sold to Tennessee," Sketchbook of Landscapes in the State of Virginia, 1853–1867, AARFA.

52. Ballard, *Dismissing the Peculiar Institution*, 14–15.

53. "Case of Violet, Slave of Sampson Sawyers, February 18, 1780," accessed July 16, 2019, http://www2.vcdh.virginia.edu/gos/countyRecords/countyIndividualRecord.php?county=augusta&year=1780&display=record&record=81.

54. *The Torch Light and Public Advertiser* (Hagerstown, MD), April 10, 1828, June 19, 1828.

55. Ibid., June 19, 1828.

56. Ibid.

57. *The Mail* (Hagerstown, MD), April 26, 1833.

58. Joseph Taper to Joseph Long, November 11, 1840, Joseph Long Papers, WRPLDU.

59. Veney, *The Narrative of Bethany Veney*, 38.

60. Simmons and Sorrells, "Slave Hire," 174; Mitchell, *Commercialism and Frontier*, 129.

61. "Map of Virginia: Showing the Distribution of Its Slave Population from the Census of 1860," accessed July 22, 2019, https://www.loc.gov/item/2010586922/.

62. Hofstra, *The Planting of New Virginia*, 222.

63. Ibid.

### Chapter 2. "The Effect Was Immediate"

1. Harris's story is recounted in Still, *The Underground Railroad*, 48–51. For further discussion of Canada as "the so-called Promised Land" see Franklin and Schweninger, *Runaway Slaves*, 116–120.

2. Link, *Roots of Secession*, 177–178.

3. Robert Young Conrad to Catherine Brooke Powell Conrad, November 27, 1859, Conrad Papers, VHS. In Conrad's letter, he places the incendiary activities of 1856–57 in the context of reported cases of arson in the aftermath of John Brown's raid on Harpers Ferry. Conrad wrote, "Several firings of barns + stockyards . . . (though not so frequent or numerous as occurred two winters ago) have excited + alarmed the people."

4. Historian David Blight convincingly argues that by the time of James Buchanan's victory in 1856, enslaved people possessed a heightened political awareness and that the tense environment in which that election occurred raised anxieties among slavery's supporters. Insurrection rumors were widespread across the South and at times met with "bloody reprisals." For further discussion see Blight, *Beyond the Battlefield*, 43.

5. Link, *Roots of Secession*, 150–151.

6. Petition from Citizens of Frederick, Jefferson, and Clarke Counties, January 1860, Legislative Petitions of the General Assembly, 1776–1865, Box 85, Folder 17, LVA.

7. *Winchester Republican*, August 7, 1857.

8. Brown, *The Original Minutes of Stephens City*, 29.

9. Link, *Roots of Secession*, 178.

10. It is not the purpose of this study to rehash all of the elements of John Brown's attack on Harpers Ferry. For additional discussion see Frye and Oliver, *Confluence*, 33–46, 62–66; Abels, *Man on Fire*, 231–299; Hearn, *Six Years of Hell*, 7–43.

11. Ambler, *When Tidewater Invaded the Valley*, 3–4.

12. Ibid.

13. Associated Press Telegram, October 17, 1859, quoted in Abels, *Man on Fire*, 273.

14. *Richmond Enquirer*, October 25, 1859.

15. Chambers, *The Truth about John Brown*, 1. One of the ways in which the Shenandoah Valley's residents immediately responded to the raid was by purchasing firearms. In the month after Brown's attack on Harpers Ferry approximately ten thousand revolvers and pistols were sold "to terrified Virginians." For additional discussion of this see Bordewich, *Bound for Canaan*, 426.

16. Robert Young Conrad to Catherine Brooke Powell, November 27, 1859, Conrad Papers, VHS.

17. Ashby, *The Valley Campaigns*, 7.

18. Ibid., 8.

19. *The National Era*, November 24, 1859.

20. Wintz, *Civil War Memoirs*, 16.

21. Elizabeth Whiting (Powell) Conrad to Holmes Conrad, October 26, 1859, Conrad Papers, VHS.

22. Out of all of the counties in the Shenandoah Valley, Clarke is unique in terms of the percentage of its population who were enslaved. According to the 1850 census 3,614 enslaved people lived in Clarke County. The same amount of whites resided there. The county included 124 free blacks, which makes the majority of Clarke's inhabitants African American, according to the 1850 census. By 1860 the number of enslaved people declined to 3,375, making the total enslaved population 47.2 percent of the county's overall population. Most counties had an enslaved population at the time of Brown's raid between 20 and 25 percent. Overall, enslaved people comprised 19.5 percent of the region's population, according to the 1850 census. For additional statistical data on the population of enslaved people and free blacks in the Shenandoah Valley in 1850 and 1860 see Koons, "'The Colored Laborers Work as Well as When Slaves,'" 233; *The National Era*, November 24, 1859. For additional discussion of Underwood see Anderson, *Blood Image*, 51–56. Also see Hickin, "John C. Underwood," 156–168.

23. Link, *Roots of Secession*, 164–167; Anderson, *Blood Image*, 57.

24. *Richmond Dispatch*, November 24, 1859. The article makes no mention of the identities or race of the individuals arrested. The article states that the "characters . . . were soon released after an examination, in which nothing was found against them." The *Shepherdstown Register* reported that John C. Underwood commanded the abolitionists, "but the report proved to be false." See *Shepherdstown Register*, November 26, 1859; Anderson, *Blood Image*, 57.

25. *New York Evening Post*, November 19, 1859.

26. Hadden, *Slave Patrols*, 169.

27. Ibid., 168–172. Hadden convincingly argues that in the aftermath of Brown's raid patrols not only increased in Virginia, but throughout the South. Oftentimes, as examples from North Carolina and South Carolina illustrate, local officials established "vigilance committees" to augment slave patrols.

28. Ibid., 168–169.

29. Charles White to John Felt, November 10, 1859, quoted in Moore, "John Brown's Raid at Harpers Ferry," 391.

30. Slave Patrol Order, June 2, 1860, Frederick County Virginia Free Black Records, Box 12, Free Negro and Slave Patrol Claims, Library of Virginia, Richmond, VA.

31. Ibid.

32. Ibid.

33. *The National Era*, November 24, 1859.

34. Ibid.

35. *New York Times*, January 7, 1860.

36. Ibid.

37. *Staunton Spectator,* January 10, 1860; *New York Times,* January 7, 1860.

38. Ibid.

39. Information about Sowers obtained from 1850 Census, Clarke County, Population Schedule, Digital Image. Ancestry.com, accessed June 1, 2018, http://ancestry.com.

40. *New York Times,* January 7, 1860.

41. Ibid.

42. Ibid.

43. *New York Times,* January 7, 1860.

44. Slave Rebellion Trial, 1860 Slave Jerry Manuscript, African American History Collection, CCHA.

45. *Staunton Spectator,* January 10, 1860.

46. Link, *Roots of Secession,* 190.

47. Ibid., 190.

48. *Richmond Enquirer,* October 28, 1859.

49. Mason, *The Public Life,* 148.

50. *Staunton Vindicator,* October 28, 1859.

51. Cartmell, *Shenandoah Valley Pioneers,* 304.

52. Reynolds, *Texas Terror,* 4–5.

53. Ibid., 4–7.

54. *Harper's Weekly,* November 26, 1859.

55. Quarles, *Allies for Freedom,* 105.

56. McFeely, *Frederick Douglass,* 196–197.

57. *Frank Leslie's Illustrated Newspaper,* November 12, 1859.

58. Frye and Oliver, *Confluence,* 10.

59. "Report, the Select Committee of the Senate Appointed to Inquire into the Late Invasion and Seizure of the Public Property at Harper's Ferry," 36th Congress, 1st Session, Report Committee No. 278, "Invasion at Harper's Ferry," 5. Note that this report is divided into two sections—the first is "Invasion at Harper's Ferry" and the second "Testimony."

60. *Shepherdstown Register,* October 29, 1859.

61. Mason Anderson to Cornelius Anderson, December 11, 1859, Anderson Letters, WRCM.

62. *Shepherdstown Register,* October 29, 1859; Quarles, *Allies for Freedom,* 103.

63. Quarles, *Allies for Freedom,* 103–104.

64. It is not the goal of this study to provide a complete treatment of Heyward Shepherd and his legacy. For additional details on how Shepherd's legacy was manipulated both at the time of Brown's raid and in the decades following the Civil War see Janney, "Written in Stone," 117–141.

65. Moore, "John Brown's Raid," 391.

66. Franklin and Schweninger, *Runaway Slaves,* 2.

67. Schwarz, *Twice Condemned,* 309.

68. *Alexandria Gazette,* November 15, 1859.

69. Ibid., November 17, 1859.

70. *Winchester Republican*, November 18, 1859.

71. *Alexandria Gazette*, November 19, 1859.

72. Robert Conrad to Catherine Brooke Powell Conrad, November 27, 1859, Conrad Papers, VHS.

73. Link, *Roots of Secession*, 317.

74. Although local white inhabitants assumed these fires were set by enslaved people, evidence, however, is not conclusive. Slave schedules for 1850 show that juror John Burns, a resident of Berkeley County, enslaved a total of nine people. While the 1850 census indicates that George Tate, a resident of Jefferson County, did not enslave people in 1850, he did enslave nine individuals at the time of the 1860 census. His mother Abigail enslaved seven people. Newspaper accounts identify the third juror as a Mr. Shirleyhall. Since no "Shirleyhall" is listed as residing in Virginia at the time, the articles must in fact be referencing Walter Shirley. Shirley, a resident of Jefferson County, enslaved thirteen people. See 1850 U.S. Census, Berkeley County, Virginia, Slave Schedule, Digital Image, Ancestry.com, accessed June 14, 2018, http://ancestry.com; 1860 U.S. Census, Jefferson County, Virginia, Population Schedule; Digital Image, Ancestry.com, accessed June 14, 2018, http://ancestry.com; 1860 U.S. Census, Jefferson County, Virginia, Slave Schedule, Digital Image, Ancestry.com, accessed June 14, 2018, http://ancestry.com. For additional discussion see *The National Era*, November 24, 1859; Berkey, "War in the Borderland," 179–180. Cases of arson not only increased in the Shenandoah Valley, but in areas that bordered the region too. For instance, white inhabitants of Loudoun County, Virginia, reported an increase in arson activity. For additional discussion see Stevenson, *Life in Black & White*, 322.

75. Link, *Roots of Secession*, 184.

76. Halstead, "The Execution of John Brown," 291. One month after Brown's raid an anonymous letter signed "Martyrs of Harpers Ferry" reached officials in Jefferson County. The letter, which noted "we are determined to put down slavery at all odds," began with one word: "Flames!" Made public, this letter intensified fears among whites. See *Shepherdstown Register*, November 19, 1859.

77. *Alexandria Gazette*, November 26, 1859.

78. *Weekly Standard* (Raleigh, NC), November 23, 1859.

79. Ibid.

80. Ibid.

81. *Cadiz Democratic Sentinel* (Ohio), December 7, 1859. The newspaper article identifies Mr. Castleman and Mr. Myers as the other two whose livestock died suddenly. Information about the amount of slaves Turner owned is derived from 1860 U.S. Census, Jefferson County, Virginia, Slave Schedule, Digital Image, Ancestry.com, accessed June 21, 2018, http://ancestry.com.

82. Quarles, *Allies for Freedom*, 108.

83. *Weekly Standard* (Raleigh, NC), November 23, 1859.

84. *Richmond Enquirer*, November 4, 1859.

85. Reynolds, *Texas Terror*, 20–21; Baum, *The Shattering of Texas Unionism*, 38.

86. Ashby, *The Valley Campaigns*, 8.

87. For further discussion on how enslaved people throughout the South employed

drinking and gambling as a means of reclaiming control, even if temporarily, see Lussana, *My Brother Slaves*, 9, 54–55.

88. Chambers, "What a School-Girl Saw," 318.

89. Ibid.

90. Ashby, *The Valley Campaigns*, 8.

91. The enslaved population is based off of figures from 1850 census in Koons, "'The Colored Laborers,'" 233.

92. Stevenson, *Life in Black & White*, 322.

93. Ashby, *The Valley Campaigns*, 8.

94. Chambers, "What a School-Girl Saw," 318.

95. Berkey, "War in the Borderland," 67.

96. Population data based on table in Koons, "'The Colored Laborers,'" 233; Population of Virginia in 1850, accessed, June 14, 2018, http://www.virginiaplaces.org/population/pop1850numbers.html; Population of Virginia in 1860, accessed June 14, 2018, http://www.virginiaplaces.org/population/pop1860numbers.html.

97. McCabe, *Freedom by Deed*, 1, 3, 7, 9, 16, 17, 24, 34, 38, 42.

98. *Shepherdstown Register*, November 5, 1859.

99. "I Was Right There When They Broke John Brown's Neck," in *The American Slave*, 18: 237.

100. Abraham Spengler to brother, November 28, 1859, SHC.

101. Ibid. In his study of African Americans in Virginia during the Civil War era, Ervin Jordan states that another accused abolitionist, David Bumgarner, made the comment about being "as good a democrat as any body." Close examination of the original document, however, shows Haines made the comment. See Jordan, *Black Confederates*, 3.

102. Abraham Spengler to brother, November 28, 1859, SHC.

103. *Shepherdstown Register*, December 3, 1859.

104. Mason Anderson to Cornelius Anderson, December 11, 1859, WRCM.

105. Chambers, "The Militia Crisis," 14.

106. Captain Samuel Brown Coyner Diary, WRCM.

107. Ashby, *The Valley Campaigns*, 8.

108. Petition of John H. Allstadt for Private Relief/Compensation, January 9, 1860, Legistlative Petitions of the General Assembly, 1776–18765, Box 127, Folder 72, LVA.

109. Ashby, *The Valley Campaigns*, 9.

110. *National Anti-Slavery Standard*, June 23, 1860.

111. Ibid.

112. Adams, *Narrative of the Life*, 6.

113. Ibid., 14, 20.

114. Ibid., 28.

115. For a broader examination of depression among enslaved individuals and thoughts of death see Piersen, "Black Martyr's Fear," 150.

116. Oakes, *Freedom National*, 88–89.

117. Adams, *Narrative of the Life*, 34.

## Chapter 3. "To Call on All the Blacks"

1. Strother, "Personal Recollections of War," 33 (June 1866): 9.

2. *National Anti-Slavery Standard*, June 8, 1861.

3. Ayers, *In the Presence of Mine Enemies*, 168.

4. Berlin et al., *Freedom*, ser. 1, vol. 1, 11.

5. The figure of $500 per enslaved person is based on the interaction Dolph White had with Newtown's Dr. John Walls. Walls's wife wrote that "Early in the war there was a slave trader in town who offered Dr. Walls a thousand dollars . . . for our two house boys, Henry Whiting and George See." See Wintz, *Civil War Memoirs*, 33. For more on Dolph White see Noyalas, *Two Peoples*, 25. The average price of slaves is derived from Jordan, *Black Confederates and Afro-Yankees*, 5. For broader discussions of how enslavers who lived on the "periphery" reacted to war's outbreak see Berlin et al., *Freedom*, ser. 1, vol. 1, 11.

6. *National Anti-Slavery Standard,* June 15, 1861.

7. Ibid., June 8, 1861.

8. Ayers, *In the Presence of Mine Enemies*, 168.

9. *National Anti-Slavery Standard*, June 15, 1861.

10. Adams, *Narrative of the Life*, 35.

11. Ashby, *The Valley Campaigns*, 41.

12. Berlin, *Generations of Captivity*, 249.

13. Berlin et al., *Slaves No More*, 12.

14. Ibid., 13.

15. Taylor, *Embattled Freedom*, 24; Gerteis, *From Contraband to Freedman*, 13–14.

16. Oakes, *Freedom National*, 98.

17. For a timeline of events surrounding Patterson's entrance into the northern Shenandoah Valley see Patterson, *A Narrative of the Campaign*, 35, 47–49; Nevins, *The War for the Union: The Improvised War, 1861–1862*, 158.

18. Strother, "Personal Recollections of the War," 33 (July 1866): 156.

19. Ibid.

20. Ibid.

21. Ibid.

22. Ibid.

23. Ibid.

24. Comey, *A Legacy of Valor*, 18–19. The assistance that Colonel George Gordon provided to refugees from slavery in the Shenandoah Valley in 1862 is discussed in the next chapter. For a full accounting of his Civil War Service in the Shenandoah Valley see Gordon, *Brook Farm to Cedar Mountain*, 101–261. While the identity of the thirteen enslaved people or all of the enslavers is not known, Gordon noted that one of the enslaved people he was "ordered in 1861 to catch and return from Harper's Ferry" was owned by Mr. John L. Ranson. See Gordon, *Brook Farm to Cedar Mountain*, 109.

25. Quint, *The Record of the Second Massachusetts Infantry*, 39.

26. Robert Gould Shaw to Sydney Howard Gay, August 1, 1861, quoted in Duncan, *Blue-Eyed Child of Fortune*, 123.

27. Quint, *The Potomac and the Rapidan*, 35.

28. *O.R.*, ser. 1, vol. 2, 662; Quint, *The Potomac and the Rapidan*, 34.

29. Strother, "Personal Recollections of the War," 33 (July 1866): 156; Berkey, "War in the Borderland," 185–186; Phillips, *The Lower Shenandoah Valley in the Civil War*, 110.

30. For a broad discussion of early Union policy toward freedom-seekers see Berlin et al., *Slaves No More*, 16–17.

31. Ibid., 16–17; Grimsley, *The Hard Hand of War*, 10; Stephen B. Oates, *With Malice Toward None*, 239.

32. Crittenden Resolution quoted in McPherson, *The Political History*, 286.

33. For a broader discussion of freedom-seekers attempting to barter with Union soldiers for their freedom see Berlin et al., *Slaves No More*, 23.

34. Robert Gould Shaw to Mother, July 21, 1861, quoted in Duncan, *Blue-Eyed Child of Fortune*, 116.

35. Stewart, *Camp, March and Battle-Field*, 19.

36. Ibid.

37. Ibid.

38. Locke, *The Story of the Regiment*, 28.

39. Ibid.

40. Ibid., 29.

41. According to Chaplain Locke he encountered George in 1863, presumably at some point during the Gettysburg Campaign. For the complete account of George's escape, including his return to the Shenandoah Valley to secure his wife Mary, see Locke, *Story of the Regiment*, 30.

42. Stewart, *Camp, March and Battle-Field*, 20.

43. For a broader examination of this see Berlin et al., *Slaves No More*, 18–19.

44. Stewart, *Camp, March and Battle-Field*, 21.

45. Letter of Major Wilder Dwight from Charles Town, July 18, 1861, quoted in *Life and Letters of Wilder Dwight*, 52.

46. Letter of Major Wilder Dwight from Harpers Ferry, July 24, 1861, quoted in ibid., 55.

47. Ibid.

48. Ibid.

49. *The American Union* (Martinsburg, VA), July 21, 1861. For a brief overview of Thomas's time in the Shenandoah Valley see Van Horne, *The Life of Major-General George H. Thomas*, 32–34.

50. James Lawrence Hooff Diary, July 21, 1861, James Lawrence Hooff Papers, VHS.

51. Stewart, *Camp, March and Battle-Field*, 21.

52. Quint, *The Potomac and the Rapidan*, 34.

53. Boyd, *Belle Boyd in Camp and Prison*, 83. Although Boyd's "negro maid" destroyed the Confederate flag, the incident escalated quickly when a Union soldier threatened Boyd's mother and Belle Boyd shot the Union soldier. For additional details about this event see ibid., 82–83.

54. Sinha, *The Slave's Cause*, 237.

55. *O.R.* ser. 2, vol. 1, 759; Gerteis, *From Contraband to Freedman*, 16; Moore and Moore, *His Brother's Blood*, 270–271.

56. Patterson, *A Narrative of the Campaign*, 85; Hollandsworth, *Pretense of Glory*, 48.

57. Hollandsworth, *Pretense of Glory*, 48; McPherson, *Tried by War*, 43.

58. McPherson, *The Political History*, 195.

59. While no evidence exists that Union soldiers in the Shenandoah Valley under Banks's command returned freedom-seekers after the First Confiscation Act, it did occur. For further discussion, see Berlin et al., *Free at Last*, 19.

60. Robert Gould Shaw to Mother, August 8, 1861, quoted in Duncan, *Blue-Eyed Child of Fortune*, 125.

61. Rev. Benjamin F. Brooke Journal, August 15, 1861, SBAHL.

62. Berlin, *Generations of Captivity*, 252.

63. "Refugees, Deserters & Contrabands, 1862 Gen. Banks' Intelligence Reports," Record Group 393, NARA. The percentages are derived from reports of contraband slaves received at Harpers Ferry from February 24, 1862, to March 9, 1862.

64. Letter of Wilder Dwight, March 9, 1862, quoted in Dwight, *Life and Letters*, 205.

65. "Refugees, Deserters & Contrabands, 1862 Gen. Banks' Intelligence Reports," Record Group 393, NARA.

66. Ibid.

67. Ibid.

68. Ibid.

69. Ibid.

70. Dwight, *Life and Letters*, 205.

71. Ibid., 206.

## Chapter 4. "The Servants . . . Could Not Be Conveniently Stored Away"

1. Mahon, *Winchester Divided*, 21.

2. Testimony of contraband slave Adam Griffith, "Refugees, Deserters & Contrabands, 1862 Gen. Banks' Intelligence Reports," Record Group 393, NARA.

3. Journal of John Peyton Clark, March 12, 1862, Louisa Morrow Crawford Collection, SBAHL.

4. Ibid. In reference to the Taylor Hotel's use for slave trading see Adams, *Narrative of the Life*, 24. Adams notes that "Taylor's Hotel" was the establishment "where all the 'big bugs' stopped; and I will tell you who else stopped there—those great and unthinking gentlemen who called themselves Negro Traders. You could see them walking around with their bags of silver and gold that they had received from selling the poor slaves." Additionally, an advertisement appeared in the June 29, 1852, issue of the *Winchester Republican*, stating that slave trader Elijah McDowell, from Baltimore, Maryland, used the Taylor Hotel as the base for his endeavor to "purchase a large number of SLAVES of both sexes, for which he will give the highest price in cash." For further discussion see Stowe, *A Key to Uncle Tom's Cabin*, 145.

5. Strother, "Personal Recollections of the War," 33 (October 1866): 182.

6. Samuel Sexton to wife, March 16, 1862, quoted in "Memoirs of Samuel Sexton," Samuel Sexton Papers, OHS.

7. Letter of Major Wilder Dwight, March 13, 1862, quoted in Dwight, *Life and Letters*, 209.

8. Ibid.

9. Berkey, "War in the Borderland," 212.

10. Letter of Major Wilder Dwight, March 13, 1862, quoted in Dwight, *Life and Letters*, 209.

11. Jordan, *Black Confederates and Afro-Yankees*, 149.

12. Mohr, *On the Threshold of Freedom*, 291.

13. Ibid., 290–291. For additional examinations of enslaved people's attachment to a particular locality see Stevenson, *Life in Black & White*, 162–163.

14. Rev. Benjamin F. Brooke Journal, March 17, 1862, SBAHL. This behavior of course is not unique. For examples of this beyond the Shenandoah Valley see Robinson, *Bitter Fruits of Bondage*, 111.

15. John Peyton Clark Journal, March 15, 1862, Louisa Morrow Crawford Collection, SBAHL.

16. Ibid.; Rev. Benjamin F. Brooke Journal, March 17, 1862, SBAHL.

17. Rev. Benjamin F. Brooke Journal, March 17, 1862, SBAHL.

18. Ibid.

19. Sternhell, "Bodies in Motion and the Making of Emancipation," 16.

20. Strader, *The Civil War Journal*, 24.

21. Robert Young Conrad to Powell Conrad, March 19, 1862, Conrad Papers, VHS.

22. In addition to Milford Thomas and Moses Williams, the other enslaved people who fled Samuel Cook were Amos Williams (age fifty), Doctor Dixon (age unknown), and Isaac Dixon (age unknown). Testimony of contraband slaves Milford Thomas and Moses Williams, "Refugees, Deserters & Contrabands, 1862 Gen. Banks' Intelligence Reports," Record Group 393, NARA.

23. Testimony of contraband slave Jno. Carter, "Refugees, Deserters & Contrabands, 1862 Gen. Banks' Intelligence Reports," Record Group 393, NARA.

24. Ayers, *In the Presence of Mine Enemies*, 247; *Staunton Spectator*, April 1, 1862; *Staunton Spectator* April 15, 1862.

25. Rev. Benjamin F. Brooke Journal, March 14, 1862, SBAHL.

26. Mahon, *Winchester Divided*, 30.

27. Rev. Benjamin F. Brooke Journal, March 17, 1862, SBAHL; Taylor, *Embattled Freedom*, 58.

28. "An Act to make an Additional Article of War," March 13, 1862, quoted in Tenney, *Military and Naval History*, 153.

29. Robert Young Conrad to Powell Conrad, March 19, 1862, Conrad Papers, VHS. When Mary Greenhow Lee learned about this new Article of War, she believed that it would further entice enslaved people to flee. On March 19, 1862, Lee wrote in her journal, "Since the passage of this new law in their Congress, forbidding the restoration of slaves, I hear every day of their renouncing their allegiance." See Strader, *The Civil War Journal*, 18.

30. Noyalas, *Stonewall Jackson's 1862 Valley Campaign*, 18.

31. Eby, *A Virginia Yankee*, 18.

32. Testimony of free blacks John William Martin and Sylvester Jordan, "Refugees, Deserters & Contrabands, 1862 Gen. Banks' Intelligence Reports," Record Group 393, NARA.

33. Testimony of free black James Sestro, "Refugees, Deserters & Contrabands, 1862 Gen. Banks' Intelligence Reports," Record Group 393, NARA. For instances of Confederates kidnapping free blacks elsewhere see Reidy, *Illusions of Emancipation*, 112–113.

34. Rev. Benjamin F. Brooke Journal, March 14, 1862, SBAHL.

35. Robert Young Conrad to Powell Conrad, March 19, 1862, Conrad Papers, VHS.

36. Mahon, *Winchester Divided*, 30.

37. Wintz, *Civil War Memoirs*, 33.

38. Ibid.

39. Ibid. According to Mary Walls, Shipley came back to Newtown after the conflict and visited the Walls. For additional information see Noyalas, *Two Peoples*, 28–29; Berkey, "In the Very Midst of the War Track," 93.

40. *National Anti-Slavery Standard*, April 12, 1862.

41. Ibid., April 19, 1862.

42. James Mason to wife, December 12, 1861, quoted in Mason, *The Public Life*, 207. For additional information on the Trent Affair see Ferris, *The Trent Affair.*

43. *National Anti-Slavery Standard*, May 3, 1862.

44. Ibid.

45. Taylor, *Embattled Freedom*, 160. In her fine study Taylor also notes that the space the group of twenty-seven worked in was donated by a white female Quaker.

46. Berkey, "War in the Borderland," 189. For a broader discussion of how Union officers dealt with this issue see Reidy, *Illusions of Emancipation*, 241. In November 1861, General John Wool issued General Order No. 34 which outlined his employment program. It consisted of organizing contrabands into two classes. The first class, which consisted of men over age eighteen, received ten dollars per month. The other class, males from ages twelve to eighteen, and those who were ill, received five dollars per month and rations. For a more detailed examination see Taylor, *Embattled Freedom*, 39.

47. The variety of tasks assigned to contrabands is based on "Lists and Reports, 1862," Nathaniel P. Banks Papers, Containers 79 and 80, LOC. An extracted list is available as "Negro Contrabands from Winchester and Frederick County Under the Occupation by Maj. Gen. N.P. Banks' V Corps, April-May 1862," Alan Tischler Collection, SBAHL.

48. Jordan, *The Civil War Journals*, 120.

49. Mahon, *Winchester Divided*, 25.

50. Strader, *The Civil War Journal*, 70.

51. Taylor, *Embattled Freedom*, 37–38.

52. Fisher, *No Cause of Offence*, 37. The story originates from *Rockingham Register*, July 7, 1862. Contrabands becoming disgruntled with broken promises, low wages, and poor working conditions compelled undetermined numbers to flee their posts. For additional discussion see Taylor, *Embattled Freedom*, 40–41; Reidy, *Illusions of Emancipation*, 241–243.

53. Letter of R. Morris Copeland to Secretary of War Edwin Stanton, May 7, 1862, quoted in *Statement of R. Morris Copeland*, 8–9.

54. Quaife, *From the Cannon's Mouth*, 73.

55. Ibid.

56. Quint, *The Potomac and the Rapidan*, 140.

57. *Acts of the General Assembly of the State of Virginia*, 34.

58. Shenandoah County: Record of Slaves that Have Escaped to the Enemy during the War [1861–1863], Runaway Slave Records, 1794, 1806–1863, Box 2, Folder 7, LVA.

59. Rockingham County: Record of Slaves that Have Escaped to the Enemy during the War [1861–1863], Runaway Slave Records, 1794, 1806–1863, Box 2, Folder 7, LVA. In addition to the seven enslaved people who escaped from Dr. Newman, six additional enslavers reported that ten enslaved people bolted in June.

60. Page County: Record of Slaves that Have Escaped to the Enemy during the War [1861–1863], Runaway Slave Records, 1794, 1806–1863, Box 2, Folder 6, LVA. The report from Page County identifies an additional sixty-two enslaved who escaped between June-August, 1862. Eleven additional enslaved people are listed as simply escaping in 1862.

61. Gordon, *Brook Farm to Cedar Mountain*, 137–138.

62. Eby, *A Virginia Yankee*, 24.

63. Eddy, *History of the Sixtieth Regiment*, 116.

64. Ibid., 120.

65. For discussions of attitudes of Union soldiers toward transforming the war for union into one of abolition at this point in the conflict see McPherson, *For Cause and Comrades*, 19. Somewhat at odds with McPherson's claim is historian Chandra Manning's conclusion that some Union soldiers, in the final months of 1861, started to recognize, as a result of their interactions with enslaved people, the necessity of destroying slavery. Evidence, as noted in this chapter, does contend that Union soldiers developed abolitionist sentiment as a result of the horrid treatment of enslaved people in the Shenandoah Valley. For more on Manning's argument see Manning, *What This Cruel War Was Over*, 44–45.

66. Quint, *The Potomac and the Rapidan*, 113.

67. Lieutenant Melzer Dutton to mother, April 9, 1862. Lieutenant Melzer Dutton Correspondence, Civil War Diaries/Letters, SBAHL.

68. Eddy, *History of the Sixtieth Regiment*, 119–121.

69. Gordon, *Brook Farm to Cedar Mountain*, 179.

70. *Hartford Courant* (Connecticut), March 18, 1862.

71. Gordon, *Brook Farm to Cedar Mountain*, 137.

72. Samuel Sexton to wife, May 3, 1862, in "Memoirs of Samuel Sexton," Samuel Sexton Papers, OHS.

73. Macon and Macon, *Reminiscences of the Civil War*, 16–19.

74. Buck, *Sad Earth, Sweet Heaven*, 81.

75. Unfortunately, neither the contraband's nor the Confederate officer's identities are known. Eddy, *History of the Sixtieth Regiment*, 114. Eddy noted that after the Confederate officer's arrest Union officials sent him to Washington, DC.

76. Quaife, *From the Cannon's Mouth*, 73.

77. *New York Times*, June 22, 1862.

78. Gordon, *Brook Farm to Cedar Mountain*, 158.

79. Mahon, *Winchester Divided*, 37.

80. McDonald, *A Diary with Reminiscences*, 79–80.

81. Strader, *The Civil War Journal*, 51.

82. Strother, "Personal Recollections," 33 (October 1866): 441.

83. Cozzens, *Shenandoah 1862*, 316.

84. Strother, "Personal Recollections," 33 (October 1866): 441.

85. It is not the purpose of this study to retrace military movements in any great detail. For further examination of the military aspects of this portion of the 1862 Valley Campaign, including the fate of Union forces commanded by Colonel John R. Kenly at Front Royal and General Banks's decision to withdraw north to Winchester, see Noyalas, *Stonewall Jackson's 1862 Valley Campaign*, 74–87.

86. Wintz, *Civil War Memoirs*, 33–34. The number of African Americans who moved north with Banks's force is based on the account of Lieutenant Melzer Dutton, 5th Connecticut Infantry. Three days after the retreat from Strasburg Dutton penned a letter to his mother and noted that "there were half as many negroes as soldiers" during the retreat from Strasburg to Winchester. At the time of the retreat Banks's command stood at approximately 10,000 men. See Lieutenant Melzer Dutton to mother, May 27, 1862, Lieutenant Melzer Dutton Correspondence, SBAHL.

87. Charles W. Boyce Journal, 74, Boyce Papers, LOC.

88. McDonald, *A Diary with Reminiscences*, 79.

89. Ibid., 79–80.

90. *National Tribune*, August 20, 1896.

91. Strother, "Personal Recollections," 33 (October 1866): 441.

92. Ibid., 445.

93. Rufus Mead Letter, May 28, 1862, from Williamsport, Maryland, Rufus Mead Papers, LOC.

94. Strother, "Personal Recollections," 33 (October 1866): 446.

95. Ibid.

96. Ibid., 445.

97. Ibid., 446.

98. Eby, *A Virginia Yankee*, 43.

99. Susan Nourse Riddle Diary, May 25, 1862, quoted in Gardiner and Gardiner, *Chronicles of Old Berkeley*, 159.

100. Hutton, *The Diary of Sarah Morgan McKown*, 31.

101. Strother, "Personal Recollections," 33 (October 1866): 446.

102. *Baltimore Sun*, June 5, 1862.

103. Taylor, *Africans-in-America of the Lower Shenandoah Valley*, 21–23; Slowe, "The Passing of George William Cook," 480.

104. Neese, *Three Years in the Confederate Horse Artillery*, 61.

105. Summers, *A Borderland Confederate*, 17.

106. Neese, *Three Years*, 61.

107. Strader, *The Civil War Journal*, 84.

108. Manuel's story is based off McDonald, *A Diary*, 80–81.

109. Ibid., 81.

110. For additional discussion of the complexities of fleeing during the conflict see Reidy, *Illusions of Emancipation*, 116.

111. In her diary McDonald does not mention the specific date of their departure, however, Manuel and his family more than likely fled on September 2, 1862, when General White evacuated Winchester. This was the first major Union evacuation of Winchester since the First Battle of Winchester. McDonald, *A Diary*, 81. For further discussion of White's occupation and evacuation of Winchester see Noyalas, *Plagued by War*, 69–73.

112. Strother, "Personal Recollections," 33 (October 1866): 724. Stonewall Jackson withdrew from Winchester on May 31, 1862, when he learned that Union forces commanded by General James Shields occupied Front Royal and General Frémont's force approached Strasburg. Fearful of being contained in the northern Shenandoah Valley, Jackson opted to withdraw from Winchester. His departure left the door open to Union occupation. For further discussion, see Noyalas, *Stonewall Jackson's 1862 Valley Campaign*, 100.

113. John Peyton Clark Journal, June 30, 1862, Louisa Morrow Crawford Collection, SBAHL.

114. Ibid., August 12, 1862.

115. Macon and Macon, *Reminiscences of the Civil War*, 27. In her account Emma Cassandra Riely noted that thirteen enslaved people left.

116. Strader, *The Civil War Journal*, 98.

117. For a broader examination of enslaved people waiting to escape until they believed they had the greatest opportunity for success see Blight, *A Slave No More*, 45.

118. In his *Narrative of the Life*, Adams states that the various points to which the family ventured during the conflict. While Elmira, New York, is not mentioned as a destination the obituary for Adams's wife, Fannie Frances Adams, states that she married John Quincy Adams on June 21, 1866, in Elmira. Interestingly, Adams's wife was the niece of John W. Jones, who aided Harriet Tubman in her efforts with the Underground Railroad. When a memorial tablet was dedicated to Tubman's memory in 1914, Adams was invited to deliver a prayer at the dedication. See Sernet, *Harriet Tubman*, 189. Additionally, newspaper accounts about his funeral state that after services in Harrisburg his body was sent to Elmira for burial. For further discussion see *Patriot* (Harrisburg, PA), July 11, 1914. For examples of his activities as an advocate for civil rights in Pennsylvania see Gasboro, "Rev. John Quincy Adams," http://civilwar.gratzpa.org/2015/02/rev-john-quincy-adams-harrisburg-preacher-civil-rights-leader-was-once-a-slave/.

119. *Telegraph* (Harrisburg, PA), January 13, 1917.

120. John Peyton Clark Journal, August 12, 1862, Louisa Morrow Crawford Collection, SBAHL. Also see Mahon, *Winchester Divided*, 51.

121. John Peyton Clark Journal, July 17, 1862, Louisa Morrow Crawford Collection, SBAHL.

122. Jordan, *Black Confederates and Afro-Yankees*, 87.

123. John Peyton Clark Journal, August 25, 1862, Louisa Morrow Crawford Collection, SBAHL.

124. Colt, *Defend the Valley*, 204, 404.

125. Ibid., 230.

126. *National Anti-Slavery Standard*, November 8, 1862.

127. Portia Baldwin Baker Diary, December 30, 1862, SBAHL.

128. For broader examinations of how news of the Emancipation Proclamation impacted slaves see Ward, *The Slaves' War*, 141; Reidy, *Illusions of Emancipation*, 30.

129. Strother, "Personal Recollections of the War," 35 (August 1867): 567.

130. Basler, *The Collected Works*, 6: 29.

131. Berlin et al., *Remembering Slavery*, 210.

**Chapter 5. "Freedom to Slaves!"**

1. Keifer, *Slavery and Four Years of War*, 1: 313. For a full biographical treatment of Milroy see Noyalas, *"My Will is Absolute Law."*

2. Keifer, *Slavery and Four Years of War*, 1:316.

3. Milroy to Mary Milroy, January 5, 1863, RHMJCPL.

4. Milroy to Mary Milroy, January 18, 1863, in ibid.

5. Hewitt, *History of the Twelfth West Virginia*, 26.

6. Strader, *Civil War Journal*, 176.

7. Mahon, *Winchester Divided*, 76.

8. McDonald, *A Diary with Reminiscences*, 130.

9. Letter of Gen. Gustave Paul Cluseret, January 7, 1863, to unidentified member of Congress, quoted in *Douglass' Monthly* (Rochester, NY), February 1863.

10. "Freedom to Slaves!" RHMJCPL.

11. For a discussion of Unionist opposition to the Emancipation Proclamation beyond the Shenandoah Valley see Myers, *Rebels Against the Confederacy*, 56.

12. Mahon, *Winchester Divided*, 63.

13. "Freedom to Slaves!," RHMJCPL.

14. For a discussion of Milroy's practices of handling civilians who presented challenges to his occupation see Noyalas, *"My Will is Absolute Law,"* 80, 84–85, 101–103.

15. Ibid., 76, 85; Strader, *Civil War Journal*, 180. For a full biographical treatment of Cluseret see Katz, *From Appomattox to Montmatre*.

16. Thomas O. Crowl to sister, January 28, 1863, Thomas O. Crowl Letter Collection, EFPSU.

17. Wild, *Memoirs and History*, 71–72.

18. Pope, *The Weary Boys*, 25.

19. "Freedom to Slaves!," RHMJCPL.

20. Basler, *Collected Works*, 6: 30; "Freedom to Slaves!," January 5, 1863, RHMJCPL; Grimsley, *The Hard Hand of War*, 144.

21. Strader, *The Civil War Journal*, 191. On February 13, 1863, Lee wrote in her diary "that the Yankee negroes left to take care of the horses in Dr. Baldwin's stable, had been burning our fence again." The following day Union authorities issued an order preventing this. Lee wrote, "orders were read last night to those negroes not to touch our fence . . . they had a bright fire to-night at some one's expense."

22. Wintz, *Civil War Memoirs*, 34.

23. Sheehan-Dean, *The Calculus of Violence*, 169.

24. Ibid.

25. Ibid., 152.

26. A. R. Boteler to Governor John Letcher, January 19, 1863, John Letcher Papers, LVA; Robinson, *Bitter Fruits of Bondage*, 48.

27. Executive Communication to the Virginia Senate and House of Delegates, January 20, 1863, John Letcher Papers, LVA.

28. Letcher informed Virginia's enslavers that they would be compensated $16 a month for the use of their enslaved laborers. Additionally, Letcher promised that if the enslaved person was captured or killed that Virginia would reimburse the enslaver for the loss. For further discussion, see Ayers, *In the Presence of Mine Enemies*, 338–339.

29. This statistical data is based on Table 3.2 in Martinez, *Confederate Slave Impressment*, 170.

30. Ibid., 166, 170.

31. Heinrich and Harding, *From Slave to Statesman*, 1–87, 104–105.

32. Martinez, *Confederate Slave Impressment*, 12, 67; Heinrich and Harding, *From Slave to Statesman*, 21.

33. Heinrich and Harding, *From Slave to Statesman*, 105–106.

34. For further discussion of enslavers' qualms with impressment, particularly negligent medical care, see Martinez, *Confederate Slave Impressment*, 55–57.

35. Journal of the Senate of Virginia, January 10, 1863, Resolution Declaring General Milroy an Outlaw in Paulus, *Papers of General Robert Huston Milroy*, 4:58.

36. Milroy to wife, February 10, 1863, in Paulus, *Papers*, 1: 237.

37. Keifer, *Slavery and Four Years of War*, 1: 318.

38. Ibid.

39. Milroy to Mary Milroy, February 10, 1863, RHMJCPL.

40. McDonald, *A Diary with Reminiscences*, 156.

41. Anna Bell Cadwallader to John Cadwallader, March 30, 1863, John N. Cadwallader Papers, VHS.

42. Bettie V. Cadwallader to John Cadwallader, February 9, 1863, John N. Cadwallader Papers, VHS.

43. *Diaries, Letters, and Recollections*, 63–64.

44. Sigismunda Stribling Kimbally Diary, February 24, 1863, CCHA.

45. *The Daily Dispatch* (Richmond, VA), February 10 and 14, 1863, quoted in Newcomer and Ramsey, *1863 Life in the Shenandoah Valley*, 49, 52.

46. Anna Bell Cadwallader to John Cadwallader, March 30, 1863, John N. Cadwallader Papers, VHS.

47. Koons, "'The Time has Come Near that We Will All Have to Learn to Work,'" 8.

48. Keifer, *Slavery and Four Years of War*, 1: 318.

49. McDonald, *A Diary with Reminiscences*, 134.

50. Milroy to Mary Milroy, February 10, 1863, RHMJCPL.

51. Ibid.

52. Keifer, *Slavery and Four Years of War*, 1: 318–319.

53. Ibid., 319.

54. Ibid., 320.

55. Ibid., 319.

56. For references to this unidentified African American cobbler see *The Diary of Margaretta "Gettie" Sperry Miller*, 6, 14, 17. It is unclear from Miller's diary if this man was born free or enslaved.

57. Milroy to General Robert C. Schenck, April 18, 1863, Robert C. Schenck Papers, UMO.

58. Strader, *The Civil War Journal*, 190.

59. McDonald, *A Diary with Reminiscences*, 135.

60. Strader, *The Civil War Journal*, 215.

61. *Weekly National Intelligencer* (Washington, DC), March 5, 1863; *The Adams Sentinel* (Gettysburg, PA), March 31, 1863.

62. Hewitt, *History of the Twelfth West Virginia*, 30–31.

63. Special Order Number 4, Record Group 393, vol. 2, Special Orders, April 1862–June 1863, NARA.

64. Hewitt, *History of the Twelfth West Virginia*, 31.

65. Ibid.

66. Stevenson, *"Boots and Saddles,"* 166.

67. For a detailed examination of Leopold's capture, trial, and execution see French, *Rebel Chronicles*, 64–112.

68. Hewitt, *History of the Twelfth West Virginia*, 34.

69. *Douglass' Monthly*, February 1863.

70. For a broader discussion of formerly enslaved people negotiating free labor contracts in areas under Union occupation see Berlin et al., *Freedom*, ser. 1., vol. 2, 23.

71. Strader, *The Civil War Journal*, 241–242; Noyalas, *"My Will is Absolute Law,"* 102–103.

72. Strader, *The Civil War Journal*, 179.

73. McDonald, *A Diary with Reminiscences*, 138.

74. Ibid., 137–138; Original Version of the Milroy Valentine, February 1863, RHMJCPL; Milroy to Mary Milroy, February 27, 1863, RHMJCPL; Noyalas, *"My Will is Absolute Law,"* 96–97. McDonald made various versions of this after the original which Milroy sent to his wife in Indiana. One of these appears in McDonald's published diary.

75. *Staunton Spectator*, January 6, 1863.

76. Ibid., April 14, 1863. For other examples of enslaved people for sale in the southern portion of the Shenandoah Valley see ibid., January 6, 1863; January 13, 1863; January 20, 1863; February 17, 1863; and March 17, 1863.

77. Ibid., January 13, 1863.

78. Ibid., May 12, 1863.

79. *Staunton Spectator*, May 19, 1863.

80. Reward for capture of Caroline and her two children quoted in Ayers, *In the Presence of Mine Enemies*, 374. This advertisement originally appeared in the *Staunton Vindicator*, April 24, 1864.

81. *Staunton Vindicator*, July 10, 1863. Pope, *The Weary Boys*, 115.

82. Noyalas, *"My Will is Absolute Law,"* 104.

83. Ibid., 104–105.

84. Buck, *Sad Earth, Sweet Heaven*, 190–191.

85. Wild, *Memoirs and History*, 53–54.

86. Colt, *Defend the Valley*, 259.

87. Ibid.

88. Wintz, *Civil War Memoirs*, 34.

89. *Diaries, Letters, and Recollections*, 77.

90. Snyder, "Suicide, Slavery, and Memory in North America," 41.

91. Colt, *Defend the Valley*, 259–260.

92. William McKenzie, undated note about case of Robert Discon, Roll 187 Unregistered Letters Received, June 1865-December 1868, Records of the Field Offices for the State of Virginia, 1865–1872, BRF&AL.

93. Mohr, *The Cormany Diaries*, 328–329.

94. For further discussion of Ewell's command capturing African Americans see Wynstra, *At the Forefront of Lee's Invasion*, 73, 81.

95. Piston, "'The Rebs are Yet Thick About Us,'" 215.

96. Captain W. S. How to Mr. Wills, August 31, 1865, in Meade Letters, CCHA.

97. McLachlan, "The Civil War Diary of Joseph H. Coit," 245, 254.

98. For an examination of this see Duncan, *Beleaguered Winchester*, 167–169.

99. *Staunton Spectator*, August 25, 1863, September 8, 1863, November 3, 1863, and December 15, 1863.

100. Lucy Maria [Grisby] Chandler to Norborne Eaton Chandler, December 25, 1863, Papers, 1745–1940 (bulk 1811–1895) of the Grisby Family of Rockbridge County, VA, VHS.

101. Runaway Notice, September 1863, "One Cent Reward" unattributed clipping in Slave Records, HRHS.

102. Runaway Notice, November 1863, "$200 Reward" in ibid.

103. For further discussion of the obstacles enslaved females confronted as compared to enslaved males see Windley, *A Profile of Runaway Slaves*, 40. For discussions of the dilemmas enslaved females confronted during the Civil War, including a lack of understanding of geography, see Champ, *Closer to Freedom*, 124–126.

104. Mahon, *Winchester Divided*, 103.

## Chapter 6. "This Causes Great Excitement"

1. *Staunton Spectator*, January 26, 1864. The advertisement noted that Oliver "had on a Yankee overcoat and jacket."

2. Ibid., March 15, 1864; March 22, 1864; March 29, 1864; April 5, 1864.

3. Ibid., February 2, 1864.

4. Ibid., March 15, 1864.

5. Lucy Maria Chandler to Norborne Eaton Chandler, March 4, 1864, Papers, 1745–1940, VHS.

6. Lucy Maria Chandler to Norborne Eaton Chandler, March 8, 1864, in ibid.

7. Wilmer et al., *History and Roster of Maryland Volunteers*, 2: 206.

8. Rickard, *Service with Colored Troops*, 9–10. The timing of this is based off Mahon, *Winchester Divided*, 138.

9. Rickard, *Service with Colored Troops*, 9–10.

10. Beach, *The First New York*, 344.

11. Summers, *19th Regiment U.S. Colored Troops*, 249; Private Benjamin Curtis, 19th USCT, Compiled Service Record, NARA.

12. Beach, *The First New York*, 344.

13. For examples of injustice perpetrated against African American troops and their white officers see Ira Berlin, *Freedom: The Black Military Experience*, 486, 509–511.

14. Ibid., 487.

15. Strader, *The Civil War Journal*, 344.

16. Ibid.

17. Mahon, *Winchester Divided*, 138.

18. For further discussion of how Confederate civilians reacted to the presence of USCT's in their communities see Lang, *In the Wake of War*, 165–169.

19. Mahon, *Winchester Divided*, 138.

20. Levin, *Searching for Black Confederates*, 55.

21. Levine, *Confederate Emancipation*, 2–3.

22. Levin, *Searching for Black Confederates*, 55; Levine, *Confederate Emancipation*, 110–111.

23. Mahon, *Winchester Divided*, 138.

24. James L. Hooff Journal, April 9, 1865, VHS.

25. Berkey, "War in the Borderland," 215.

26. Rickard, *Service with Colored Troops*, 12.

27. Berkey, "War in the Borderland," 215–216; John W. Douglass, 19th USCT, Compiled Service Record, NARA.

28. Stevenson, *A History of the First Volunteer Cavalry*, 257.

29. John Able, 19th USCT, Compiled Service Record, NARA.

30. Henry Harrison, 19th USCT, Compiled Service Record, NARA.

31. Lowe, "Battle on the Levee," 108.

32. Luke and Smith, *Soldiering for Freedom*, 45–46.

33. For further discussion of the many considerations African Americans confronted as they considered joining USCT's see Gary Kynoch, "Terrible Dilemmas," 1: 116–124; Levin, *Remembering the Battle of the Crater*, 28–32.

34. Glatthaar, *Forged in Battle*, 156.

35. This statistical data is based on analysis of information extracted from brief biographical sketches in Shenandoah Valley Black Heritage Project, *We Honor Those Who Served*, 105–221. Jefferson County is excluded from this publication. For information on the 128 African Americans who enlisted in USCT's from Jefferson County see Surkamp, "128 African Sons of Jefferson County . . . In Blue Coats," accessed May 10, 2019, http://civilwarscholars.com/2013/12/154-african-sons-of-jefferson-county-in-blue-coats/.

36. Wilmer et al., *History and Roster of Maryland Volunteers*, 2: 233–234, 251.

37. Edward Hall, 30th USCT, Compiled Service Record, NARA; Edward Hall, 30th USCT, Pension File, NARA.

38. Edward Hall, Certificate of Death, Virginia Death Records, 1912–2014, Virginia Department of Health, Richmond, VA.

39. Jesse Scott, 43rd USCT, Compiled Service Record, NARA.

40. William Bird, 25th USCT, in ibid.

41. Knight, *Valley Thunder*, 48; Engle, *Yankee Dutchman*, 178–179.

42. Eby, *A Virginia Yankee*, 222.

43. *Staunton Spectator*, January 26, 1864; February 2, 1864; March 15, 1864; March 29, 1864; April 12, 1864.

44. *Staunton Spectator*, April 26, 1864; May 10, 1864; May 17, 1864; May 31, 1864.

45. Engle, *Yankee Dutchmen*, 194.

46. Patchan, *The Battle of Piedmont*, 35–36.

47. Eby, *A Virginia Yankee*, 254.

48. Ibid.

49. Edgar Peirce to William Peirce, July 14, 1864, Peirce Letters, LVA.

50. Eby, *A Virginia Yankee*, 258.

51. Keyes, *The Military History*, 73.

52. Edgar Peirce to William Peirce, July 14, 1864, Peirce Letters, LVA.

53. Eby, *A Virginia Yankee*, 275.

54. *Wheeling Intelligencer*, July 12, 1864.

55. For an overview of Hunter's operations in the Valley at this time see Miller, *Lincoln's Abolitionist General*, 164–198.

56. Joseph Waddell Diary, June 6, 1864, "Valley of the Shadow Project," accessed April 22, 2019, http://valley.lib.virginia.edu/papers/AD1500.

57. *New York Tribune*, June 23, 1864. For additional information on the Asylum's operations during the conflict see Wood, *Dr. Francis T. Stribling*, 159–171.

58. *New York Tribune*, June 23, 1864.

59. Miller, *Lincoln's Abolitionist General*, 189.

60. Ibid., 190.

61. Eby, *A Virginia Yankee*, 248.

62. Stark, "The Great Skedaddle," 87.

63. Joseph Waddell Diary, June 18, 1864, "Valley of the Shadow Project," accessed April 22, 2019, http://valley.lib.virginia.edu/papers/AD1500.

64. Ibid., June 6, 1864.

65. *Wheeling Intelligencer*, July 12, 1864.

66. Cranmer, *History of Wheeling City*, 191.

67. *Wheeling Intelligencer*, July 12, 1864.

68. Sheridan, *Personal Memoirs*, 1: 499–500.

69. Basler, *The Collected Works*, 7: 548.

70. For additional information about Rebecca Wright's role see Noyalas, "That Woman," 43–49.

71. General George Crook to Colonel Theo. W. Bean, September 26, 1886, quoted in *The Loyal Girl of Winchester*, 7; *New York Times*, July 28, 1912; Sheridan, *Personal Memoirs*, 2:4.

72. Austin, "A Quiet Man," 36–37.

73. Thomas Laws to James Taylor, September 26, 1894, quoted in Taylor, *With Sheridan up the Shenandoah*, 355.

74. For examples of the important work African Americans played in intelligence-gathering during the conflict see Brasher, *The Peninsula Campaign*, 86, 90–91, 155.

75. Waller, *Lincoln's Spies*, 134.

76. Sheridan, *Personal Memoirs*, 2: 3.

77. Taylor, *With Sheridan up the Shenandoah*, 355.

78. Sheridan, *Personal Memoirs*, 2: 3–4.

79. Burr and Hinton, *The Life of Gen. Philip H. Sheridan*, 198.

80. Ibid.

81. Rebecca Wright to Charles Carleton Coffin, May 3, 1890, Charles Coffin Papers, HLHU.

82. Ibid.

83. Burr and Hinton, *The Life of Gen. Philip H. Sheridan*, 198.

84. Ibid., 199.

85. *New York Times*, July 28, 1912; Rebecca Wright to Charles Carlton Coffin, May 1, 1890, Charles Coffin Papers, HLHU.

86. Mahon, *Winchester Divided*, 21, 165; Some accounts state that Wright's father died shortly after his arrest, however, other sources indicate that he died on August 27, 1865. He is buried in the Friends' Cemetery at Ridge Meeting, Virginia. Some sources indicate that the conditions of his incarceration exacerbated health problems that quickened his demise. See *The Loyal Girl of Winchester*, 5; *Cincinnati Daily Gazette*, July 18, 1873.

87. Rebecca Wright to Charles Carleton Coffin, May 1, 1890, Charles Coffin Papers, HLHU; *The Times* (Washington, DC), October 5, 1902.

88. Burr and Hinton, *The Life of Gen. Philip H. Sheridan*, 199; Noyalas, "That Woman," 45.

89. Wright to Sheridan, September 16, 1864, quoted in Charles Carleton Coffin, *Freedom Triumphant: The Fourth Period of the War of the Rebellion* (New York: Harper and Brothers, 1890), 17; *The Times* (Washington, DC), October 5, 1902.

90. For the most detailed treatment of the Third Battle of Winchester see Patchan, *The Last Battle of Winchester*.

91. *New York Times*, July 28, 1912.

92. *New Hampshire Sentinel*, February 14, 1867.

93. *New York Times*, July 28, 1912.

94. On February 20, 1867, all of Winchester learned about Wright's role when the *Winchester Times* announced that she had "received as a present from General 'Barn burning,' Sheridan, and elegant gold watch, and exquisitely wrought chain, a brooch and charms . . . The present it is said, was made in recognition of an act, which for the sake of Virginia women shall be nameless in these columns." For additional information regarding Wright see Noyalas, "That Woman," 43–49.

95. *Morning Star* (Washington, DC), July 12, 1888.

96. Ibid.

97. *New York Times*, July 28, 1912; *The United States Treasury Register*, 41. When Wright received her position she initially earned an annual salary of $900.

98. Worsham, *One of Jackson's Foot Cavalry*, 267.

99. Wray, *History of the Twenty-Third Pennsylvania*, 169.

100. Rhodes, *All for the Union*, 179; Taylor, *With Sheridan up the Shenandoah*, 83.

101. Stephenson, *Headquarters in the Brush*, 330.

102. *Ironton Register* (Ohio), November 25, 1886; Stephenson, *Headquarters in the Brush*, 170.

103. A roster of the Union dead buried in the Winchester National Cemetery denotes that the individual buried in grave 2001, killed on November 18, 1864, was "Colored." For further information see *Roll of Honor (No. XV): Names of Soldiers Who Died*, 236.

104. Publication Committee of the Regimental Association, *History of the Eighteenth*, 57.

105. Heatwole, *The Burning*, 97.

106. Ibid., 51, 122.

107. Stevens, *Three Years in the Sixth Corps*, 411–412.

108. Joseph Waddell Diary, October 8, 1864, "Valley of the Shadow Project," accessed April 22, 2019, http://valley.lib.virginia.edu/papers/AD1500.

109. Ibid.

110. Mottelay and Copeland, *The Soldier in Our Civil War*, 2: 352.

111. Ibid.

112. Heatwole, *The Burning*, 38.

113. Wenger and Rodes, *Unionists and the Civil War Experience*, 6: 38, 42–43, 45.

114. Savery Iverson, Claim No. 4983, Southern Claims Commission Records, NARA.

115. Taylor Thornton, Claim No. 55264, in ibid.

116. Meshack Johnson, Claim No. 17570, in ibid.

117. Milford Jones, Claim No. 41794, in ibid.

118. Kenyette Spencer, "Serena, Henrietta and Abe Spencer, Free Blacks Account of Battle of Cedar Creek" accessed June 13, 2019, https://www.genealogy.com/forum/surnames/topics/spencer/9094/.

119. Johnson, *Battleground Adventures*, 414.

120. For a broader discussion of Union soldiers' attacks on and rape of African American women see Murphy, *I Had Rather Die*, 63–86.

121. Johnson, *Battleground Adventures*, 406, 415.

122. Ibid., 395.

123. Varon, "The Last Hour of the Slaveholders' Rebellion," 254.

124. Ibid.

### Chapter 7. John Brown's "Soul Is Still Marching On"

1. Johnson, *The Twentieth Century Biographical Dictionary*, 10: 211.

2. Trowbridge, *The South*, 69.

3. Ibid., iii.

4. Ibid., 489.

5. Ibid., 69.

6. Watkins James served as assistant United States assessor in the war's aftermath in Frederick, Shenandoah, and Warren Counties. He was a native of Maryland, but moved to Virginia and the Shenandoah Valley in 1844. Report on the Joint Committee, pt. 2: 40–41.

7. Ibid., 109.

8. Ashby, *The Valley Campaigns*, 165.

9. Ibid., 166.

10. Report on the Joint Committee, 109.

11. Trowbridge, *The South*, 68.

12. Ibid.

13. *Staunton Spectator*, August 8, 1865.

14. Seeking the protection of Union troops in the war's immediate aftermath was the response of African Americans across the former Confederacy. For a discussion of this beyond the Shenandoah Valley see Manning, *Troubled Refuge*, 243.

15. Waddell, *Annals*, 337.

16. Ibid.

17. Ibid.

18. Trowbridge, *The South*, 67.

19. Mr. and Mrs. C. C. Harris were tasked with finding employment for African Americans in New York and Rhode Island while Mr. O. S. B. Wall, who served as an officer in the 104th USCT during the conflict, sought individuals to emigrate to Ohio. For additional discussion see Stealey, III, "The Freedmen's Bureau in West Virginia," 32.

20. Carrie Bushong to Frank Bushong, March 20, 1870, quoted in Koons, "'The Colored Laborers,'" 242. Bushong also wrote in the letter that various white families from the area around New Market headed for various points west and south.

21. For a broader discussion of how freed people journeyed to other areas in the former Confederacy because of the prospect of acquiring land as a result of the Southern Homestead Act see Lanza, "'One of the Most Appreciated Labors of the Bureau,'" 67–87.

22. Carrie Bushong to Frank Bushong, March 20, 1870, quoted in Koons, "'The Colored Laborers,'" 241–242. The statistical analysis of the reduction in the African American population is based on Koons. What is difficult to determine, based on comparisons of census data, is precisely at what moment in the span between 1860 and 1870 African Americans departed the Shenandoah Valley. As has been argued in previous chapters, African Americans departed at various points during the war and in its immediate aftermath. Nonetheless, Bushong's letter offers some evidence that even five years after the conflict African Americans still departed the region.

23. Letter of General Isaac Duval to General Alfred T. A. Torbert, June 9, 1865, Roll 187 Unregistered Letters Received, June 1865–December 1868, BRF&AL.

24. An Act to Establish a Bureau for the Relief of Freedmen and Refugees, March 3, 1865, in Journal of the House of Representatives of the United States; Being the Second Session of the Thirty-Eighth Congress, 482–483. For Howard's perspective on the challenges he confronted see Howard, Autobiography, 2: 215–233. For a full overview of the Freedmen's Bureau's operations see Cimbala, The Freedmen's Bureau, 3–108.

25. Lowe, *Republicans and Reconstruction in Virginia*, 29; Farmer, "'Because They Are Women,'" 164.

26. Directive from Colonel Orlando Brown, August 8, 1865, Roll 187, Unregistered Letters Received, June 1865–December 1868, Records of the Field Office for the State of Virginia, Bureau of Refugees, Freedmen and Abandoned Lands, 1865–1872, BRF&AL.

27. *Shepherdstown Register*, June 15, 1865.

28. Manning, *Troubled Refuge*, 267.

29. Wintz, *Civil War Memoirs*, 33.

30. Ashby, *The Valley Campaigns*, 311–312.

31. Ibid., 312.

32. Case of Emma Morris against Jno. Lupton, Roll 192, Records: Subordinate Field Offices, Winchester Assistant Sub-Assistant Commissioner & Woodstock Assistant Sub-Assistant Commissioner, BRF&AL.

33. McConnell, *Negroes and Their Treatment in Virginia*, 34. House Document 120, Thirty-Ninth Congress, First Session in Executive Documents Printed by Order of the House of Representatives During the First Session of the Thirty-Ninth Congress, 16.

34. The range of monthly salaries is based on contracts negotiated for the year 1866 in Frederick and Clarke Counties. Roll 192, Freedmen's Bureau Contracts and Indentures, Winchester Sub-Assistant Commissioner, BRF&AL.

35. Labor contract between Calvin Hall and Miss Mannie McCole, May 12, 1866, Roll 192, Freedmen's Bureau Contracts and Indentures, Winchester Sub-Assistant Commissioner, BRF&AL.

36. Labor contract between Patrick Tracy and Jasco Thompson, April 11, 1866, in ibid.

37. Article of Agreement between William F. Snapp and George Washington, April 12, 1866, Roll 176, Contracts, Bills of Lading, Receipts and Miscellaneous Records, 1865–1868, Staunton assistant-sub assistant commissioner, BRF&AL.

38. According to historian Ralph Shlomowitz, most sharecropping agreements signed between 1865 and 1868 included the stipulation that laborers receive one-third of the crop, unless the employer provided rations. If rations were provided, then sharecroppers received one-quarter of the crop. For additional discussion see Ralph Shlomowitz, "The Origins of Southern Sharecropping," 203.

39. For a discussion of why African Americans preferred sharecropping see Foner, *Reconstruction*, 174–175.

40. This percentage is based off an examination of contracts executed at the Freedmen's Bureau office in Staunton. Of the sixty-five total contracts filed between 1865 and 1868 only two of them offered a share of crops as compensation. The remainder offered wages. See Labor Contracts, Roll 176, Contracts, Bills of Lading, Receipts and Miscellaneous Records, 1865–1868, Staunton assistant-subassistant commissioner, BRF&AL.

41. *Staunton Vindicator*, October 30, 1868.

42. Koons, "'The Colored Laborers,'" 250–251; Kerr-Ritchie, *Freedpeople in the Tobacco South*, 103–104.

43. Foner, *Reconstruction*, 174.

44. For a discussion of this see Thorp, *Facing Freedom*, 74.

45. General Oliver O. Howard, Circular on Apprenticeship, October 4, 1865, Roll 192, Freedmen's Bureau Contracts and Indentures, Winchester-Sub-Assistant Commissioner, BRF&AL. For an excellent case study of apprenticeship laws and the challenges they presented to freed people in the war's aftermath see Barry A. Crouch, "'They Enslave the Rising Generation,'" 263–274.

46. Indenture of Robert to Jordan Pifer, November 10, 1865, Roll 192, Freedmen's

Bureau Contracts and Indentures, Winchester-Sub-Assistant Commissioner, BRF&AL. The Jordan Pifer referenced in the indenture might in fact be J. W. Pifer, who according to the 1860 slave schedules enslaved three people, all of whom in 1860 were under the age of fifteen. J. W. Pifer enslaved two males, aged thirteen and nine and one female aged fifteen. The enslaved male aged nine in the 1860 slave schedule might be Robert. See Bureau of the Census, Eighth Census of the United States, 1860, NARA.

47. Indenture of Robert to Jordan Pifer, November 10, 1865, Roll 192, Freedmen's Bureau Contracts and Indentures, Winchester Sub-Assistant Commissioner, BRF&AL. While freed people throughout the South frequently complained about the terms of Freedmen's Bureau contracts, nothing stirred greater ire among African Americans than the apprenticeship system. Freed people believed this not only afforded former enslavers an opportunity to take advantage of orphaned children, but also, as Eric Foner noted in his magisterial study of Reconstruction, to seize "upon the consequences of slavery—the separation of families and the freedmen's poverty." For additional discussion of the ways in which the apprenticeship system created a new kind of slavery see Foner, *Reconstruction*, 201–202. For a discussion beyond the Shenandoah Valley of how white employers further manipulated the apprenticeship system see O'Donovan, *Becoming Free*, 155–156.

48. Jonathan Berkey notes for example that in December 1865 more than half of the complaints registered with the Freedmen's Bureau in Winchester involved disputes over pay. See Berkey, "War in the Borderland," 296.

49. Complaint of David Jefferson against Robert McCampbell, Roll 192, Records: Subordinate Field Offices, Winchester Assistant Sub-Assistant Commissioner and Woodstock Assistant Sub-Assistant Commissioner, BRF&AL.

50. Case of Aaron Green Against George Rodgers, December 5, 1865, in ibid.

51. Ibid.

52. Letter of E. C. Clarkhurst to Captain William Stover How, August 8, 1865, Roll 187 Unregistered Letters Received, June 1865–December 1868, Records of the Field Office for the State of Virginia, Bureau of Refugees, Freedmen and Abandoned Lands, 1865–1872, BRF&AL. Captain William Stover How served as superintendent of the Sixth District from August 1865–May 1866.

53. Ayers, *The Thin Light of Freedom*, 431–432; 434–435; Dabney, *Virginia*, 367; Documents of the Constitutional Convention of the State of Virginia, 6.

54. Wallenstein, *Cradle of America*, 222.

55. Monthly report of Captain E. H. Ripley, November 30, 1867, Roll 89, Letters Sent, May 1866–December 1868, BRF&AL; Wallenstein, *Cradle of America*, 222.

56. Report of Thomas Jackson quoted in Ayers, *The Thin Light of Freedom*, 436–437.

57. Monthly report of Captain E. H. Ripley, November 30, 1867, Roll 89, Letters Sent, May 1866–December 1868, BRF&AL.

58. Monthly report of Captain E. H. Ripley, May 30, 1868, in ibid.

59. Ibid.

60. Monthly report of Captain E. H. Ripley, November 30, 1867, in ibid.

61. Ayers, *The Thin Light of Freedom*, 431.

62. Monthly report of Captain E. H. Ripley, January 31, 1868, Roll 89, Letters Sent, May 1866–December 1868, BRF&AL.

63. Monthly report of Captain E. H. Ripley, March 30, 1868, in ibid.

64. Report of Captain T. A. McDonell to General Orlando M. Brown, April 30, 1867, Roll 188, Reports Forwarded to Assistant Commissioner and Received from Subordinates (cont.) Nov. 1866–May 1867, BRF&AL.

65. Ibid.

66. Report of Freedmen's Schools for month of December 1865, Roll 12, Monthly Statistical Reports of District Superintendents July 1865–April 1869 and January 1878. BRF&AL. The schools were established at Lexington, Staunton, Woodstock, Harrisonburg, Luray, Winchester, Harpers Ferry, Martinsburg, and Charles Town. Five of the schools were supported by the American Missionary Association, one by the Old School Presbyterians Church of Pittsburgh, Pennsylvania, and the remaining three by the New England Baptist Society.

67. Ibid.

68. Reilly, *Sarah Jane Foster*, 34.

69. Ibid., 35.

70. Ibid., 56.

71. Ibid., 36.

72. Monthly Report of Captain E. H. Ripley, July 30, 1867, Roll 89, Letters Sent, May 1866–December 1868, BRF&AL.

73. School Report for April 1868, 1st Division, 9th Sub-District. Roll 13, Reports of Superintendents of Education for the State of Virginia, 1865–1870, BRF&AL.

74. Fox, "The Labor of a Free Man," 29. Brackett was a native of Maine and served as an agent with the United States Christian Commission during the Civil War. It was in that capacity that he saved the unidentified Confederate soldier who intervened on his behalf in Charles Town.

75. School Report for April 1868, 1st Division, 9th Sub-District. Roll 13, Reports of Superintendents of Education for the State of Virginia, 1865–1870, BRF&AL.

76. Rev. D. A. Mills is listed as the teacher for the school at Woodstock in the December 1865 monthly school report, therefore, based on the time of Watkins James's testimony to Congress on February 2, 1866, the incident James described likely involved Rev. Mills. See Report of Freedmen's Schools for the month of December 1865, Roll 12, Monthly Statistical School Reports of District Superintendents July 1865–April 1869; January 1878, BRF&AL.; Testimony of Watkins James, Report on the Joint Committee, 42.

77. Testimony of Watkins James, Report on the Joint Committee, 42.

78. As is the case with Mills this account is based on the testimony of Watkins James. Although James offered no names the timing of the event suggests that it was Mr. G. Hammond. See Report of Freedmen's Schools for the month of December 1865, Roll 12, Monthly Statistical School Reports of District Superintendents July 1865–April 1869; January 1878, BRF&AL.; Testimony of Watkins James, Report on the Joint Committee, 43.

79. Testimony of Watkins James, Report on the Joint Committee on Reconstruction, 43.

80. Reilly, *Sarah Jane Foster*, 54.

81. Ibid., 51. In his essay on West Virginia's Reconstruction experience, Randall S. Gooden paints a very different picture of the African American experience than that

portrayed by Foster. Gooden notes: "Strife over the status and roles of African Americans did not erupt as it did in the South." While this might be true of the experience in other parts of West Virginia, evidence indicates that was not the case in the state's eastern panhandle. See Gooden, "'Neither War nor Peace,'" 211.

82. Reilly, *Sarah Jane Foster*, 36, 52–53. Although Hoke refused to rent her a room out of fear of reprisals against her property, Foster quickly found a place to reside while teaching in Martinsburg—the residence of Mr. and Mrs. Adam Bayles. Mrs. Bayles even assisted Foster with her teaching duties after Hoke displaced her.

83. Howard, *Autobiography*, 2: 329; Richardson, "Architects of a Benevolent Empire," 124.

84. Reilly, *Sarah Jane Foster*, 56.

85. Monthly School Report, June 1868, Roll 13, Reports of Superintendent of Education for the State of Virginia, BRF&AL.

86. Monthly School Report, January 1868, in ibid. The six teachers listed were Martha J. Stowers, Emily E. Deering, Sarah J. Percival, James W. Washington, Matilda Robinson, and Isabella Steele. Stowers, Deering, and Percival were white, while Washington, Robinson, and Steele were African American. A survey of the 1860 census reveals that only Percival and Washington resided in Winchester. Eighth Census of the United States, 1860, NARA.

87. Teachers Monthly Report, January 1868, Roll 15, Teacher's Monthly Reports, November 1865–April 1869, BRF&AL. According to the 1870 census Percival's residence and school was located at 336 South Braddock Street. The structure no longer stands. She died in May 1884 and is buried in Mount Hebron Cemetery in Winchester, Old Plot 274, Grave 1.

88. Wenger and Rodes, *Unionists and the Civil War*, 6: 214–215. Scanlon also supported the construction of an African American church in the war's aftermath. He even reportedly paid the final payment to the church's builder after the congregation could not make payment. Additionally, he "provided free of charge the wine for communion and never charged for anything he did for the colored church."

89. Stealey, "The Freedmen's Bureau in West Virginia," 46.

90. Case of Chas. W. Barbour, January 1868, Roll 59, Records Relating to Murders and Outrages, BRF&AL.

91. Case of Lizzie Harper, August 1868, in ibid.

92. Case of Sarah Brown, June 1868, in ibid.

93. Statement of Watkins James, Feb. 2, 1866, in Report on the Joint Committee, 40.

94. Statement of assault against "a colored boy" in Lexington, Virginia, June 14, 1866, Roll 183, Endorsements Sent, November 1865-June 1866, BRF&AL. In 1845 Brockenbrough was appointed judge for the United States District Court for the Western Virginia District of Virginia by President James K. Polk. He held that post until 1861. For additional biographical information see Warner and Yearns, *Biographical Register*, 33.

95. Case of Caesar Griffin, May 1868, Roll 59, Records Relating to Murders and Outrages, BRF&AL.

96. Case of Lucy Forge (child of Fletcher), June 1868, Roll 59, Records Relating to Murders and Outrages, BRF&AL.

97. Case of John Burns, April 1868, in ibid.

98. In addition to Douglass Grove, African American communities existed near Gerrardstown, Darkesville, and Bunker Hill. For a full treatment of the Douglass Grove community see Planchon, "Free Blacks in Berkeley County and the Black Community of Douglass Grove," 35–43.

99. Ehrenpreis, *Picturing Harrisonburg*, 66.

100. Jones, *An African American Community of Hope*, 20.

101. Sometimes identified as Crossroads, this community might predate the Civil War, with a small number of free black families reportedly purchasing land there as early as 1853. The community grew in the Civil War's aftermath and was inhabited by at least nine families. For additional information on the prewar exchange of land see Frederick County Virginia Deed Book, 80: 367, 486 and Frederick County Virginia Deed Book 81: 192; in addition to Freetown, Frederick County was home to at least two additional African American communities, Cedar Hill and Leetown. For additional information on these two communities see Kalbian, *Frederick County Virginia*, 81; Noyalas, *Two Peoples*, 52.

102. Kalbian, *Clarke County*, 29; Josephine City Historic District, National Register of Historic Places Registration Form, VDHR File No. 168–5029, 28–31. The report notes that in addition to Josephine City, Clarke County was home to four additional African American communities—Browntown, Claytonville, Lewisville, and Webbtown. *Clarke Courier*, October 12, 1870.

103. Burks and Morris, "Through the Shadow," 84–85.

104. *Staunton Spectator*, Dec. 26, 1865; *Valley Virginian*, January 10, 1866.

105. *Valley Virginian*, Aug. 1, 1866; September 26, 1866; November 21, 1866; March 27, 1867; and August 7, 1867; *Staunton Vindicator*, September 23, 1870.

106. History Matters, *History of Orrick Chapel*, 5; *Baltimore Sun*, July 9, 1902. Orrick was enslaved prior to the Civil War, but enjoyed a lucrative career as a preacher and livery owner in Winchester after the conflict. An obituary published in the *Baltimore Sun* on July 9, 1902, noted of Orrick: "He was a man of impressive appearance and magnetism, and one of the most eloquent ministers of his race in this section, and amassed a fortune in the livery business."

107. DuBois, *The Negro Church*, 5; Richardson, *Christian Reconstruction*, 157–158.

108. *The National Anti-Slavery Standard*, March 13, 1869.

109. The percentage of African American males registered to vote is based on statistical evidence presented in Williams, *I Freed Myself*, 222. In his study Williams notes that by the fall of 1867 more than 90 percent of African American males eligible to vote registered. The only former Confederate state below 90 percent was Mississippi, which had 83 percent registered.

110. *Spirit of Jefferson*, February 23, 1869.

111. Lowe, *Republicans and Reconstruction in Virginia*, 173.

112. *Staunton Spectator*, June 15, 1869.

113. Ibid.

114. Ibid.

115. Ibid., July 13, 1869.

116. For example, in Rockbridge County 78 percent of registered African American voters turned out to vote. While significant, 85 percent of the county's registered white voters came to the polls on July 6, 1869. See Lowe, *Republicans and Reconstruction in Virginia*, 176.

117. For information on the statewide election returns see Lowe, *Republicans and Reconstruction in Virginia*, 177. The election numbers for the Shenandoah Valley are based on the election returns reported in the *Staunton Spectator*, July 20, 1869.

118. *Staunton Spectator*, July 13, 1869.

119. Lowe, *Republicans and Reconstruction in Virginia*, 178.

120. Ashby, *The Valley Campaigns*, 108.

121. The situation continued to deteriorate for African Americans after the election of 1869. For further discussion of redemption in Virginia see Dabney, *Virginia*, 372–379; Lowe, *Republicans and Reconstruction in Virginia*, 180–183.

122. Historian William Blair notes that the earliest celebrations of emancipation occurred in some locales the moment the Emancipation Proclamation went into effect. In Norfolk approximately five hundred African Americans participated in a parade that included formerly enslaved individuals trampling Confederate flags and burning an effigy of Confederate president Jefferson Davis. For further discussion of celebrations of emancipation during the conflict see Blair, *Cities of the Dead*, 26. This conclusion, about the first emancipation celebrations not occurring in the Shenandoah Valley until the summer of 1869, is based on an examination of Shenandoah Valley newspapers published in Shepherdstown, Charles Town, Winchester, Woodstock, and Staunton.

123. *Shepherdstown Register*, September 4, 1869.

124. Ibid.

125. *Spirit of Jefferson* (Charles Town, WV), October 26, 1869.

126. Ibid.

127. For further discussion of the variety of dates for Emancipation celebrations see Janney, *Remembering the Civil War*, 214.

128. *Shepherdstown Register*, August 21, 1869; September 4, 1869; September 13, 1873; September 20, 1873; September 27, 1873; August 18, 1877; September 10, 1881; October 7, 1882; *Spirit of Jefferson* (Charles Town, WV), September 7, 1869; September 28, 1869; October 26, 1869; September 26, 1871; September 16, 1873; August 9, 1887; *Shenandoah Herald* (Woodstock, VA), September 25, 1878; August 29, 1890; *Staunton Spectator*, October 1, 1878; October 22, 1890; *Virginia Free Press* (Charles Town, WV), August 11, 1887.

129. Blair, *Cities of the Dead*, 23–24.

130. *Spirit of Jefferson* (Charles Town, WV), September 28, 1869.

131. *Shenandoah Herald* (Woodstock, VA), September 25, 1878.

132. Blair, *Cities of the Dead*, 41.

133. *Shepherdstown Register*, August 18, 1877.

134. Ibid., September 27, 1873. For additional discussion of how some correspondents downplayed attendance at Emancipation celebrations see Blair, *Cities of the Dead*, 41.

135. *Spirit of Jefferson* (Charles Town, WV), September 7, 1869.

136. Blair, *Cities of the Dead*, 144–145, 161–170.

137. *Shenandoah Herald*, August 29, 1890.

138. Heinrich and Harding, *From Slave to Statesman*, 65.

139. *Staunton Spectator*, October 22, 1890.

140. Blair, *Cities of the Dead*, 166.

141. *Clarke Courier* (Berryville, Virginia), October 14, 1903.

142. *Valley Virginian* (Staunton, Virginia); Heinrich and Harding, *From Slave to Statesman*, 64; Blight, *Race and Reunion*, 66–70.

143. Pollard, *The Lost Cause*, 70.

144. Douglass, *John Brown*, 10, 16.

145. Ibid., 14.

146. *Winchester Evening Star*, July 9, 1902.

147. Ibid., August 14, 1907; Mildred G. Brumback, "Aunt Caroline," Unpublished Paper, Middletown Heritage Society, Middletown, VA.

148. 1870 U.S. Census, Opequon District, Frederick County, VA (Middletown Post Office), population schedule, digital image, accessed September 5, 2019, http://ancestry.com.

149. 1870 U.S. Census, Staunton, VA, population schedule, digital image, accessed September 5, 2019, http://ancestry.com.

150. 1870 U.S. Census, Winchester, VA, population schedule, digital image, accessed September 5, 2019, http://ancestry.com.

## Conclusion

1. Painter, *Creating Black Americans*, ix.

2. Ibid.

3. James H. Cone quoted in Croft, *The Motif of Hope*, 10, 41.

# BIBLIOGRAPHY

**Archives and Newspapers**

Abby Aldrich Rockefeller Folk Art Museum, Colonial Williamsburg Foundation, Williamsburg, VA
> Sketchbook of Landscapes in the State of Virginia, 1853–1867

Clarke County Historical Association, Berryville, VA
> African American History Collection
> Meade Letters
> Sigismunda Stribling Kimball Diary

Frederick County Judicial Center, Winchester, VA
> Frederick County Deed Book 80
> Frederick County Deed Book 81

Harrisonburg-Rockingham Historical Society, Dayton, VA
> Slave Records

Historical Collections and Labor Archives, Eberly Family Special Collections Library, Pennsylvania State University, State College, PA
> Thomas O. Crowl Letter Collection

Houghton Library, Harvard University, Cambridge, MA
> Charles Coffin Papers

Jasper County Public Library, Rensselaer, IN
> General Robert H. Milroy Papers

Library of Congress, Washington, DC
> Boyce Papers
> Nathaniel P. Banks Papers
> Rufus Mead Papers

Library of Virginia, Richmond, VA
> Frederick County, Virginia Free Black Records
> John Letcher Papers
> Legislative Petitions of the General Assembly, 1776–1865
> Peirce Letters
> Runaway Slave Records, 1794, 1806–1863

National Archives and Records Administration, Washington, DC
> Compiled Service Records

Contracts, Bills of Lading, Receipts and Miscellaneous Records, 1865–1868, Bureau of Refugees, Freedmen, and Abandoned Lands

Letters Sent, May 1866–December 1868, Bureau of Refugees, Freedmen, and Abandoned Lands

Monthly Statistical Reports of District Superintendents July 1865–April 1869 and January 1878, Bureau of Refugees, Freedmen, and Abandoned Lands

Record Group 393, Refugees, Deserters & Contrabands, 1862

Record Group 393, Special Orders, April 1862–June 1863

Records of the Fields Offices for the State of Virginia, Bureau of Refugees, Freedmen, and Abandoned Lands, 1865–1872.

Records Relating to Murders and Outrages, Bureau of Refugees Freedmen, and Abandoned Lands

Records: Subordinate Field Offices, Bureau of Refugees, Freedmen, and Abandoned Lands

Reports of Superintendents of Education for the State of Virginia, 1865–1870, Bureau of Refugees Freedmen, and Abandoned Lands

Southern Claims Commission Records

Teacher's Monthly Reports, November 1865–April 1869, Bureau of Refugees Freedmen, and Abandoned Lands

Newtown History Center, Stephens City, VA

Joseph Long Papers

Ohio Historical Society, Columbus, OH

Samuel Sexton Papers

Stewart Bell, Jr. Archives, Handley Regional Library, Winchester, VA

Alan Tischler Collection

Lieutenant Melzer Dutton Correspondence, Civil War Diaries/Letters

Louisa Morrow Crawford Collection

Portia Baldwin Baker Diary

Rev. Benjamin F. Brooke Journal

University of Miami, Ohio, Oxford, OH

Robert C. Schenck Papers

University of North Carolina, Chapel Hill, NC

Southern Historical Collection, Abraham Spengler Letter

Virginia Department of Health, Richmond, VA

Virginia Death Records, 1912–2014.

Virginia Historical Society, Richmond, VA

Conrad Papers

James Lawrence Hooff Papers

John N. Cadwallader Papers

Papers, 1745–1940 (bulk 1811–1895)

Warren Rifles Confederate Museum, Front Royal, VA

Anderson Letters

Samuel Coyner Papers

William R. Perkins Library, Duke University, Durham, NC
    Joseph Long Papers
Winchester-Frederick County Joint Judicial Center, Winchester, VA
    Frederick County Will Book 22

*Alexandria Gazette*
*Baltimore Sun*
*Cadiz Democratic Sentinel* (Cadiz, OH)
*Cincinnati Daily Gazette*
*Clarke Courier* (Berryville, VA)
*Douglass' Monthly* (Rochester, NY)
*Frank Leslie's Illustrated Newspaper*
*Harper's Weekly*
*Hartford Courant* (Hartford, CT)
*Ironton Register* (Ironton, OH)
*Morning Star* (Washington, DC)
*National Anti-Slavery Standard*
*National Tribune*
*New Hampshire Sentinel*
*New York Evening Post*
*New York Times*
*New York Tribune*
*Patriot* (Harrisburg, PA)
*Richmond Dispatch*
*Richmond Enquirer*
*Shenandoah Herald* (Woodstock, VA)
*Shepherdstown Register*
*Spirit of Jefferson* (Charles Town, WV)
*Staunton Spectator*
*Staunton Vindicator*
*Telegraph* (Harrisburg, PA)
*The Adams Sentinel* (Gettysburg, PA)
*The American Union* (Martinsburg, VA)
*The Mail* (Hagerstown, MD)
*The National Era* (Washington, DC)
*The Times* (Washington, DC)
*The Torch Light and Public Advertiser* (Hagerstown, MD)
*Valley Virginian*
*Virginia Free Press* (Charles Town, WV)
*Weekly National Intelligencer* (Washington, DC)
*Weekly Standard* (Raleigh, NC)
*Wheeling Intelligencer*
*Winchester Evening Star*

Winchester Republican

Winchester Times

**Primary Sources**

*Acts of the General Assembly of the State of Virginia, Passed at Called Session, 1862, in the Eighty-Seventh Year of the Commonwealth.* Richmond, VA: William F. Ritchie, Public Printer, 1862.

Adams, John Quincy. *Narrative of the Life of John Quincy Adams: When in Slavery, and Now as a Freeman.* Harrisburg, PA: Sieg, Printer and Stationer, 1872.

Ambler, Lucy Johnston. *When Tidewater Invaded the Valley: A Tribute to the Men of Lower Virginia in the Days of John Brown's Raid.* Charlestown, WV: Sprit of Jefferson Press, 1934.

Ashby, Thomas A. *The Valley Campaigns: Being the Reminiscences of a Non-Combatant While Between the Lines in the Shenandoah Valley During the War of the States.* New York: The Neale Publishing Co., 1914.

Basler, Roy P., ed. *The Collected Works of Abraham Lincoln.* Vol. 6. New Brunswick, NJ: Rutgers University Press, 1953.

Beach, William H. *The First New York (Lincoln) Cavalry: From April 19, 1861 to July 7, 1865.* New York: The Lincoln Cavalry Association, 1902.

Berlin, Ira, Marc Favreau, and Steven F. Miller. *Remembering Slavery: African Americans Talk About Their Personal Experiences of Slavery and Emancipation.* New York: The New Press, 1998.

Berlin, Ira, Barbara J. Field, Steven F. Miller, Joseph P. Reidy, and Leslie S. Rowland. *Free at Last: A Documentary History of Slavery, Freedom, and the Civil War.* Edison, NJ: The Blue & Grey Press, 1992.

Berlin, Ira, Steven F. Miller, Joseph P. Reidy, and Leslie S. Rowland. *Freedom: A Documentary History of Emancipation 1861–1867.* Ser. 1, Vol. 1. Cambridge: Cambridge University Press, 1985.

Berlin, Ira, Joseph P. Reidy, and Leslie S. Roland. *Freedom: A Documentary History of Emancipation, 1861–1867: The Black Military Experience.* Ser. 2. Cambridge: Cambridge University Press, 1982.

Boyd, Belle. *Belle Boyd in Camp and Prison.* Baton Rouge: Louisiana State University Press, 1998.

Brown, Helen Sue, comp. *The Original Minutes of Stephens City (Newtown/Stephensburg), Virginia, 1842–1899.* n.p., n.d.

Buck, Lucy Rebecca. *Sad Earth, Sweet Heaven: The Diary of Lucy Rebecca Buck.* Birmingham, AL: Buck Publishing Co., 1992.

Case of Violet, Slave of Sampson Sawyers, February 18, 1780. http://www2.vcdh.virginia.edu/gos/countyRecords/countyIndividualRecord.php?county=augusta&year=1780&display=record&record=81, accessed July 16, 2019.

Chambers, Jennie. *The Truth about John Brown by an Eye-Witness.* Pioneer Historical Society, n.d.

Chambers, Jennie. "What a School-Girl Saw of John Brown's Raid." *Harper's Monthly*

*Magazine: December, 1901 to May, 1902*. New York: Harper and Brothers Publishers, 1902.

Clarke County Population Schedule, 1850. http://ancestry.com, accessed June 1, 2018.

Colt, Margaretta Barton. *Defend the Valley: A Shenandoah Family in the Civil War*. Oxford: Oxford University Press, 1994.

Comey, Lyman Richard, ed. *A Legacy of Valor: The Memoirs and Letters of Captain Henry Newton Comey, 2nd Massachusetts Infantry*. Knoxville: University of Tennessee Press, 2004.

Copeland, Robert Morris. *Statement of R. Morris Copeland*. Boston: Prentiss & Deland, 1864.

*Diaries, Letters, and Recollections of the War Between the States*. Winchester, VA: Winchester-Frederick County Historical Society, 1955.

*Documents of the Constitutional Convention of the State of Virginia*. Richmond, VA: Office of the New Nation, 1867.

Douglass, Frederick. *John Brown: An Address by Frederick Douglass, at the Fourteenth Anniversary of Storer College, Harper's Ferry, West Virginia, May 30, 1881*. Dover, NH: Morning Star Job Printing House, 1881.

Duncan, Russell, ed. *Blue-Eyed Child of Fortune: The Civil War Letters of Colonel Robert Gould Shaw*. Athens: University of Georgia Press, 1992.

Dwight, Wilder. *Life and Letters of Wilder Dwight, Lieut-Col. Second Mass. Inf. Vols*. Boston: Ticknor and Fields, 1868.

Eby, Cecil D., Jr., ed. *A Virginia Yankee in the Civil War: The Diaries of David Hunter Strother*. Chapel Hill: University of North Carolina Press, 1961.

Eddy, Richard. *History of the Sixtieth Regiment New York State Volunteers*. Philadelphia: Published by the Author, 1864.

*Executive Documents Printed by Order of the House of Representatives During the First Session of the Thirty-Ninth Congress, 1865-'66*. Washington, DC: Government Printing Office, 16.

Farrar, Samuel Clarke. *The Twenty-Second Pennsylvania Cavalry and the Ringgold Battalion, 1861–1865*. Pittsburgh, PA: Twenty-Second Pennsylvania Ringgold Cavalry Association, 1911.

Gasboro, Norman. "Rev. John Quincy Adams—Harrisburg Preacher and Civil Rights Leader was Once a Slave." *Civil War Blog: A Project of a PA Historian* (blog). http://civilwar.gratzpa.org/2015/02/rev-john-quincy-adams-harrisburg-preacher-civil-rights-leader-was-once-a-slave/. February 13, 2015.

Gordon, George H. *Brook Farm to Cedar Mountain: In the War of the Great Rebellion, 1861–62*. Boston: Houghton Mifflin & Co., 1885.

Greer, Matthew C. "Cather and Enslaved Life in the Northern Shenandoah Valley." Paper Presented at 17th International Willa Cather Seminar, Shenandoah University, June 17, 2019.

Halstead, Murat. "The Execution of John Brown." *Ohio Archaeological and Historical Publications* 30 (1921): 290–299.

Howard, Oliver O. *Autobiography of Oliver Otis Howard*. New York: Baker and Taylor, 1908.

Hewitt, William. *History of the Twelfth West Virginia Volunteer Infantry: The Part It Took in the War of the Rebellion 1861–1865.* Published by the Twelfth West Virginia Infantry Association, 1892.

Hutton, James V., Jr., comp. *The Diary of Sarah Morgan McKown, 1860–1899.* Self-published, n.d.

Johnson, Clifton. *Battleground Adventures: The Stories of Dwellers on the Scenes of Conflict in Some of the Most Notable Battles of the Civil War.* Boston: Houghton Mifflin, 1915.

Jordan, William B., Jr., ed. *The Civil War Journals of John Mead Gould 1861–1866.* Baltimore: Butternut & Blue, 1997.

"Joseph Waddell Diary." Valley of the Shadow Project. http://valley.lib.virginia.edu/papers/AD1500. Accessed April 22, 2019.

*Journal of the House of Representatives of the United States: Being the Second Session of the Thirty-Eighth Congress; Begun and Held at the City of Washington, December 5, 1864, in the Eighty-Ninth Year of Independence of the United States.* Washington, DC: Government Printing Office, 1865.

Keyes, Charles M. *The Military History of the 123d Regiment Ohio Volunteer Infantry.* Sandusky, OH: Register Steam Press, 1874.

Kiefer, Joseph Warren. *Slavery and Four Years of War: A Political History of Slavery in the United States Together with a Narrative of the Campaigns and Battles of the Civil War in Which the Author Took Part: 1861–1865.* 2 vols. New York: G. P. Putnam's Sons, 1900.

Locke, William Henry. *The Story of the Regiment.* Philadelphia: J. B. Lippincott, 1888.

Macon, Emma Cassandra Riely, and Reuben Conway Macon. *Reminiscences of the Civil War.* Cedar Rapids, IA: The Torch Press, 1911.

Mahon, Michael, ed. *Winchester Divided: The Civil War Diaries of Julia Chase & Laura Lee.* Mechanicsburg, PA: Stackpole Books, 2002.

"Map of Virginia: Showing the Distribution of Its Slave Population from the Census of 1860." https://www.loc.gov/item/2010586922/. Accessed July 22, 2019.

Mason, Virginia. *The Public Life and Diplomatic Correspondence of James M. Mason with Some Personal History.* New York: The Neale Publishing Co., 1906.

McDonald, Cornelia. *A Diary with Reminiscences of the War and Refugee Life in the Shenandoah Valley, 1860–1865.* Nashville, TN: Cullom & Ghertner, 1934.

McLachlan, James, ed. "The Civil War Diary of Joseph H. Coit." *Maryland Historical Magazine* 60 (September 1965): 245–260.

McPherson, Edward. *The Political History of the United States of America during the Great Rebellion.* Washington, DC: Philp & Solomons, 1865.

Mohr, James C., ed. *The Cormany Diaries: A Northern Family in the Civil War.* Pittsburgh: University of Pittsburgh Press, 1982.

Moore, Rayburn S., ed. "John Brown's Raid at Harpers Ferry: An Eyewitness Account." *Virginia Magazine of History and Biography* 67 (October 1959): 387–395.

Moore, William F., and Jane Ann Moore, eds. *His Brother's Blood: Speeches and Writings, 1838–64.* Urbana: University of Illinois Press, 2004.

Morris, Mary T., and Ned Burks, eds. "Through the Shadow: A Boy's Memories of the

Civil War in Clarke County." *Proceedings of the Clarke County Historical Association* 24 (1989–1990): 1–89.

Mottelay, Paul F., and T. Campbell Copeland, eds. *The Soldier in Our Civil War: A Pictorial History of the Conflict, 1861–1865.* Vol. 2. New York: Stanley Bradley Publishing Co., 1890.

National Register of Historic Places Registration Form for Josephine City, Virginia Department of Historic Resources File No. 168–5029. Richmond: Virginia Department of Historic Resources.

Neese, George M. *Three Years in the Confederate Horse Artillery.* New York: The Neale Publishing Co., 1911.

Newcomer, Elsie Renalds, and Janet Renalds Ramsey. *1863 Life in the Shenandoah Valley: A Compilation of the Journal of Simon Peter Henkel, The Letter Collection of Casper Coiner Henkel, M.D., The Richmond Daily Dispatch of Richmond, Virginia.* Mechanicsville, VA: Hills and Mills, 2013.

Patterson, Robert. *A Narrative of the Campaign in the Shenandoah in 1861.* Philadelphia: Sherman & Co., Printers, 1865.

Paulus, Margaret B., comp. *Papers of General Robert Huston Milroy.* 4 vols. Self-published, 1965.

Perdue, Charles L., Jr., Thomas E. Barden, and Robert K. Phillips, eds. *Weevils in the Wheat: Interviews with Virginia Ex-Slaves.* Charlottesville: University Press of Virginia, 1976.

Piston, William Garret, ed. "'The Rebs are Yet Thick About Us': The Civil War Diary of Amos Stouffer of Chambersburg," *Civil War History* 38 (September 1992): 210–231.

Pollard, Edward A. *The Lost Cause: A New Southern History of the War of the Confederates.* New York: E. B. Treat & Co., 1867.

Population of Virginia in 1790. http://www.virginiaplaces.org/population/pop1790numbers.html. Accessed June 1, 2019.

Population of Virginia in 1800. http://www.virginiaplaces.org/population/pop1800numbers.html. Accessed June 1, 2019.

Population of Virginia in 1810. http://www.virginiaplaces.org/population/pop1810numbers.html. Accessed June 1, 2019.

Population of Virginia in 1820. http://www.virginiaplaces.org/population/pop1820numbers.html. Accessed June 1, 2019.

Population of Virginia in 1830. http://www.virginiaplaces.org/population/pop1830numbers.html. Accessed June 1, 2019.

Population of Virginia in 1840. http://www.virginiaplaces.org/population/pop1840numbers.html. Accessed June 1, 2018.

Population of Virginia in 1850. http://www.virginiaplaces.org/population/pop1850numbers.html. Accessed June 1, 2018.

Population of Virginia in 1860. http://www.virginiaplaces.org/population/pop1860numbers.html. Accessed June 1, 2018.

Publication Committee of the Regimental Association, comp. *History of the Eighteenth Regiment of Cavalry Pennsylvania Volunteers (163d Regiment of the Line) 1862–1865.* New York: Wynkoop Hallenbek Crawford Co., 1909.

Quaife, Milo M., ed. *From the Cannon's Mouth: The Civil War Letters of General Alpheus S. Williams*. Lincoln: University of Nebraska Press, 1995.

Quint, Alonzo H. *The Potomac and the Rapidan: Army Notes, from the Failure at Winchester to the Reenforcement of Rosecrans, 1861–3*. Boston: Crosby and Nicols, 1864.

Quint, Alonzo H. *The Record of the Second Massachusetts Infantry, 1861–65*. Boston: James P. Walker, 1867.

Rawick, George P., ed. *The American Slave: A Composite Autobiography*. Vol. 18. Westport, CT: Greenwood Publishing Co., 1972.

Reilly, Wayne E., ed. *Sarah Jane Foster: Teacher of the Freedmen: A Diary and Letters*. Charlottesville: University Press of Virginia, 1990.

*Report of the Joint Committee on Reconstruction at the First Session of the Thirty-Ninth Congress*. Pt. 2. Washington, DC: Government Printing Office, 1866.

*Report, the Select Committee of the Senate Appointed to Inquire into the Late Invasion and Seizure of the Public Property at Harper's Ferry*. Washington, DC: n.p., 1860.

Rickard, James H. *Services with Colored Troops in Burnside's Corps*. Providence, RI: Published by the Society, 1894.

Rhodes, Robert Hunt, ed. *All for the Union: The Civil War Diary and Letters of Elisha Hunt Rhodes*. New York: Vintage Books, 1985.

*Roll of Honor (No. XV): Names of Soldiers Who Died in Defence of the American Union, Entered in the National Cemeteries at Antietam (Maryland), and at Arlington, (Additional), Culpeper Court-House, Cold Harbor, Winchester, Staunton, and Various Scattered Localities in Virginia*. Washington, DC: Government Printing Office, 1868.

Sheridan, Philip H. *Personal Memoirs of P.H. Sheridan*. 2 vols. New York: Charles L. Webster, 1888.

Spencer, Kenyette. "Serena, Henrietta and Abe Spencer, Free Blacks Account of Battle of Cedar Creek." https://www.geneaology.com/forum/surnames/topics/spencer/9094/. June 13, 2019.

Stark, William. "The Great Skedaddle." *The Atlantic Monthly* 162 (July 1938): 86–94.

Stevens, George T. *Three Years in the Sixth Corps: A Concise Narrative of Events in the Army of the Potomac, From 1861 to the Close of the Rebellion, April 1865*. Albany, NY: S. R. Gray Publisher, 1866.

Stevenson, James H. *"Boots and Saddles": A History of the First Volunteer Cavalry of the War, Known as the First New York (Lincoln) Cavalry, and Also as the Sabre Regiment*. Harrisburg, PA: Patriot Publishing Company, 1879.

Stewart, Rev. A. M. *Camp, March and Battle-Field: Or Three Years and a Half with the Army of the Potomac*. Philadelphia: Jas. B. Rodgers, Printer, 1865.

Still, William. *The Underground Railroad: A Record of the Facts, Authentic Narratives, Letters, & c., Narrating the Hardships Hair-breadth Escapes and Death Struggles of the Slaves in their Efforts for Freedom*. Philadelphia: People's Publishing Co., 1871.

Stowe, Harriet Beecher. *A Key to Uncle Tom's Cabin: Presenting the Original Facts and Documents Upon Which the Story is Founded. Together with Corroborative Statements Verifying the Truth of Her Work*. Boston: John P. Jewett & Co., 1853.

Strader, Eloise C., ed. *The Civil War Journal of Mary Greenhow Lee (Mrs. Hugh Holmes*

*Lee) of Winchester, Virginia*. Winchester, VA: Winchester-Frederick County Historical Society, 2011.

Strother, David Hunter. "Personal Recollections of the War." *Harper's New Monthly Magazine* 33 (June 1866): 1–25.

Strother, David Hunter. "Personal Recollections of the War." *Harper's New Monthly Magazine* 33 (July 1866): 137–160.

Strother, David Hunter. "Personal Recollections of the War." *Harper's New Monthly Magazine* 33 (October 1866): 545–567.

Strother, David Hunter. "Personal Recollections of the War." *Harper's New Monthly Magazine* 35 (August 1867): 273–295.

Summers, Festus P., ed. *A Borderland Confederate*. Pittsburgh: University of Pittsburgh Press, 1962.

Surkamp, Jim. "128 African Sons of Jefferson County . . . In Blue Coats." http://civilwarscholars.com/2013/12/154-african-sons-of-jefferson-county-in-blue-coats/. May 10, 2019.

Taylor, James E. *With Sheridan up the Shenandoah Valley in 1864: Leaves from a Special Artist's Sketchbook and Diary*. Dayton, OH: Morningside House, Inc., 1989.

Tenney, W. J. *Military and Naval History of the Rebellions in the United States*. New York: D. Appleton & Co., 1865.

*The Diary of Margaretta "Gettie" Sperry Miller, March 23, 1863–September 19, 1863*. Winchester, VA: Godfrey Miller Historic Home and Fellowship Center, 2008.

*The United States Treasury Register: Containing a List of all Persons Employed in the Treasury Department*. Washington, DC: Government Printing Office, 1873.

Trowbridge, John T. *The South: A Tour of Its Battle-fields and Ruined Cities, A Journey Through the Desolated States, and Talks with the People*. Hartford, CT: L. Stebbins, 1866.

U.S. War Department, comp. *War of the Rebellion: A Compilation of the Official Records of the Union and Confederate Armies*. 128 vols. Washington, DC: Government Printing Office, 1880–1901.

Veney, Bethany. *The Narrative of Bethany Veney: A Slave Woman*. Worcester, MA: Press of A. P. Bicknell, 1890.

Waddell, Joseph A. *Annals of Augusta County Virginia*. Richmond, VA: Wm. Ellis Jones, Book & Job Printer, 1886.

Wenger, Norman R., and David S. Rodes, comps. *Unionists and the Civil War Experience in the Shenandoah Valley*. Vol. 6. Dayton, VA: The Valley Research Associates and the Valley Brethren-Mennonite Heritage Center, 2012.

Wild, Frederick W. *Memoirs and History of Capt. F. W. Alexander's Baltimore Battery of Light Artillery U.S.V.* Baltimore: Frederick W. Wild, 1912.

Wintz, William D., ed. *Civil War Memoirs of Two Rebel Sister*. Charleston, WV: Pictorial Histories Publishing Co., 1989.

Worsham, John H. *One of Jackson's Foot Cavalry: His Experiences and What He Saw During the War, 1861–1865*. New York: Neale Publishing Co., 1912.

Wray, William J., comp. *History of the Twenty-Third Pennsylvania Infantry*. Philadelphia, PA: Survivors Association Twenty-Third Regiment Pennsylvania Volunteers, 1903–1904.

## Other Published Sources

Abels, Jules. *Man on Fire: John Brown and the Cause of Liberty*. New York: Macmillan, 1971.

*American Slavery As It Is: Testimony of a Thousand Witnesses*. New York: Published by the American Anti-Slavery Society, 1839.

Anderson, Paul Christopher. *Blood Image: Turner Ashby in the Civil War and the Southern Mind*. Baton Rouge: Louisiana State University Press, 2002.

Austin, William H. "A Quiet Man." *Civil War Times* 58 (February 2019): 36–37.

Ayers, Edward L. *In the Presence of Mine Enemies: War in the Heart of America, 1859–1863*. New York: Norton, 2003.

Ayers, Edward L. *The Thin Light of Freedom: The Civil War and Emancipation in the Heart of America*. New York: Norton, 2017.

Baldau, Catherine, ed. *"To Emancipate the Mind and Soul": Storer College, 1867–1955*. Harpers Ferry, WV: Harpers Ferry Park Association, 2017.

Ballard, Charles C. *Dismissing the Peculiar Institution: Assessing Slavery in Page and Rockingham Counties, Virginia*. Luray, VA: Page County Heritage Association, 1999.

Berkey, Jonathan M. "In the Very Midst of the War Track: The Valley's Civilians and the Shenandoah Campaign." In *The Shenandoah Valley Campaign of 1862*, edited by Gary W. Gallagher, 86–114. Chapel Hill: University of North Carolina Press, 2003.

Berkey, Jonathan M. "War in the Borderland: The Civilians' War in Virginia's Lower Shenandoah Valley." PhD diss., Pennsylvania State University, 2003.

Berlin, Ira. *Generations of Captivity: A History of African-American Slaves*. Cambridge, MA: Harvard University Press, 2003.

Berlin, Ira., Barbara J. Fields, Steven F. Miller, Joseph P. Reidy, and Leslie S. Rowland. *Slaves No More: Three Essays on Emancipation*. Cambridge, MA: Cambridge University Press, 1992.

Blair, William. *Cities of the Dead: Contesting the Memory of the Civil War in the South, 1865–1914*. Chapel Hill: University of North Carolina Press, 2004.

Blight, David W. *A Slave No More: Two Men Who Escaped to Freedom*. Orlando, FL: Harcourt, 2007.

Blight, David W. *Beyond the Battlefield: Race, Memory, and the American Civil War*. Amherst: University of Massachusetts Press, 2002.

Blight, David W. *Race and Reunion: The Civil War in American Memory*. Cambridge, MA: The Belknap Press of Harvard University Press, 2001.

Bordewich, Fergus M. *Bound for Canaan: The Underground Railroad and the War for the Soul of America*. New York: Amistad, 2005.

Burr, Frank A., and Richard J. Hinton. *The Life of Gen. Philip H. Sheridan: Its Romance and Reality*. Providence, RI: J. A. & R. A. Reid, Publishers, 1888.

Brasher, Glenn David. *The Peninsula Campaign and the Necessity of Emancipation: African Americans and the Fight for Freedom*. Chapel Hill: University of North Carolina Press, 2012.

Breen, Patrick H. *The Land Shall be Deluged in Blood: A New History of the Nat Turner Revolt*. Oxford: Oxford University Press, 2015.

Brundage, Fitzhugh. "Shifting Attitudes Towards Slavery in Antebellum Rockbridge County." *Proceedings of the Rockbridge Historical Society* 10 (1980–1989): 333–344.

Cartmell, Thomas K. *Shenandoah Valley Pioneers and Their Descendants*. Berkeley, WV: Eddy Press Corporation, 1909.

Chambers, Moreau B. C. "The Militia Crisis." *Virginia Cavalcade* 16, no. 4 (1967): 10–14.

Champ, Stephanie M. H. *Closer to Freedom: Enslaved Women and Everyday Resistance in the Plantation South*. Chapel Hill: University of North Carolina Press, 2004.

Cimbala, Paul A. *The Freedmen's Bureau: Reconstructing the American South after the Civil War*. Malabar, FL: Kriger Publishing, 2005.

Cimbala, Paul A., and Randall M. Miller, eds. *The Freedmen's Bureau and Reconstruction: Reconsiderations*. New York: Fordham University Press, 1999.

Cozzens, Peter. *Shenandoah 1862: Stonewall Jackson's 1862 Valley Campaign*. Chapel Hill: University of North Carolina Press, 2008.

Cranmer, Gibson Lamb, ed. *History of Wheeling City and Ohio County, West Virginia and Representative Citizens*. Apollo, PA: Apollo Press, 1994.

Crouch, Barry A. "'To Enslave the Rising Generation': The Freedmen's Bureau and the Texas Slave Code." In *The Freedmen's Bureau and Reconstruction: Reconsiderations*, edited by Paul A. Cimbala and Randall M. Miller, 261–287. New York: Fordham University Press, 1999.

Dabney, Virginius. *Virginia: The New Dominion: A History from 1607 to the Present*. Garden City, NY: Doubleday, 1971.

Davis, Julia. *The Shenandoah*. New York: Rinehart & Co., 1945.

Denkler, Ann. *Sustaining Identity, Recapturing Heritage: Exploring Issues of Public History, Tourism, and Race in a Southern Town*. Lanham, MD: Lexington Books, 2007.

DuBois, W.E.B. *The Negro Church*. Atlanta: Atlanta University Press, 1903.

Dunaway, Wilma A. *Slavery in the American Mountain South*. Cambridge: Cambridge University Press, 2003.

Duncan, Richard R. *Beleaguered Winchester: A Virginia Community at War, 1861–1865*. Baton Rouge: Louisiana State University Press, 2007.

Engle, Stephen D. *Yankee Dutchman: The Life of Franz Sigel*. Baton Rouge: Louisiana State University Press, 1993.

Ehrenpreis, David. *Picturing Harrisonburg: Visions of a Shenandoah Valley City Since 1828*. Staunton, VA: George F. Thompson Publishing, 2017.

Farmer, Mary J. "'Because They Are Women': Gender and the Virginia Freedmen's Bureau's 'War on Dependency.'" In *The Freedmen's Bureau and Reconstruction: Reconsiderations*, edited by Paul A. Cimbala and Randall M. Miller, 161–192. New York: Fordham University Press, 1999.

Ferris, Norman B. *The Trent Affair: A Diplomatic Crisis*. Knoxville: University of Tennessee Press, 1977.

Fisher, Lewis F. *No Cause of Offence: A Virginia Family of Union Loyalists Confronts the Civil War*. San Antonio, TX: Maverick Publishing, 2012.

Foner, Eric. *Reconstruction: America's Unfinished Revolution, 1863–1877.* New York: Harper and Row, 1988.

Fox, David. "The Labor of a Free Man." In *"To Emancipate the Mind and Soul": Storer College 1867–1955*, edited by Catherine Baldau, 29–34. Harpers Ferry, WV: Harpers Ferry Park Association, 2017.

Franklin, John Hope, and Loren Schweninger. *Runaway Slaves: Rebels on the Plantation.* Oxford: Oxford University Press, 1999.

French, Steve. *Rebel Chronicles: Raiders, Scouts, and Train Robbers of the Upper Potomac.* New Wilmington, PA: New Horizons Publishing, 2012.

Frye, Dennis E., and Catherine Magi Oliver. *Confluence: Harpers Ferry as Destiny.* Harpers Ferry, WV: Harpers Ferry Park Association, 2019.

Gallagher, Gary W., ed. *The Shenandoah Valley Campaign of 1862.* Chapel Hill: University of North Carolina Press, 2003.

Gardiner, Mabel Henshaw, and Ann Henshaw Gardiner. *Chronicles of Old Berkeley: A Narrative History of a Virginia County from Its Beginnings to 1926.* Durham, NC: The Seeman Press, 1938.

Geier, Clarence R., and Stephen R. Potter, eds. *Archaeological Perspectives on the American Civil War.* Gainesville: University Presses of Florida, 2000.

Gerteis, Louis S. *From Contraband to Freedman: Federal Policy Toward Southern Blacks 1861–1865.* Westport, CT: Greenwood Press, 1973.

Glatthaar, Joseph T. *Forged in Battle: The Civil War Alliance of Black Soldiers and White Officers.* New York: Free Press, 1990.

Gooden, Randall S. "'Neither War nor Peace': West Virginia's Reconstruction Experience." In *Reconstructing Appalachia: The Civil War's Aftermath*, edited by Andrew L. Slap, 211–236. Lexington: University Press of Kentucky, 2010.

Greenberg, Martin H., and Charles G. Waugh, eds. *The Price of Freedom: Slavery and the Civil War.* 2 vols. Nashville, TN: Cumberland House, 2000.

Grimsley, Mark. *The Hard Hand of War: Union Military Policy Toward Southern Civilians 1861–1865.* Cambridge: Cambridge University Press, 1995.

Hadden, Sally E. *Slave Patrols: Law and Violence in Virginia.* Cambridge, MA: Harvard University Press, 2001.

Hale, Laura Virginia. *Four Valiant Years in the Lower Shenandoah Valley: 1861–1865.* Strasburg, VA: Shenandoah House Publishing, 1968.

Hearn, Chester G. *Six Years of Hell: Harpers Ferry During the Civil War.* Baton Rouge: Louisiana State University Press, 1996.

Heatwole, John L. *The Burning: Sheridan in the Shenandoah Valley.* Charlottesville, VA: Rockbridge Publishing, 1998.

Heinrich, Robert, and Deborah Harding. *From Slave to Statesman: The Life of Educator, Editor, and Civil Rights Activist Willis M. Carter of Virginia.* Baton Rouge: Louisiana State University Press, 2016.

Hickin, Patricia. "John C. Underwood and the Antislavery Movement in Virginia, 1847–1860." *Virginia Magazine of History and Biography* 73 (April 1965): 156–168.

History Matters, *History of Orrick Chapel Methodist Church in Stephens City, Virginia.* Washington, DC: History Matters, 2006.

Hofstra, Warren R. *The Planting of New Virginia: Settlement and Landscape in the Shenandoah Valley.* Baltimore: Johns Hopkins University Press, 2004.

Hollandsworth, James G., Jr. *Pretense of Glory: The Life of General Nathaniel P. Banks.* Baton Rouge: Louisiana State University Press, 1998.

Janney, Caroline E., ed. *Petersburg to Appomattox: The End of the War in Virginia.* Chapel Hill: University of North Carolina Press, 2018.

Janney, Caroline E. *Remembering the Civil War: Reunion and the Limits of Reconciliation.* Chapel Hill: University of North Carolina Press, 2013.

Janney, Caroline E. "Written in Stone: Gender, Race, and the Heyward Shepherd Memorial." *Civil War History* 52 (June 2006): 117–141.

Johnson, Rossiter, ed. *The Twentieth Century Biographical Dictionary of Notable Americans.* Vol. 10. Boston: The Biographical Society, 1904.

Jones, Nancy Bondurant. *An African American Community of Hope: Zenda: 1869–1930.* McGaheysville, VA: Long's Chapel Preservation Society, 2007.

Jordan, Ervin L., Jr. *Black Confederates and Afro-Yankees in Civil War Virginia.* Charlottesville: University Press of Virginia, 1995.

Kalbian, Maral S. *Clarke County.* Charleston, SC: Arcadia Publishing, 2011.

Kalbian, Maral S. *Frederick County Virginia: History Through Architecture.* Winchester, VA: Winchester-Frederick County Historical Society, 1999.

Katz, Philip M. *From Appomattox to Montmatre: Americans and the Paris Commune.* Cambridge, MA: Harvard University Press, 1998.

Kerr-Ritchie, Jeffrey R. *Freedpeople in the Tobacco South: Virginia, 1860–1900.* Chapel Hill: University of North Carolina Press, 1999.

Knight, Charles R. *Valley Thunder: The Battle of New Market and the Opening of the Shenandoah Valley Campaign, May 1864.* New York: Savas Beatie, 2010.

Koons, Kenneth E. "'The Colored Laborers Work as Well as When Slaves': African Americans in the Breadbasket of the Confederacy, 1850–1880." In *Archaeological Perspectives on the American Civil War,* edited by Clarence R. Geier and Stephen R. Potter, 229–252. Gainesville: University Presses of Florida, 2000.

Koons, Kenneth E. "'The Time has Come Near that We Will All Have to Learn to Work': Elite Farm Women of the Lower Shenandoah Valley and Their Slaves During the Civil War." *Journal of the Shenandoah Valley During the Civil War Era* 1 (2018): 3–13.

Koons, Kenneth E., and Warren R. Hofstra. *After the Backcountry: Rural Life in the Great Valley of Virginia 1800–1900.* Knoxville: University of Tennessee Press, 2000.

Kynoch, Gary. "Terrible Dilemmas: Black Enlistment in the Union Army During the American Civil War." In *The Price of Freedom: Slavery and the Civil War,* vol. 1, *The Demise of Slavery,* edited by Martin H. Greenberg and Charles G. Waugh, 107–127. Nashville, TN: Cumberland House, 2000.

Lang, Andrew F. *In the Wake of War: Military Occupation, Emancipation, and Civil War America.* Baton Rouge: Louisiana State University Press, 2017.

Lanza, Michael L. "'One of the Most Appreciated Labors of the Bureau': The Freedmen's Bureau and the Southern Homestead Act." In *The Freedmen's Bureau and Reconstruction: Reconsiderations,* edited by Paul A. Cimbala and Randall M. Miller, 67–92. New York: Fordham University Press, 1999.

Levin, Kevin M. *Remembering the Battle of the Crater: War as Murder*. Lexington: University Press of Kentucky, 2012.

Levin, Kevin M. *Searching for Black Confederates: The Civil War's Most Persistent Myth*. Chapel Hill: University of North Carolina Press, 2019.

Levine, Bruce. *Confederate Emancipation: Southern Plans to Free and Arm Slaves during the Civil War*. New York: Oxford University Press, 2007.

Link, William A. *Roots of Secession: Slavery and Politics in Antebellum Virginia*. Chapel Hill: University of North Carolina Press, 2003.

Link, William A., and James J. Broomall, eds. *Rethinking American Emancipation: Legacies of Slavery and the Quest for Black Freedom*. New York: Cambridge University Press, 2016.

Longenecker, Stephen L. *Shenandoah Religion: Outsiders and the Mainstream, 1716–1865*. Waco, TX: Baylor University Press, 2002.

Lowe, Richard. "Battle on the Levee: The Fight at Milliken's Bend." In *Black Soldiers in Blue: African American Troops in the Civil War Era*, edited by John David Smith, 107–135. Chapel Hill: University of North Carolina Press, 2002.

Lowe, Richard. *Republicans and Reconstruction in Virginia, 1856–1870*. Charlottesville: University Press of Virginia, 1991.

Luke, Bob, and John David Smith. *Soldiering for Freedom: How the Union Army Recruited, Trained, and Deployed the U.S. Colored Troops*. Baltimore: Johns Hopkins University Press, 2014.

Lussana, Sergio A. *My Brother Slaves: Friendship, Masculinity and Resistance in the Antebellum South*. Lexington: The University Press of Kentucky, 2016.

Mahon, Michael G. *The Shenandoah Valley, 1861–1865: The Destruction of the Granary of the Confederacy*. Mechanicsburg, PA: Stackpole Books, 1999.

Manning, Chandra. *Troubled Refuge: Struggling for Freedom in the Civil War*. New York: Knopf, 2016.

Manning, Chandra. *What This Cruel War Was Over: Soldiers, Slavery, and the Civil War*. New York: Vintage, 2007.

Martinez, Jaime Amanda. *Confederate Slave Impressment in the Upper South*. Chapel Hill: University of North Carolina Press, 2013.

McCabe, Susan L., ed. *Freedom by Deed: An Index to Emancipation and Manumissions in the Winchester and Frederick County, VA Deed Books, 1752–1862*. Winchester, VA: Shenandoah Valley Geneaological Society, 2007.

McConnell, John Preston. *Negroes and their Treatment in Virginia from 1865–1867*. Pulaski, VA: B. D. Smith & Brothers, 1910.

McFeely, William S. *Frederick Douglass*. New York: Norton, 1991.

McPherson, James M. *For Cause and Comrades: Why Men Fought in the Civil War*. New York: Oxford University Press, 1997.

McPherson, James M. *Tried by War: Abraham Lincoln as Commander in Chief*. New York: Penguin Press, 2008.

Miller, Edward A., Jr. *Lincoln's Abolitionist General: The Biography of David Hunter*. Columbia: University of South Carolina Press, 1997.

Mitchell, Robert D. *Commercialism and Frontier: Perspectives on the Early Shenandoah Valley.* Charlottesville: University Press of Virginia, 1977.

Mohr, Clarence L. *On the Threshold of Freedom: Masters and Slaves in Civil War Georgia.* Baton Rouge: Louisiana State University Press, 1986.

Murphy, Kim. *I Had Rather Die: Rape in the Civil War.* Afton, VA: Coachlight Press, 2014.

Myers, Barton A. *Rebels Against the Confederacy: North Carolina's Unionists.* New York: Cambridge University Press, 2014.

Nevins, Allan. *The War for the Union: The Improvised War, 1861–1862.* New York: Charles Scribner's Sons, 1959.

Nieman, Donald G., ed. *From Slavery to Sharecropping: White Land and Black Labor in the Rural South 1865–1890.* New York: Garland Publishing, 1994.

Noyalas, Jonathan A. *"My Will is Absolute Law": A Biography of Union General Robert H. Milroy.* Jefferson, NC: McFarland, 2006.

Noyalas, Jonathan A. *Plagued by War: Winchester, Virginia, During the Civil War.* Leesburg, VA: Gauley Mount Press, 2003.

Noyalas, Jonathan A. *Stonewall Jackson's 1862 Valley Campaign: When War Comes to the Home Front.* Charleston, SC: History Press, 2010.

Noyalas, Jonathan A. "That Woman was Worth a Whole Brigade." *Civil War Times* 52 (June 2012): 43–49.

Noyalas, Jonathan A. *Two Peoples, One Community: The African American Experience in Newtown (Stephens City), Virginia, 1850–1870.* Stephens City, VA: Stone House Foundation, 2007.

Oakes, James. *Freedom National: The Destruction of Slavery in the United States, 1861–1865.* New York: Norton, 2013.

Oates, Stephen B. *With Malice Toward None: The Life of Abraham Lincoln.* New York: Harper & Row, 1977.

O'Donovan, Susan Eva. *Becoming Free in the Cotton South.* Cambridge, MA: Harvard University Press, 2007.

Painter, Nell Irvin. *Creating Black Americans: African American History and Its Meanings, 1619 to the Present.* Oxford: Oxford University Press, 2006.

Patchan, Scott C. *The Battle of Piedmont and Hunter's Raid on Staunton: The 1864 Shenandoah Campaign.* Charleston, SC: History Press, 2011.

Patchan, Scott C. *The Last Battle of Winchester: Phil Sheridan, Jubal Early, and the Shenandoah Valley Campaign, August 7–September 19, 1864.* El Dorado Hills, CA: Savas Beatie, 2013.

Phillips, Edward H. *The Lower Shenandoah Valley in the Civil War: The Impact of War Upon the Civilian Population and Upon Civil Institutions.* Lynchburg, VA: H. E. Howard, 1993.

Piersen, William D. "Black Martyr's Fear, Depression and Religious Faith as Causes of Suicide Among New Slaves." *Journal of Negro History* 62 (April 1977): 147–159.

Planchon, Paul. "Free Blacks in Berkeley County and the Black Community of Douglass Grove." *The Berkeley Journal* 32 (2006): 35–43.

Pope, Thomas E. *The Weary Boys: Colonel J. Warren Keifer and the 110th Ohio Volunteer Infantry.* Kent, OH: Kent State University Press, 2002.

Quarles, Benjamin. *Allies for Freedom & Blacks on John Brown*. New York: DaCapo Press, 1974.

Reidy, Joseph P. *Illusions of Emancipation: The Pursuit of Freedom & Equality in the Twilight of Slavery*. Chapel Hill: University of North Carolina Press, 2019.

Reynolds, Donald E. *Texas Terror: The Slave Insurrection Panic of 1860 and the Secession of the Lower South*. Baton Rouge: Louisiana State University Press, 2007.

Rhea, Gordon C. *Carrying the Flag: The Story of Private Charles Whilden, the Confederacy's Most Unlikely Hero*. New York: Basic Books, 2004.

Richardson, E. Allen. "Architects of a Benevolent Empire: The Relationship between the American Missionary Association and the Freedmen's Bureau in Virginia, 1865–1872." In *The Freedmen's Bureau and Reconstruction: Reconsiderations*, edited by Paul A. Cimbala and Randall M. Miller, 119–139. New York: Fordham University Press, 1999.

Richardson, Joe M. *Christian Reconstruction: The American Missionary Association and the Southern Blacks, 1861–1890*. Athens: University of Georgia Press, 1986.

Robinson, Armstead L. *Bitter Fruits of Bondage: The Demise of Slavery and the Collapse of the Confederacy, 1861–1865*. Charlottesville: University of Virginia Press, 2005.

Savitt, Todd L. *Medicine and Slavery: The Diseases and Health Care of Blacks in Antebellum Virginia*. Urbana: University of Illinois Press, 1978.

Schwarz, Philip J. *Twice Condemned: Slaves and the Criminal Laws of Virginia, 1705–1865*. Union, NJ: The Lawbook Exchange, 1998.

Sernet, Milton C. *Harriet Tubman: Myth, Memory, and History*. Durham, NC: Duke University Press, 2007.

Sheehan-Dean, Aaron. *The Calculus of Violence: How Americans Fought the Civil War*. Cambridge: MA: Harvard University Press, 2018.

Shenandoah Valley Battlefields Foundation, *Shenandoah Valley Battlefields National Historic District: Final Management Plan*. New Market, VA: Shenandoah Valley Battlefields Foundation, 2000.

Shenandoah Valley Black Heritage Project. *We Honor Those Who Served*. Harrisonburg, VA: Shenandoah Valley Black Heritage Project, 2015.

Shlomowitz, Ralph. "The Origins of Southern Sharecropping." In *From Slavery to Sharecropping: White Land and Black Labor in the Rural South 1865–1890*, edited by Donald G. Nieman, 199–217. New York: Garland Publishing, 1994.

Silber, Nina. *This War Ain't Over: Fighting the Civil War in New Deal America*. Chapel Hill: University of North Carolina Press, 2018.

Simmons, J. Susanne, and Nancy T. Sorrells. "Slave Hire and the Development of Slavery in Augusta County, Virginia." In *After the Backcountry: Rural Life in the Great Valley of Virginia, 1800–1900*, edited by Kenneth E. Koons and Warren R. Hofstra, 169–184. Knoxville: University of Tennessee Press, 2000.

Sinha, Manisha. *The Slave's Cause: A History of Abolition*. New Haven, CT: Yale University Press, 2016.

Slap, Andrew L., ed. *Reconstructing Appalachia: The Civil War's Aftermath*. Lexington: University Press of Kentucky, 2010.

Slowe, Lucy D. "Notes: The Passing of George William Cook." *Journal of Negro History* 16 (October 1931): 480–482.

Smith, John David, ed. *Black Soldiers in Blue: African American Troops in the Civil War Era*. Chapel Hill: University of North Carolina Press, 2002.

Snyder, Terri L. "Suicide, Slavery, and Memory in North America." *Journal of American History* 97 (June 2010): 39–62.

Stealey, John E., III. "The Freedmen's Bureau in West Virginia." *Magazine of the Jefferson County Historical Society* 48 (December 2002): 19–73.

Stephenson, Darl L. *Headquarters in the Brush: Blazer's Independent Union Scouts*. Athens: Ohio University Press, 2001.

Sternhell, Yael E. "Bodies in Motion and the Making of Emancipation." In *Rethinking American Emancipation: Legacies of Slavery and the Quest for Black Freedom*, edited by William A. Link and James J. Broomall, 15–41. New York: Cambridge University Press, 2016.

Stevenson, Brenda E. *Life in Black and White: Family and Community in the Slave South*. New York: Oxford University Press, 1996.

Stowe, Harriet Beecher. *Uncle Tom's Cabin*. London: John Casseli, Ludgate Hill, 1852.

Summers, Robert K. *19th Regiment U.S. Colored Troops: Profiles in Courage*. Self-published, 2016.

Tanner, Robert. *Stonewall in the Valley: Thomas J. "Stonewall" Jackson's Shenandoah Valley Campaign, Spring 1862*. Garden City, NY: Doubleday, 1976.

Taylor, Amy Murrell. *Embattled Freedom: Journeys through the Civil War's Slave Refugee Camps*. Chapel Hill: University of North Carolina Press, 2018.

Taylor, James L. *Africans-in-America of the Lower Shenandoah Valley: 1700–1900*. Self-published, 1999.

*The Loyal Girl of Winchester: September 1864*. n.p., n.d.

Thorp, Daniel B. *Facing Freedom: An African American Community in Virginia from Reconstruction to Jim Crow*. Charlottesville: University Press of Virginia, 2017.

Van Horne, Thomas Budd. *The Life of Major-General George H. Thomas*. New York: Charles Scribner's Sons, 1882.

Varon, Elizabeth. "The Last Hours of the Slaveholders' Rebellion: African American Discourse on Lee's Surrender." In *Petersburg to Appomattox: The End of the War in Virginia*, edited by Caroline E. Janney, 254–284. Chapel Hill: University of North Carolina Press, 2018.

Wallenstein, Peter. *Cradle of America: Four Centuries of Virginia History*. Lawrence: University Press of Kansas, 2007.

Waller, Douglas. *Lincoln's Spies: Their Secret War to Save a Nation*. New York: Simon & Schuster, 2019.

Ward, Andrew. *The Slaves' War*. Boston: Mariner Books, 2008.

Warner, Ezra J., and W. Buck Yearns. *Biographical Register of the Confederate Congress*. Baton Rouge: Louisiana State University, 1975.

Wayland, John Walter. *The German Element of the Shenandoah Valley of Virginia*. Charlottesville, VA: The Michie Co., 1907.

Whitman, T. Stephen. *The Price of Freedom: Slavery and Manumission in Baltimore and Early National Maryland*. Lexington: University Press of Kentucky, 1997.

Williams, David. *I Freed Myself: African American Self-Emancipation in the Civil War Era*. New York: Cambridge University Press, 2014.

Willis, Deborah, and Barbara Krauthamer. *Envisioning Emancipation: Black Americans and the End of Slavery*. Philadelphia: Temple University Press, 2013.

Wilmer, L. Allison, J. H. Jarrett, and George W. F. Vernon. *History and Roster of Maryland Volunteers, War of 1861–5*. Vol. 2. Baltimore: Press of Guggenheimer, Weil, & Co., 1899.

Windley, Lathan A. *A Profile of Runaway Slaves in Virginia and South Carolina from 1730–1787*. New York: Routledge, 1995.

Wood, Alice Davis. *Dr. Francis T. Stribling and Moral Medicine: Curing the Insane at Virginia's Western State Hospital, 1836–1874*. Waynesboro, VA: Galileo Gianniny Publishing, 2004.

Wynstra, Robert J. *At the Forefront of Lee's Invasion: Retribution, Plunder, and Clashing Cultures on Richard S. Ewell's Road to Gettysburg*. Kent, OH: Kent State University Press, 2018.

Zaborney, John J. *Slaves for Hire: Renting Enslaved Laborers in Antebellum Virginia*. Baton Rouge: Louisiana State University Press, 2012.

Zambone, Louis. *Daniel Morgan: A Revolutionary Life*. Yardley, PA: Westholme Publishing, 2018.

Zigler, D. H. *History of the Brethren in Virginia*. Elgin, IL: Brethren Publishing House, 1914.

# INDEX

Jonathan A. Noyalas is director of Shenandoah University's McCormick Civil War Institute. He is the author or editor of fourteen books and has contributed more than a hundred articles, essays, book chapters, and reviews to a variety of scholarly and popular publications. He is the recipient of numerous awards for his scholarship and teaching including Shenandoah University's teaching excellence award for the first-year seminar and the highest honor that can ever be bestowed upon a professor teaching at a college/university in the Commonwealth of Virginia: the State Council for Higher Education in Virginia's Outstanding Faculty Award.

Printed in the United States
By Bookmasters